POSTCARD HISTORY SERIES

Traverse City in Vintage Postcards

POSTCARD HISTORY SERIES

Traverse City

IN VINTAGE POSTCARDS

C.S. Wright

ARCADIA
PUBLISHING

ISBN 978-0-7385-3182-3

Published by Arcadia Publishing
Charleston, South Carolina

Printed in the United States of America

Library of Congress Catalog Card Number: 2003110754

For all general information contact Arcadia Publishing at:
Telephone 843-853-2070
Fax 843-853-0044
E-mail sales@arcadiapublishing.com
For customer service and orders:
Toll-Free 1-888-313-2665

Visit us on the Internet at www.arcadiapublishing.com

Contents

My grandparents not only lived much of the early history of the Grand Traverse area, but also gave me a sense of what Traverse City and the Old Mission Peninsula were like in days gone by, and for leaving me such a rich legacy,

I would like to dedicate this book to:

Dr. Johnson Kent Wright and Gwendolyn Santo Wright

and

Elmer and Katherine McManus

Introduction

This book offers a perspective on the early history, as well as the natural wonders that abound in the Grand Traverse region, one that will hopefully complement other books on the subject. Focusing on the geographical area and including such areas as the Old Mission Peninsula, Antrim, Kalkaska, Leelanau, Wexford, Charlevoix, and Emmett counties, provides a much more comprehensive view of the area's history and natural beauty. Essentially, while this book does concern itself for the most part with Traverse City, the general focus is on the "Gold Coast" of Michigan.

In closing, it is only fitting to acknowledge the advice of local historian Lawrence Wakefield, as well as the assistance of my good friend, R.D. Anderson. Lastly, writing this book would not have been possible if it were not for the patience and dedication of my wife and children, and of course, Mom and Dad.

One

Logging, Farming, and the Asylum

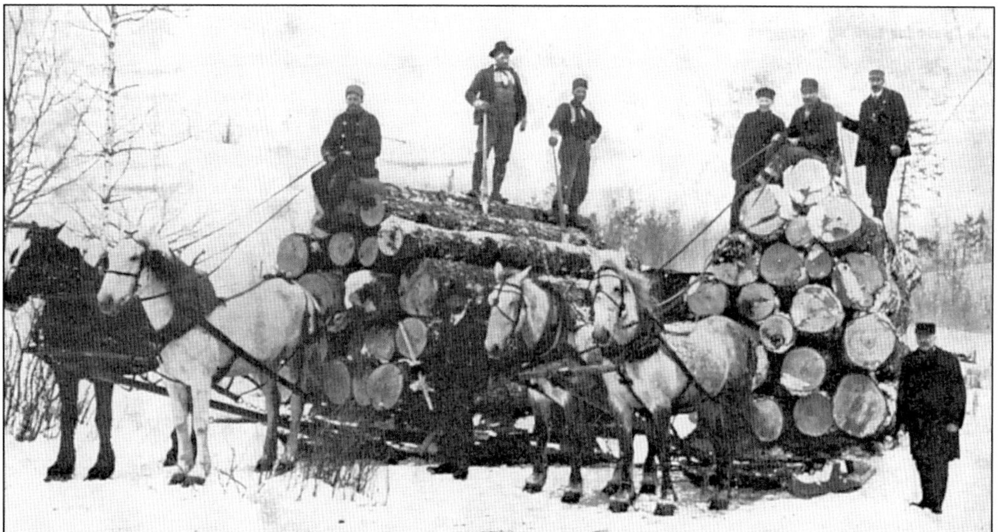

During the winter months, the rivers and lakes filled with ice, making it all but impossible to drive logs down the waterway to the mill. In fact, the more timber that was cut, the further and further it ended up from the waterways. This posed a real problem, and the solution was to haul the lumber on horse-drawn sleds. Most of the men employed as lumberjacks worked long hours and earned a pittance considering the conditions that they endured. In the 1880s and 1890s, the average wage for a lumberjack was between $20 and $25 a month, including room and board. Between the years of 1851 and 1886, Hannah & Lay Lumber Company harvested more than 350 million board feet of lumber.

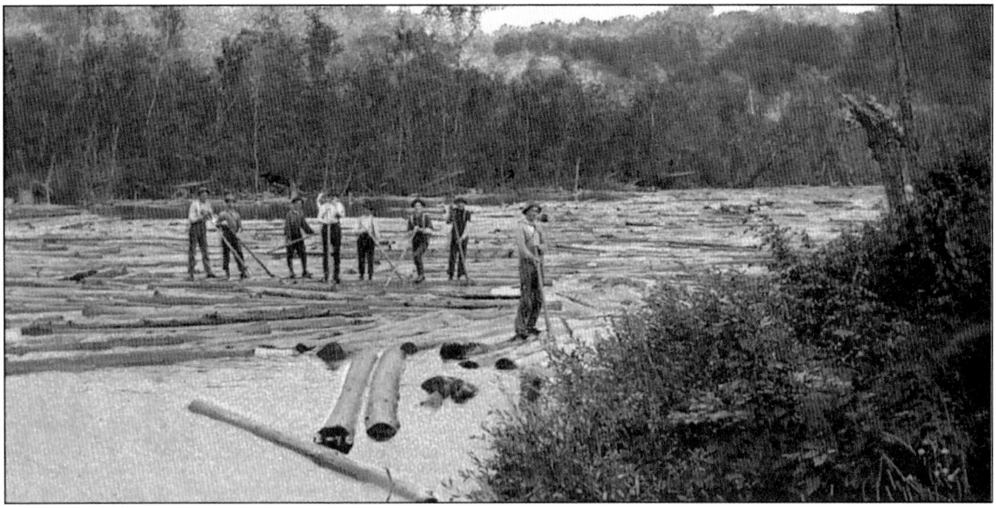

A good winter snowfall provided a spring runoff that would allow log drivers, such as these men, to steer the cut timber downstream to the sawmill. The task was not an easy one, breaking up log jams, building and tearing down dams, and essentially trying to control the flow of the river in an effort to get the logs to head in the right direction. Log drives, while prevalent in the spring, took place all year long. Horace Boardman built the first sawmill in Traverse City in 1847, although Perry Hannah, Tracy Lay, and James Morgan purchased the Boardman Mill in 1851.

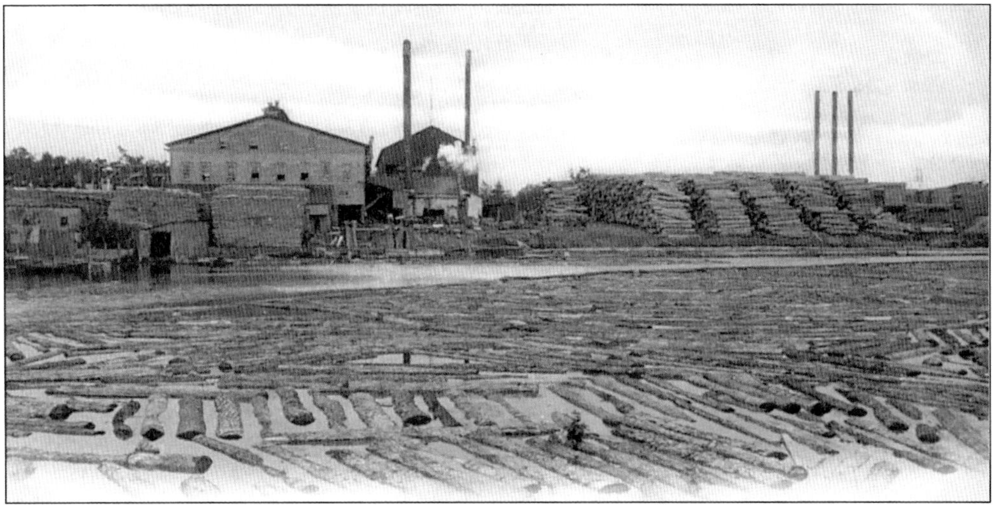

In 1847, Horace Boardman built the first a saw mill in Traverse City on what is now known as Kid's Creek, and in 1851, Perry Hannah, Tracy Lay, and James Morgan purchased the Boardman Mill along with an additional 200 hundred acres of land. Over the next 35 years, over 400 million board feet of timber, primarily white pine, was harvested from the local forests. The lumber business peaked in 1893, a year when approximately 250 million board feet of timber was cut down. The railroads and the invention of logging wheels, as well as the introduction of mechanized steam saws, not only increased the efficiency of lumber operations, but also sealed their fate. By the turn of the century, much of the land had been clear-cut, leaving it virtually useless. The lumber business declined dramatically in 1915, and the days of the lumber barons were all but over.

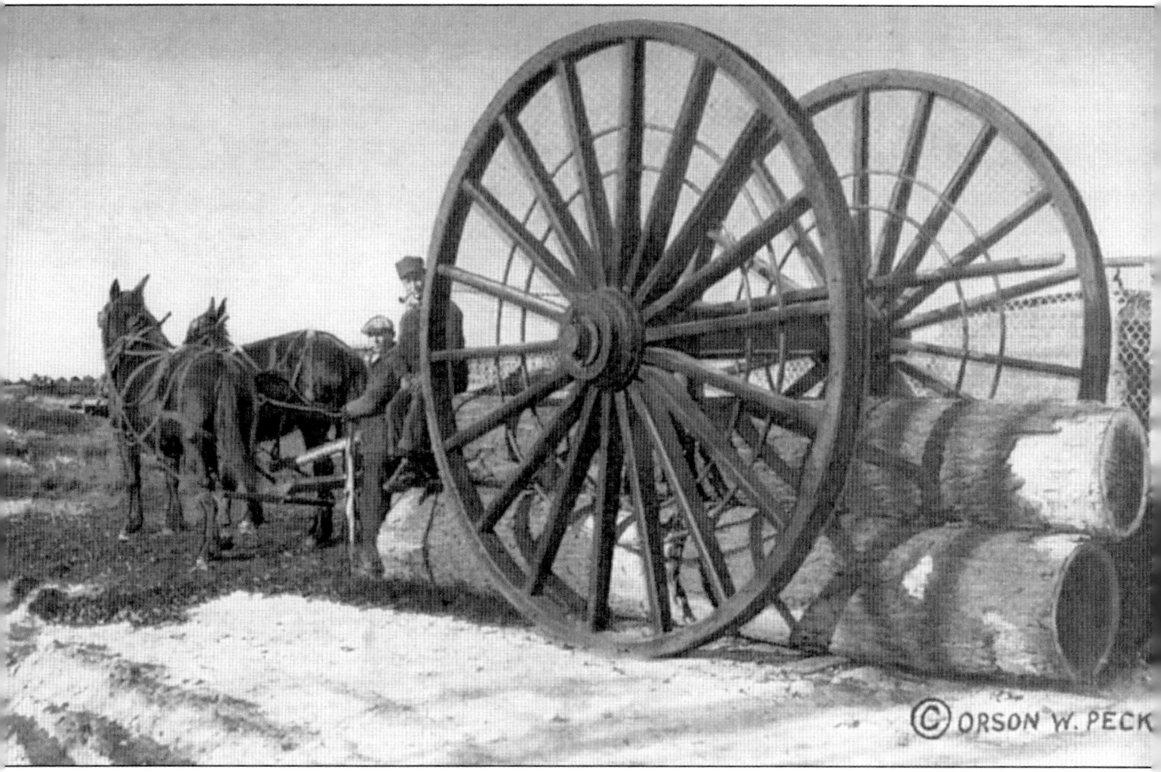

Logging in Michigan was a seasonal business in its early years, primarily due to the rugged terrain. Winter was the season for logging, making it easier to slide timber down across the frozen ground to the riverbank. Then, in spring, they would slide the massive timbers into the river and begin the log drive to the sawmill. That was until 1893, when Silas C. Overpack of Manistee exhibited his "big wheels" at the Columbian Exposition in Chicago. The logging wheels, as they came to be known, changed the face of the lumber industry in Traverse City and around the world. It was no longer necessary to rely on ice and snow to transport logs, now the horse-driven logging wheels—capable of carrying 12- to 100-foot timbers, up to 2,000 board feet of logs in a single load—made lumbering a year round business.

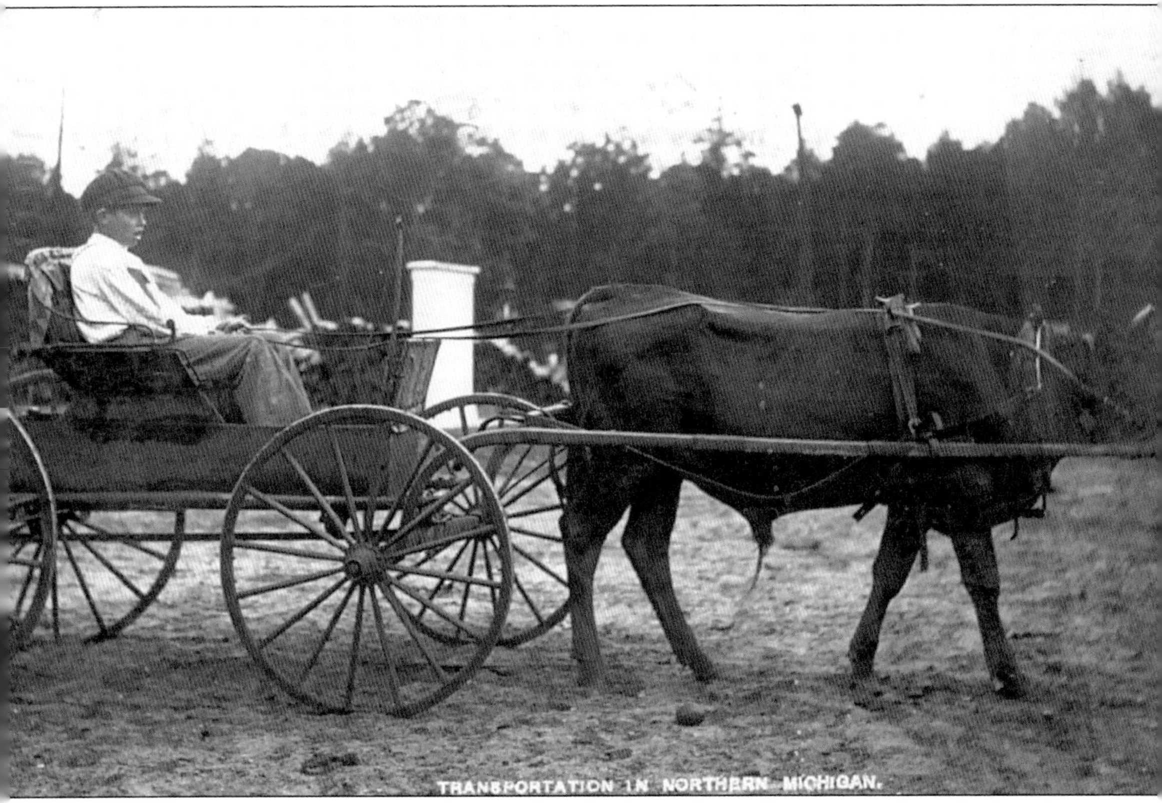

Transportation in Traverse City has significantly changed over the years. In the early days, it was common to see a family riding into town in a buggy or carriage—although a bull pulling one of these is quite unusual, even at the turn of the century. Despite the fact that mass production of the automobile came in the early 1900s, most people in the Traverse City area could not afford to purchase one. Horse-drawn wagons were a common sight in the Grand Traverse region into the 1920s.

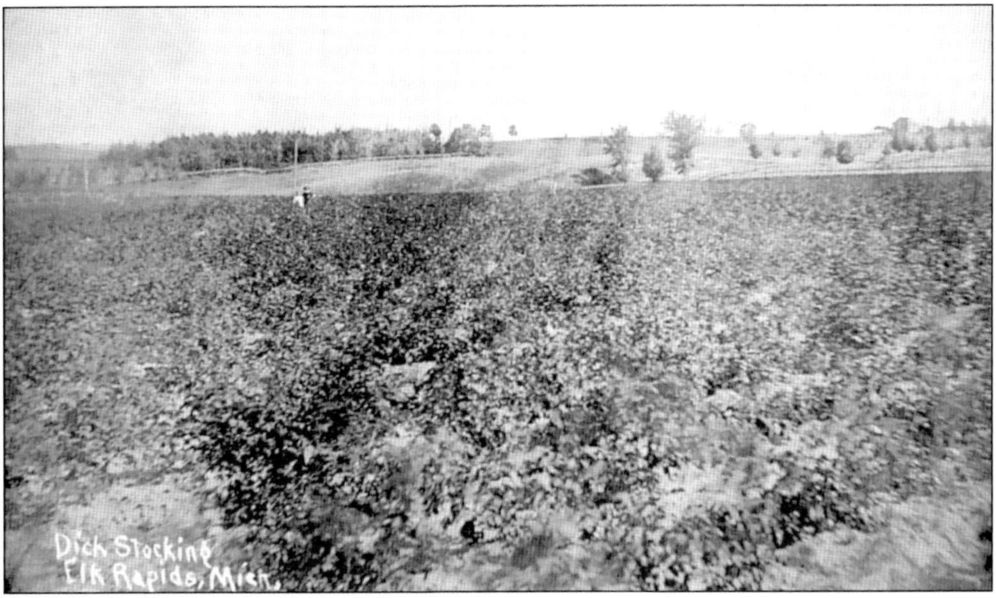

In an effort to find a crop that would grow in the short season of the Grand Traverse region, some farmers turned to potatoes. While potatoes grew, they did not flourish in amounts sufficient enough to be considered as a cash crop. Like peaches, plums, and apples, the market and weather conditions were not conducive to their growth. Despite the fact that the cherry became Traverse City's crop of choice, the potato is Michigan's leading produce commodity.

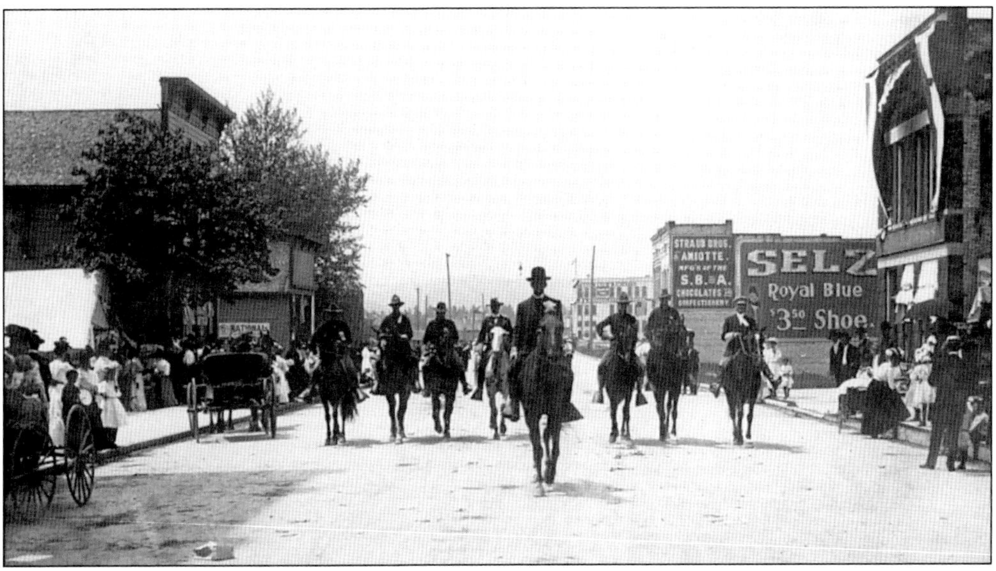

This sheriff's turn-of-the-century posse may be looking to crack down on lawbreakers, or they could be merely parading down Front Street. While Traverse City was never the Wild West, there was a need for law and order. In 1881, the same year that the town was incorporated as a village, a law was enacted forbidding cows to roam free in the streets. The town's population boomed from only 300 people in 1862 to over 4,000 in 1885. Soon afterward, in 1889, a speed limit was set for horses: 8 miles per hour on Front Street and 12 miles per hour on Union Street.

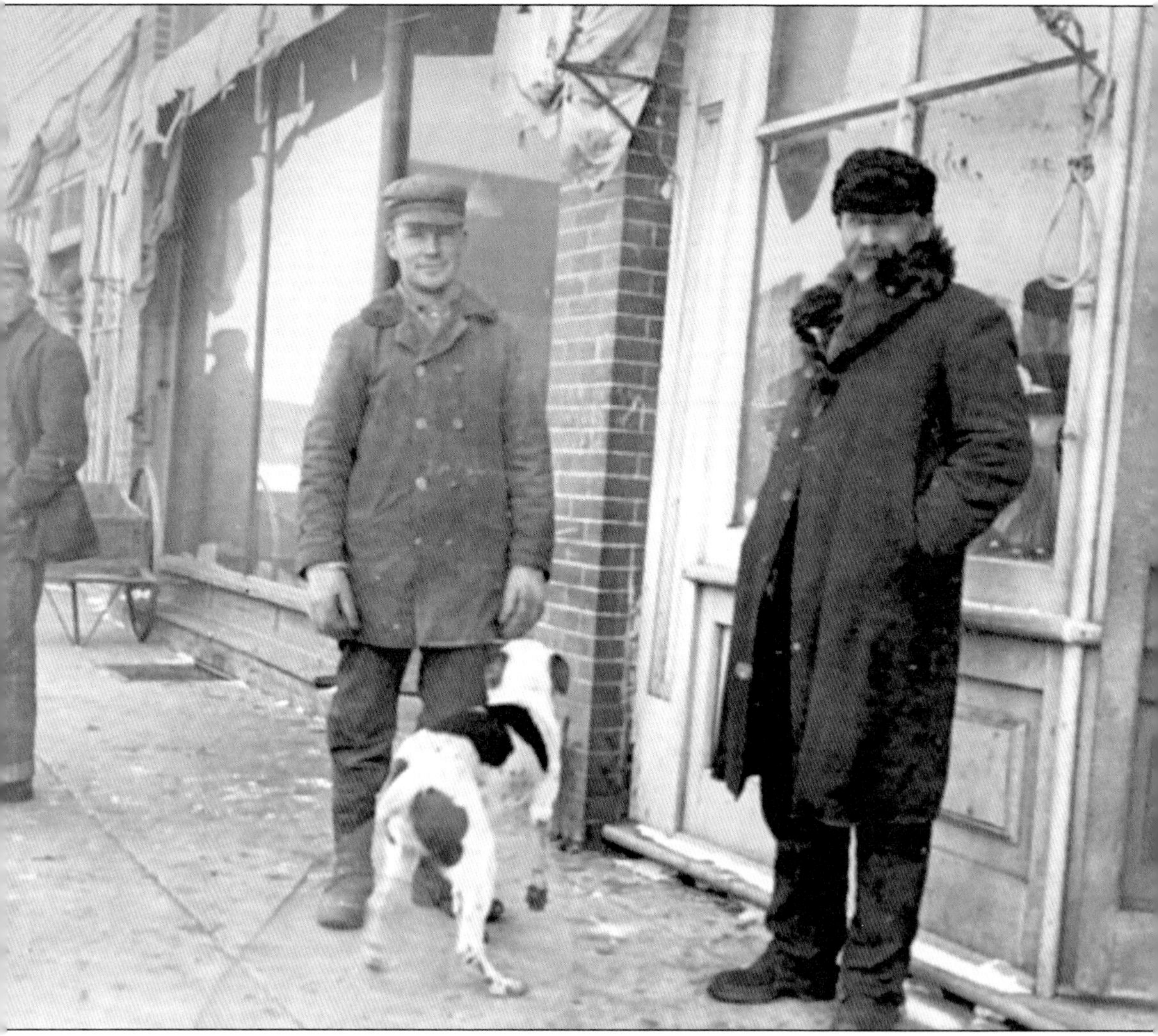

For most people, life was difficult in turn-of-the-century Traverse City, although every now and then there were opportunities to relax and enjoy the day. Leisure time was at a premium, and for those fortunate enough to have steady employment, the days were long and the work was hard. The largest employers in the area were the Oval Wood Dish Factory and the Hannah & Lay Lumber Mill. Outside of these two firms there were relatively few good jobs available in Traverse City. Over the next two decades, Traverse City's economic base would change dramatically, from relying primarily on lumber and its byproducts, to an agricultural and resort town.

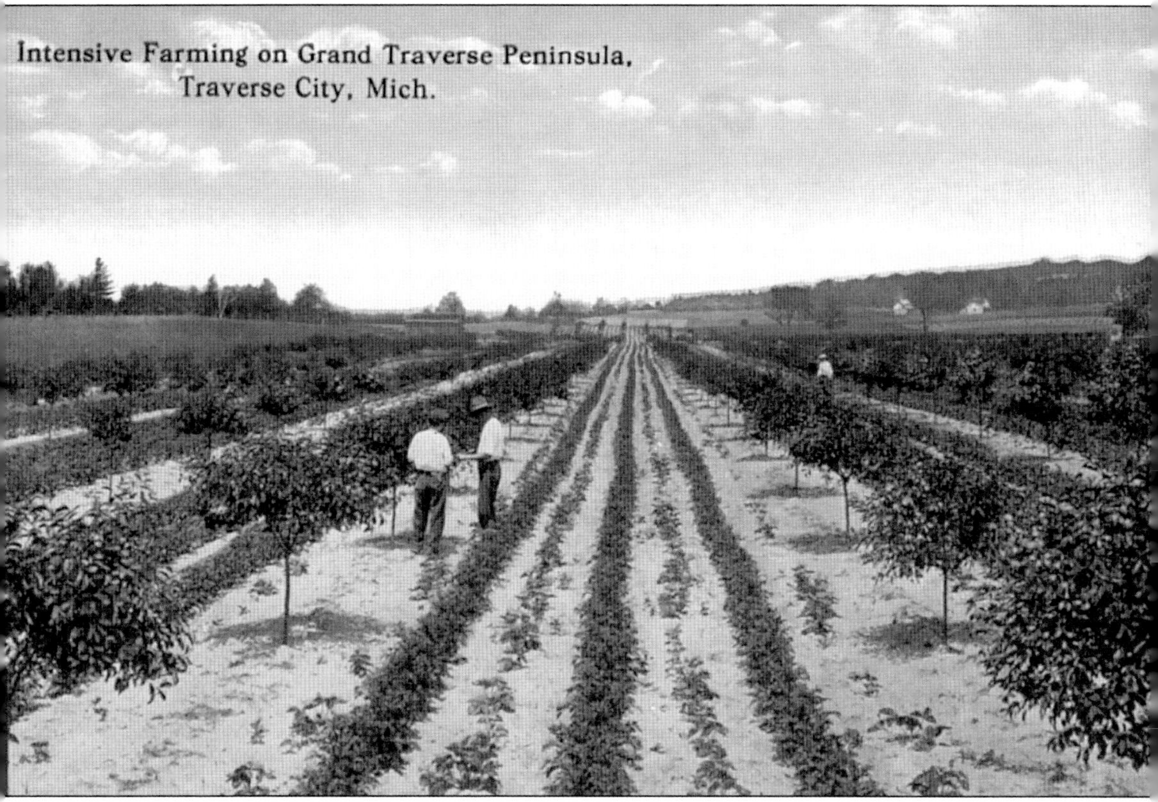

Intensive farming on the Old Mission Peninsula was initially—and still remains—integral to success. Every successful orchard is a blend of saplings, which need to be nurtured and cared for, as well as more mature trees. Planting young trees, pruning, and spraying for insects and disease are all necessary in order to maintain a healthy orchard. Dedication and hard work help to ensure that there will be a successful crop year after year, but then again there is no way to plan for the elements. Wind, rain, frost, and drought are only a few of the natural disasters, only one of which need happen to alter the outcome of an entire harvest.

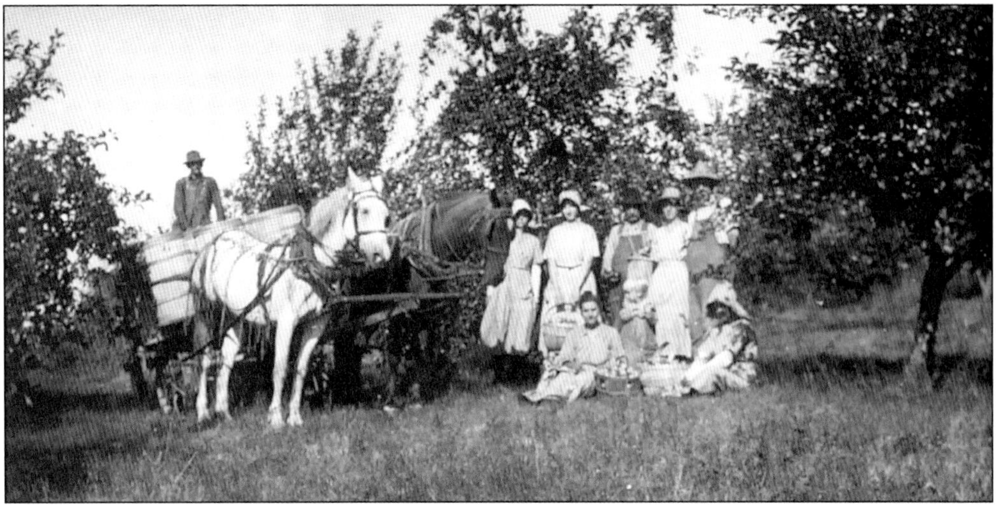

Almost gone are the days when families, native or migrant, worked in the orchards, hand picking cherries from the trees. Yet, many locals can recall the days when scenes such as this one were not all that uncommon. While families have always worked together in the orchards, there was a time when teachers spent summers picking cherries in order to supplement their incomes. Later on, families of migrant workers, moving from town to town harvesting various crops, made the Traverse City area one of their regular stops. As might be expected, that is not all that has changed; the horse and the wagon have also been replaced in favor of automation.

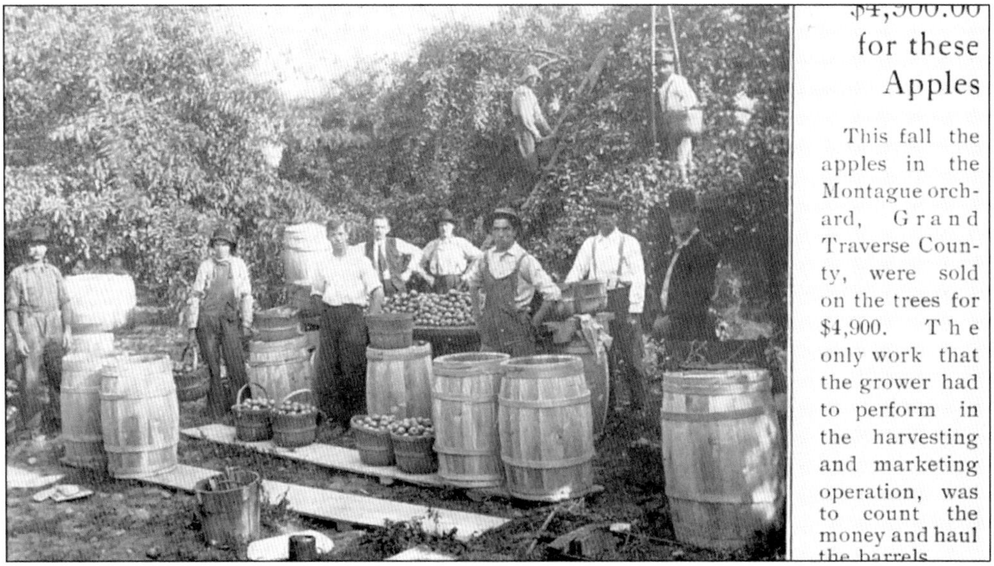

Montague Orchards, like many of the other family farms on the Old Mission Peninsula, grows not only cherries, but apples as well. In fact, prior to cherries becoming the agricultural mainstay in the Grand Traverse region, apples, peaches, and numerous other crops were grown, all with varying degrees of success. According to this advertising card published by the Traverse City Board of Trade, the Montague's apple crop was sold on the trees for $4,900. As far as the harvesting and marketing was concerned, the only thing that the grower had to do was to count out the money and haul away the barrels.

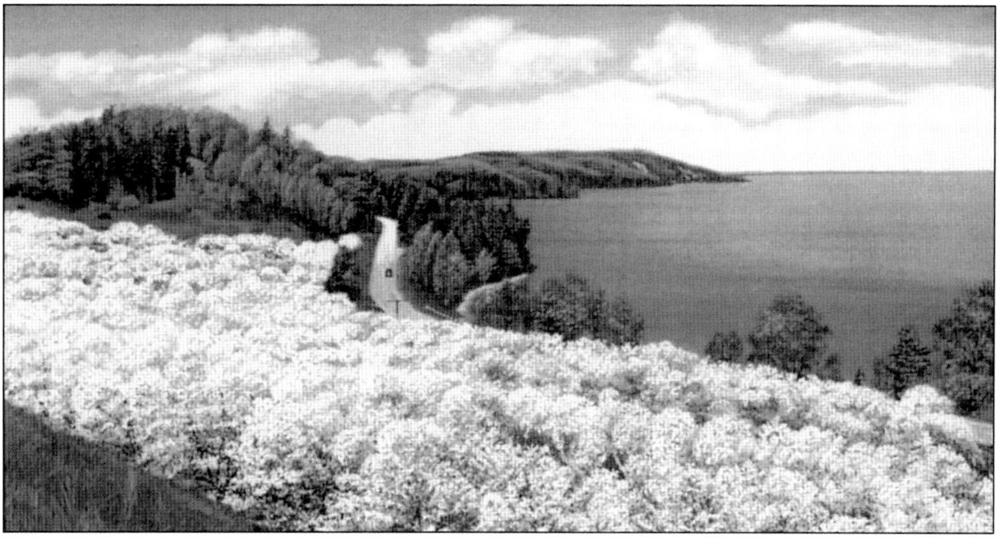

A sweeping view of cherry trees in full blossom, the Old Mission Peninsula, the Bluffs, and the East Arm of Grand Traverse Bay in the background, its sheer natural beauty provides proof to those individuals who claim this to be "God's Country." Few sights can even begin to compare with the natural beauty found in Northern Michigan, where locals and tourists alike concur that there is nothing more beautiful than the Old Mission Peninsula when the cherry trees are in full blossom. It is here, on the Old Mission Peninsula, that the Blessing of the Blossoms takes place each May prior to the National Cherry Festival.

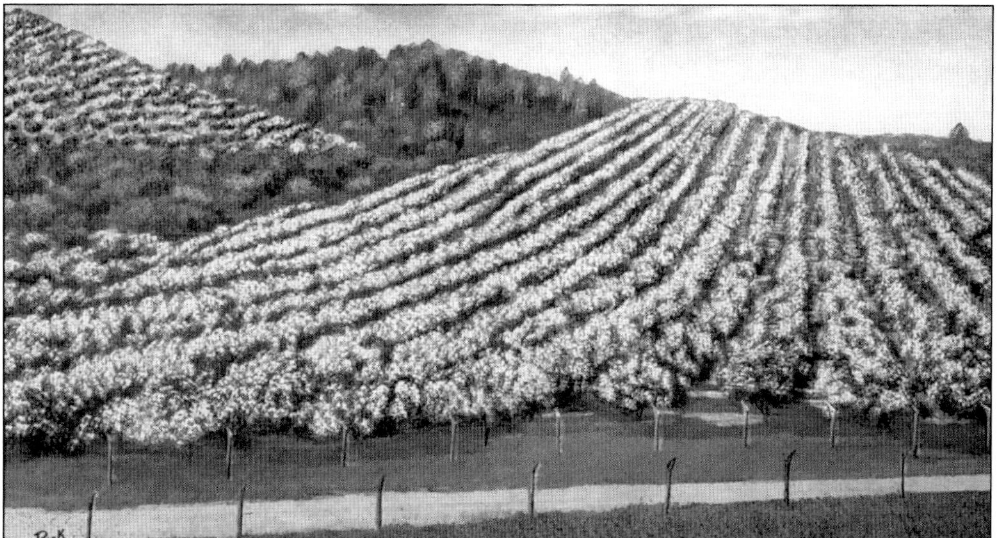

Cherry trees in full blossom portend a sign of things to come on the Old Mission Peninsula. Breathtaking panoramic views such as this one fill the countryside throughout the Grand Traverse and Leelanau region during the spring months and are a harbinger of things to come. An orchard in full bloom in the spring will normally translate into trees laden with cherries during the summer, and most probably, a harvest worthy of the farmer's long hours and hard labor. The Morgan Orchard, pictured here, provides a glimpse of what most orchards look like when the trees are in full bloom.

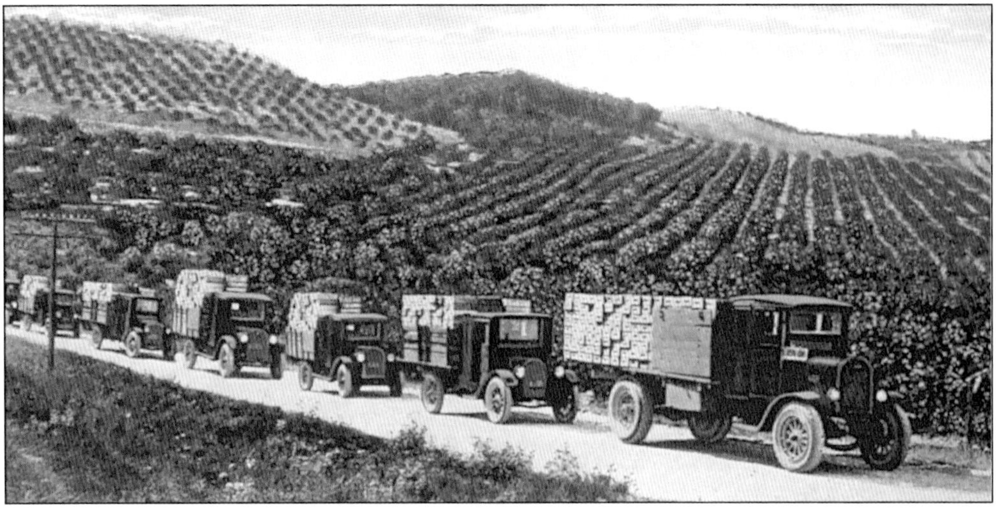

Morgan Orchards, as one of the largest cherry growers in the Grand Traverse area, was also one of the busiest. In the foreground is a caravan of Napoleon trucks loaded down with lugs of cherries and headed for the processing plant. The Morgan family was at one time the partial owner of their own cherry processing plant, located down in the area of the Open Space Project on West Bay. In the background are row upon row of cherry trees as far as the eye can see. The Napoleon Motor Car Company, which produced both cars and trucks, was located in Traverse City until its demise in the late 1920s.

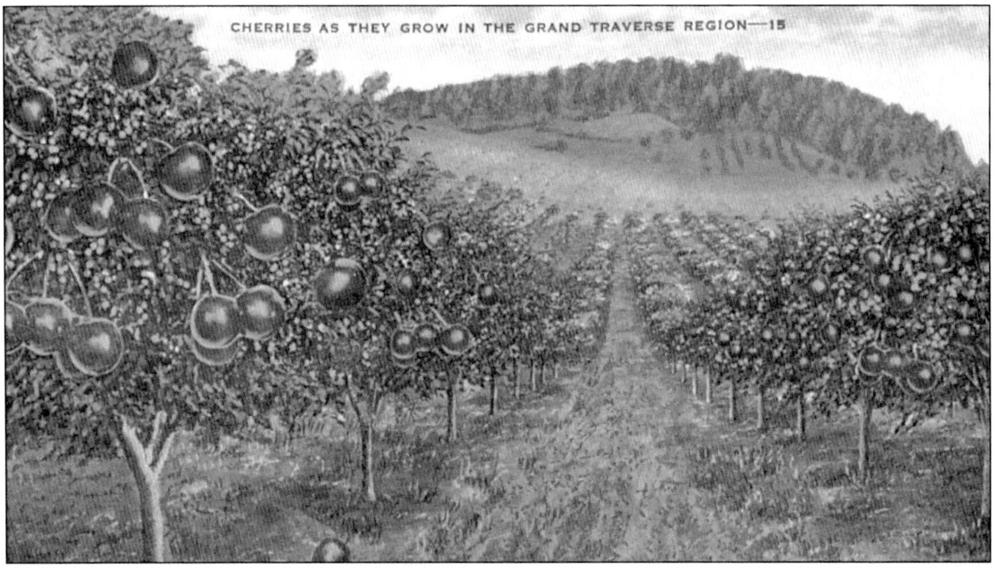

Row upon row of trees laden with cherries bring both a feeling of satisfaction and of consternation to every cherry grower. Virtually everyone in the Traverse City area is, in some way, affected by the outcome of the harvest. The farmer, hoping for a bumper crop, such as the one depicted here, must now hope that the weather will remain calm, that the spray which has been applied to the fruit will repel insects, and that he is able to harvest the fruit before it starts to turn bad. Other factors come into play as well, such as the fact that some varieties of cherries ripen before others, and it is essential that each variety be harvested as it ripens, enabling the grower to move on to the next one. Timing is of the essence, and for many, this is their livelihood.

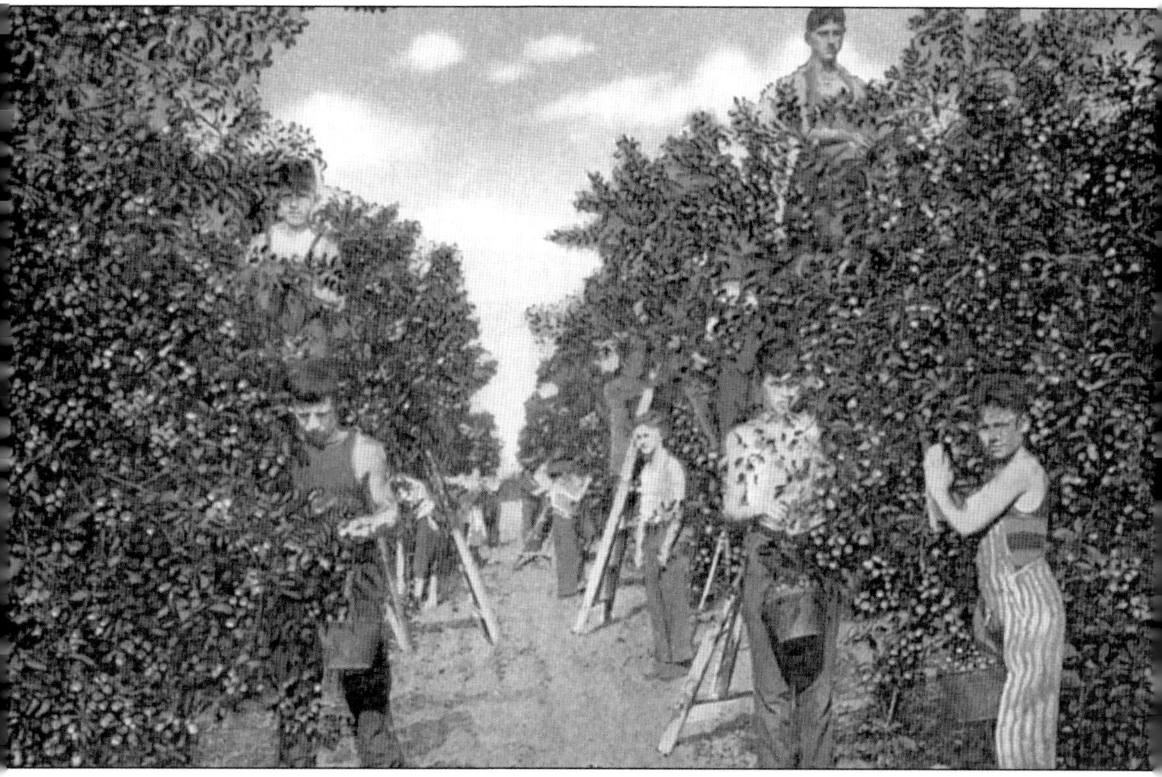

The cherry harvest, which has traditionally been a labor-intensive effort, has become more efficient in recent years with the introduction of the cherry shaker. These people, most of whom appear to be working diligently, are from a time long past when migrant workers traveled from crop to crop, not only in Michigan, but also throughout the United States. They hand-picked cherries, allowing them to drop into buckets that were hung about the neck, and then dumped the contents of a full bucket into a lug—a rectangular wooden box usually supplied by the fruit exchange. As the trees were picked, the lugs were stacked to the side of the rows, allowing for the farmer to drive the tractor down the rows, cross-stacking the lugs on the tractor trailer. These would then be stacked onto a truck bed, and when it was full, shipped off to the fruit exchange.

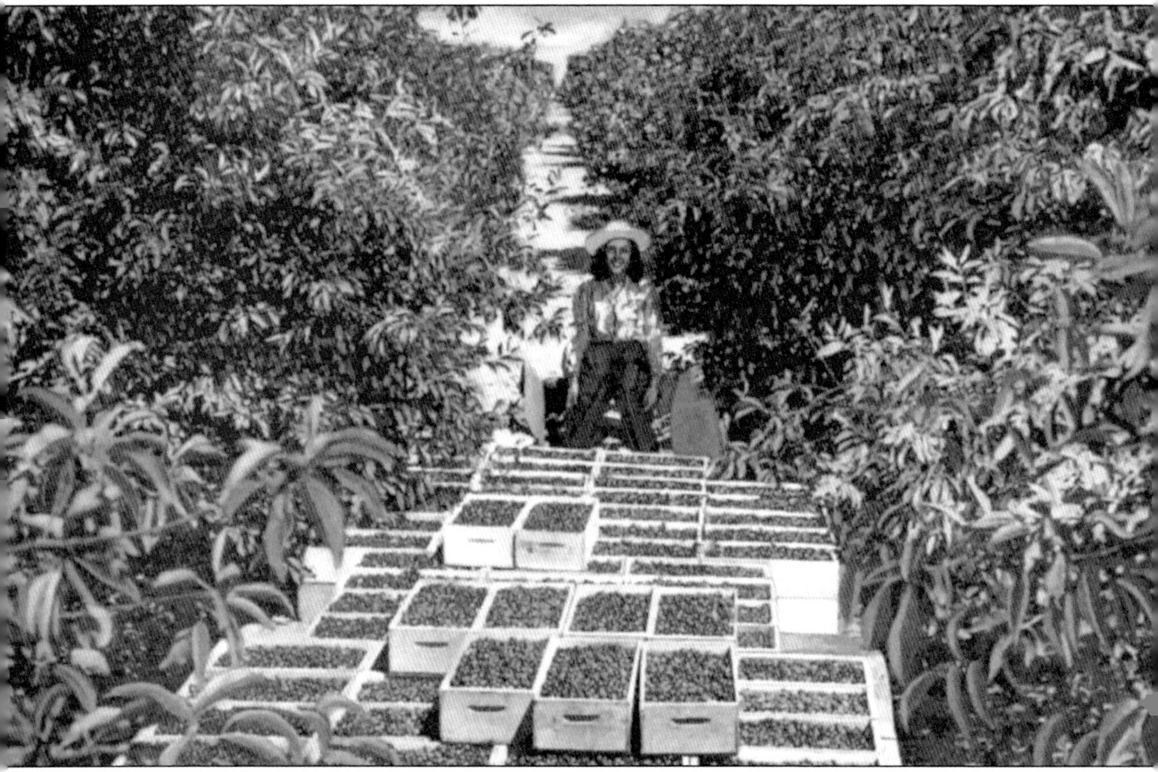

One of the many cherry orchards on the Old Mission Peninsula serves as the backdrop for this young lady, as she proudly displays lugs brimming with freshly picked sour cherries. Hand picking cherries and placing them in lugs is, for the most part, a thing of the past. Advances in agricultural technology have replaced the cherry picker and the lugs with a mechanical cherry shaker, which is pulled behind a tractor, and actually shakes the fruit off of the tree and onto tarps, which when rolled up place the cherries on a conveyor belt. The cherries move along the belt until they are dropped into a crate, where they are stored until taken to the fruit exchange.

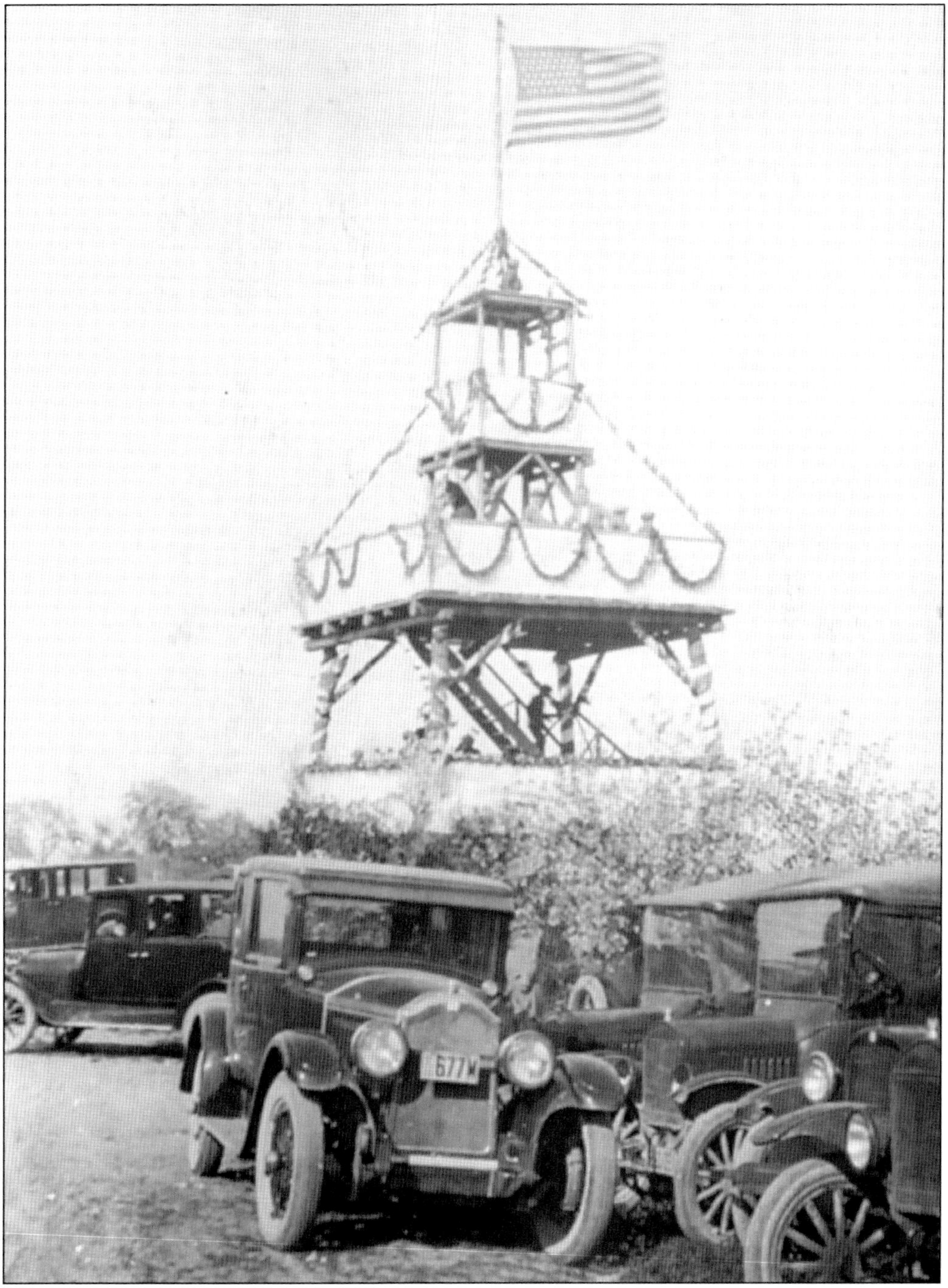

Traverse City is known as the Cherry Capital of the World, although few people know that this festival started with a celebration called the "Blessing of the Blossoms." The first of these celebrations took place in 1924 at Frederick's Tower, a structure that rose out of the orchards, making it one of the highest points on the Old Mission Peninsula. The first "Blessing of the Blossoms" attracted approximately 3,000 people, less than one percent of the visitors in attendance at today's National Cherry Festival.

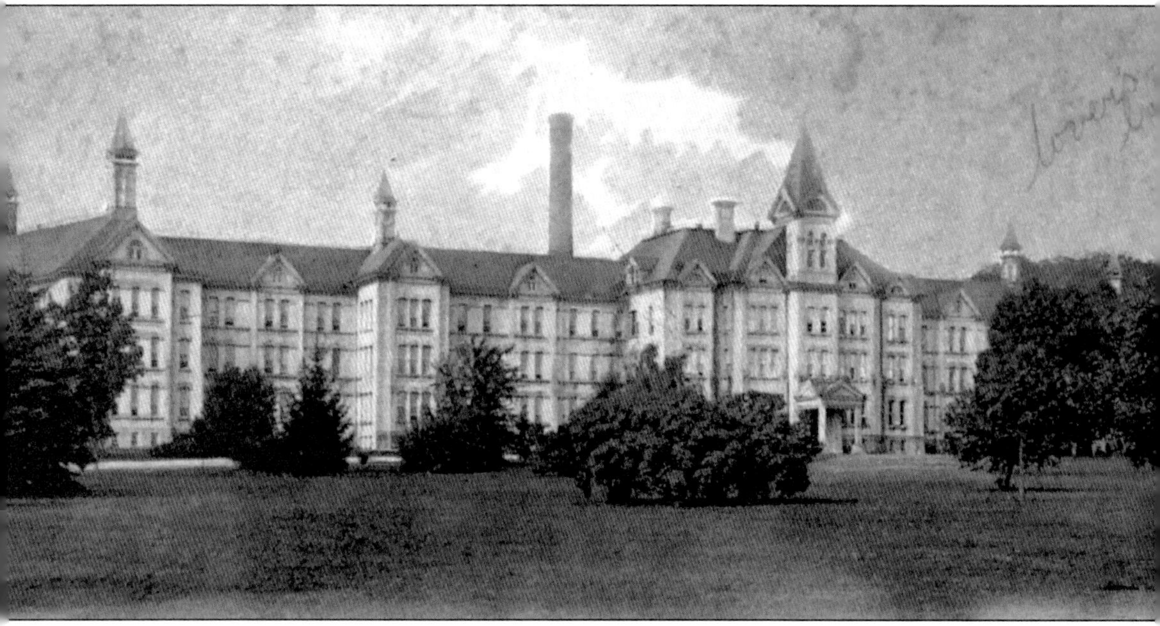

In 1881, Perry Hannah lobbied for and succeeded in bringing the Northern Michigan Asylum to Traverse City. Opening its doors in 1885, the asylum, also known as Willow Lake State Hospital, Northern Michigan State Hospital, Traverse City State Hospital, and Traverse City Regional Psychiatric Hospital, was initially placed under the direction of Dr. James Decker Munson. Located to the west of Elmwood Street, between Seventh Street to the north and Silver Lake Road to the south, are the sprawling grounds of the state hospital, which once housed up to several thousand patients. Michigan's mental health department oversaw operations and funding of the hospital until 1989, and in the 1990s it came under the control of local government agencies. Now called the Village at Grand Traverse Commons, many of the Victorian-Italianate buildings have been or are in the process of being refurbished for multi-purpose business and residential use.

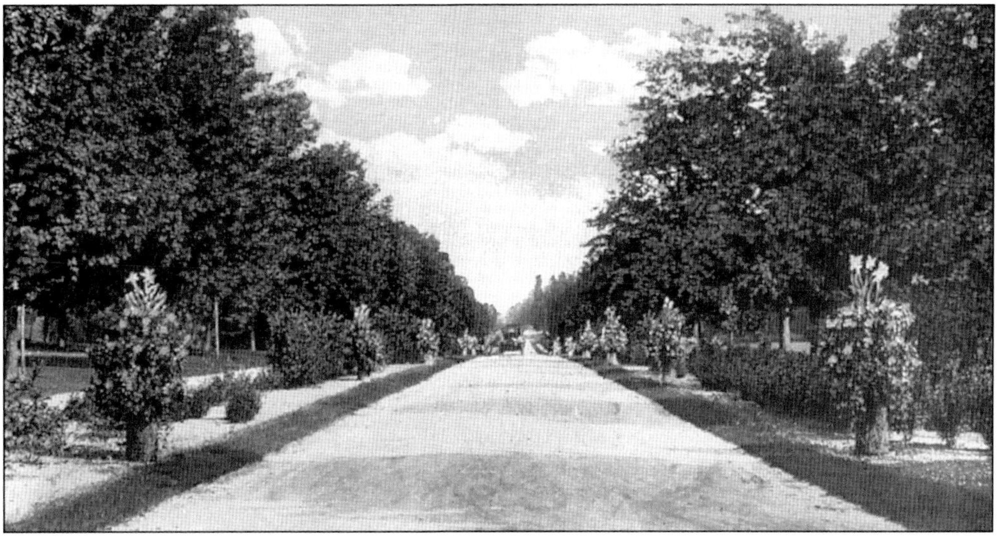

The Traverse City State Hospital features a myriad of avenues, streets, and boulevards that wind their way through the sprawling grounds of the institution. Landscaping efforts did not even start until 1901, a full 26 years after the hospital was built—although Dr. James Decker Munson, first superintendent of the hospital, ensured that it was done properly. Dr. Munson, a world traveler, brought a variety of exotic flora and fauna back with him from his journeys. Legend has it that he would walk the grounds with the manager of the farm, a handful of stones in his pocket and, when he found a site suitable for planting, mark it with one of the stones. As a result, the grounds of the old hospital feature a number of trees and plants found nowhere else in Northern Michigan.

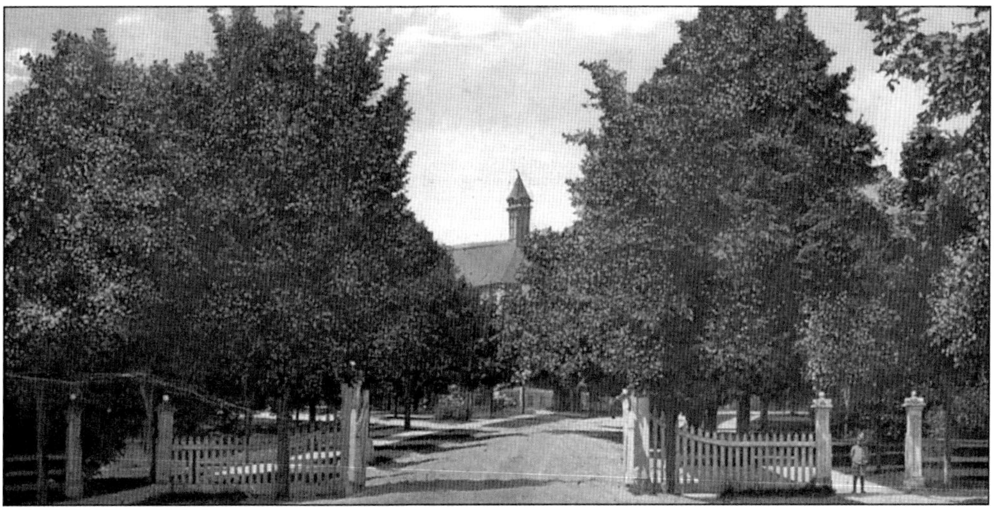

Gables loom high above the stone structures just inside the main gateway of the Traverse City State Hospital. The buildings were designed according to the Kirkbride Plan, a popular design for institutions during the latter part of the nineteenth century. While the hospital operated for over a century—from 1885 until 1989—changes in the treatment of the mentally ill, as well as a lack of federal and state funding, forced its closure. The buildings, through the actions of a number of concerned citizen groups, have gained a new lease on life and are currently being refurbished.

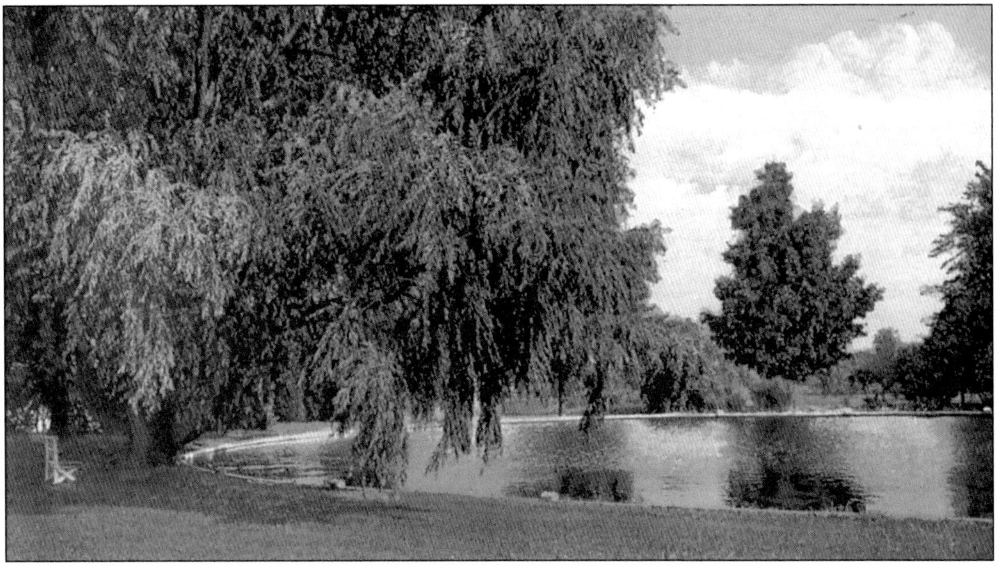

Willow Lake was located on the grounds of the Traverse City State Hospital—or as it was called in earlier times, the Northern Michigan State Hospital. To a great extent, Dr. James Decker Munson provided the landscape design for grounds of the hospital, including Willow Lake. Dr. Munson, somewhat of a pioneer, was an advocate of relaxation therapy and felt that pleasant surroundings would benefit the healing process. Its shores surrounded by weeping willows, as well as other more exotic trees that Dr. Munson had brought back from his travels, Willow Lake provided just such an atmosphere.

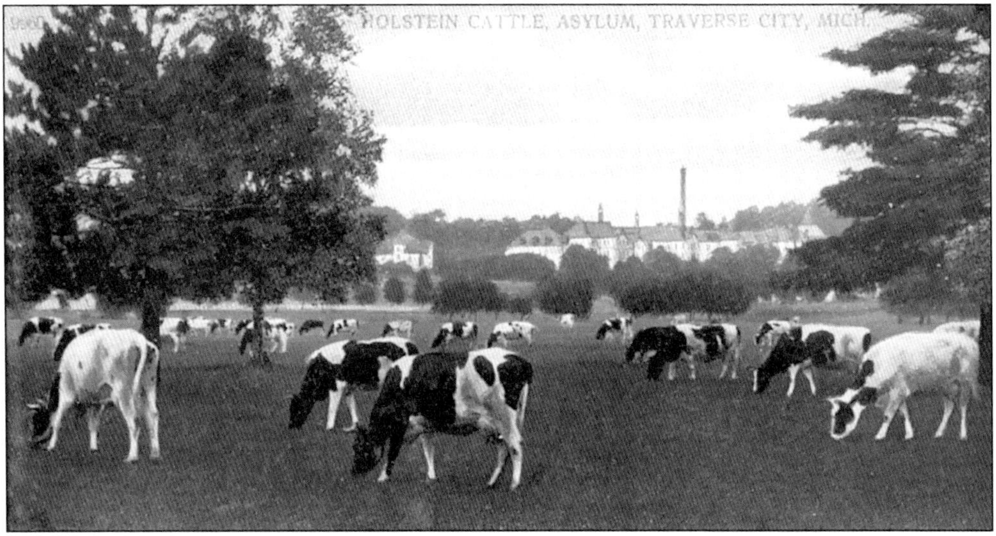

The Traverse City State Hospital, like many mental institutions, usually lacked sufficient funding. As a result, the farm buildings located just off of Silver Lake Road to the south not only provided food for the patients, but in many respects were also considered a part of their therapy. It was here that Traverse Colantha Walker was raised, a grand champion cow who produced 200,144 of pounds of milk and 7,525 pounds of butterfat in her lifetime. While there were other cattle, as well as chicken, horses, and pigs, Traverse Corantha Walker is the only one memorialized with a gravestone on the grounds of the former hospital.

Two

Downtown and the Clinch Park Zoo

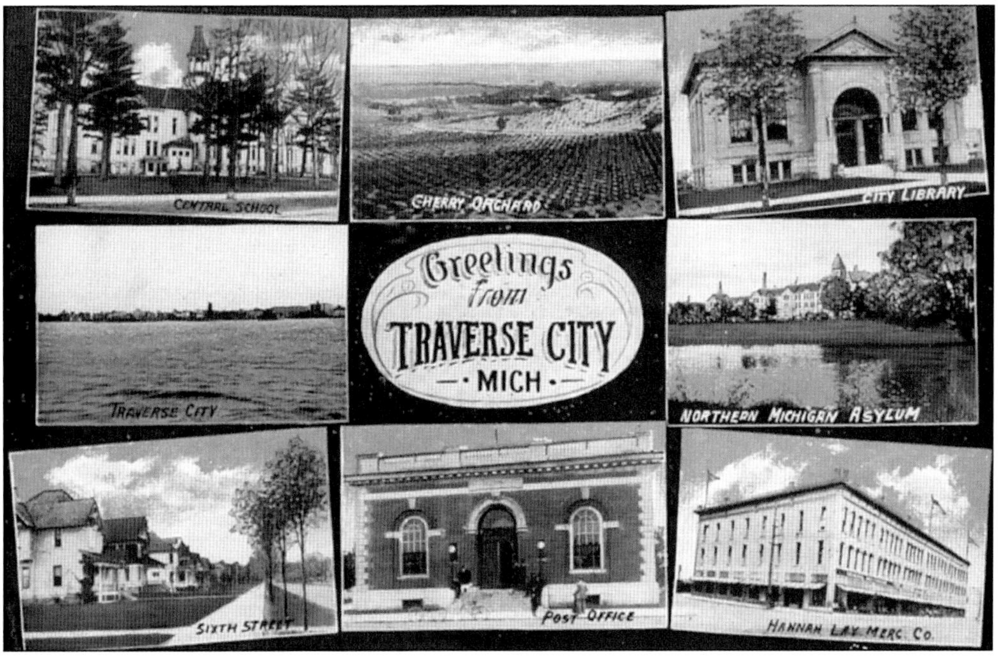

Greetings from an urbane, modern, yet quaint city. Starting at the top left hand corner is a picture of the old Traverse City Central High School on Seventh Street, and going clockwise to its right is a panoramic view of a cherry orchard. At the top right is the Traverse City Public Library and below it is the Northern Michigan Asylum with Willow Lake in the foreground. Hannah & Lay Mercantile Company, located on the northeast corner of Front and Union Streets, is at the lower right and the Traverse City Post Office is at the bottom center of the postcard. At the lower left is a picture of Sixth Street and, lastly, above that is a view of the town from Grand Traverse Bay.

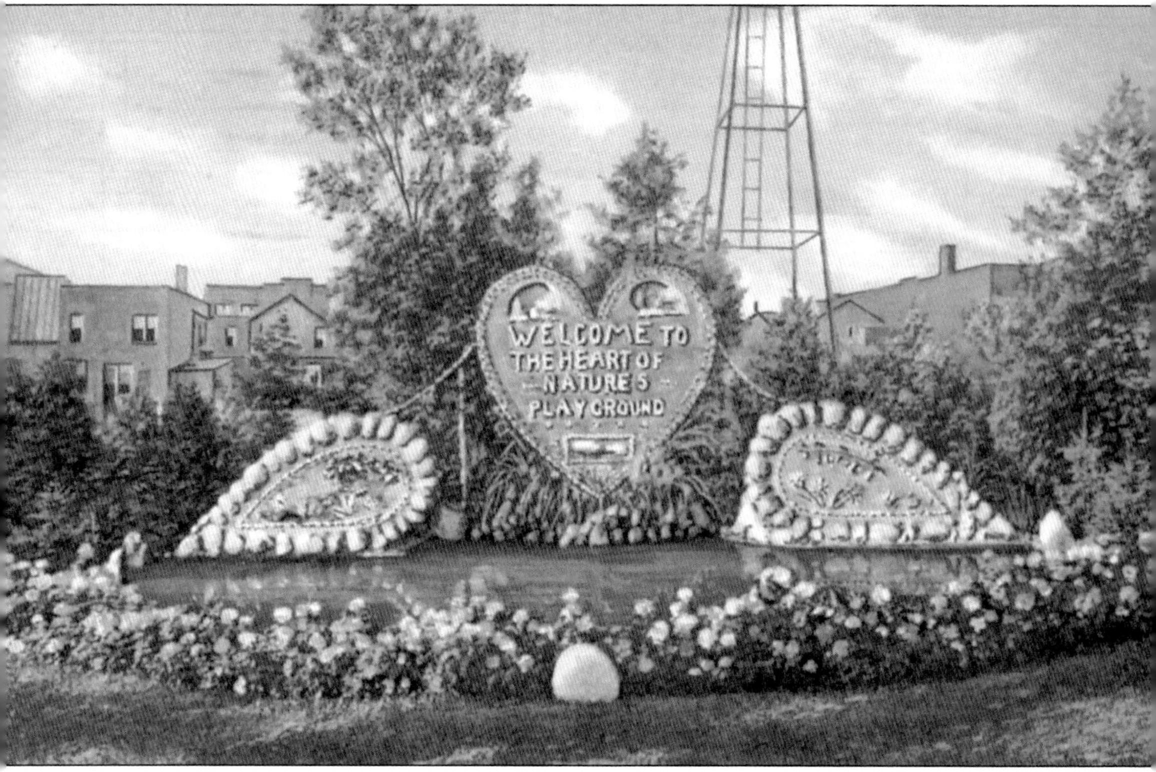

Traverse City has gone by many names since the European settlers first arrived here, although "Heart of Nature's Playground" probably best exemplifies the area. A floral landscape design from the 1940s, one exalting the virtues of the Grand Traverse region, signals to the world that this little town in Northern Michigan has found its way. By that time, the cherry industry was in full production, the summer resorts were packed with guests, and the National Cherry Festival had gained worldwide acclaim. It was only a matter of time before cross country and downhill skiing, as well as ice fishing, sledding, and snowmobiling would make the Grand Traverse region a year-round playground.

(*Opposite, bottom*) The original Grand Traverse County Courthouse was built in 1854, although the wooden structure was destroyed by fire in 1862. It was not until 1898 that the county accepted architectural plans and began building a new courthouse. Designed by Rush, Bowman & Rush, an architectural firm from Grand Rapids, the new courthouse was completed in 1900. Built on the same site as the first courthouse at the corner of Boardman Avenue and Washington Streets, the new building originally cost Grand Traverse County taxpayers slightly under $36,000. In 1981, the building was renovated at a cost of $1.7 million. While the old courthouse is still being utilized, the newer City-County Governmental Center, completed in 1979, is located just around the corner on Boardman Avenue and has allowed for the expansion of services.

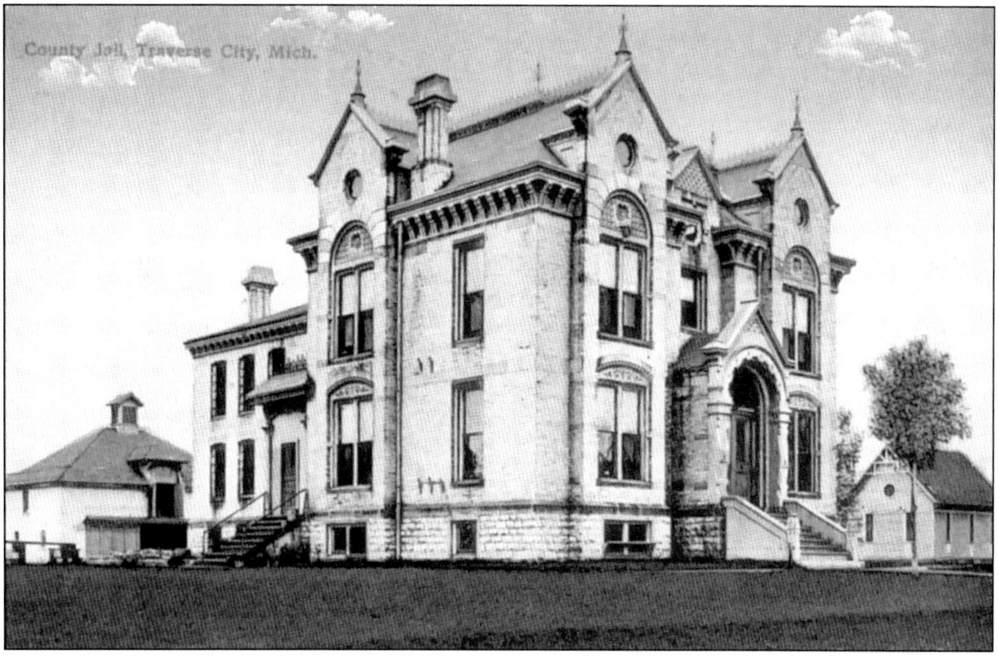

(*Above*) In 1882, the Grand Traverse County Board of Supervisors found it necessary to build not only a jail, but also a sheriff's residence as well. The brick building was completed in 1884, and all of the county offices were moved into the building. By 1898, it was determined that a courthouse be built on the same grounds as the Grand Traverse County Jail. Known as "Courthouse Square," the complex was finished in 1899. While the sheriff's office and county jail have been moved to newer quarters, they are still located on Washington Street.

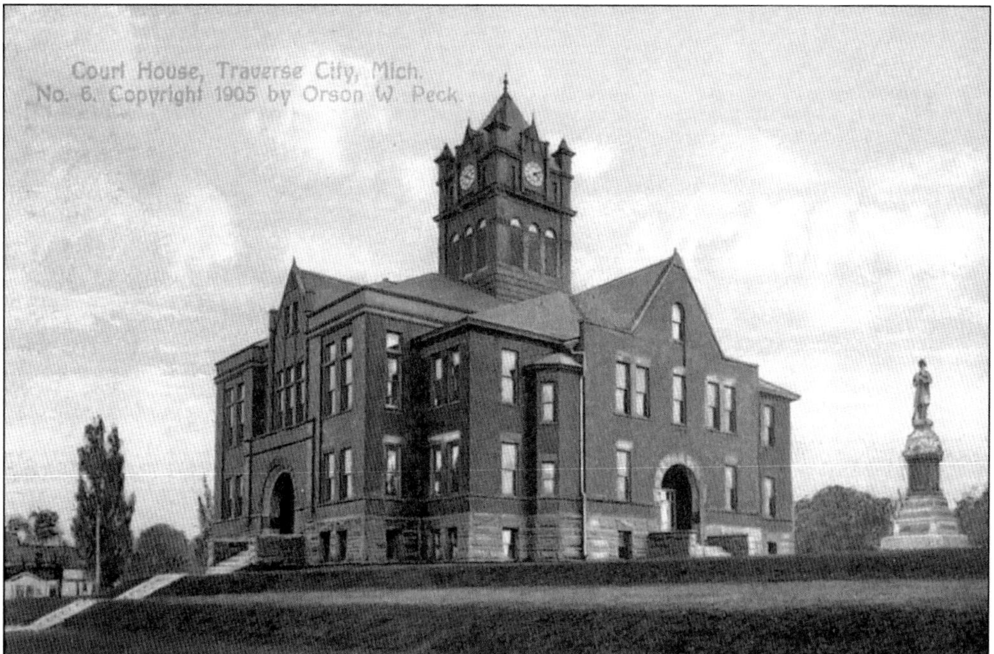

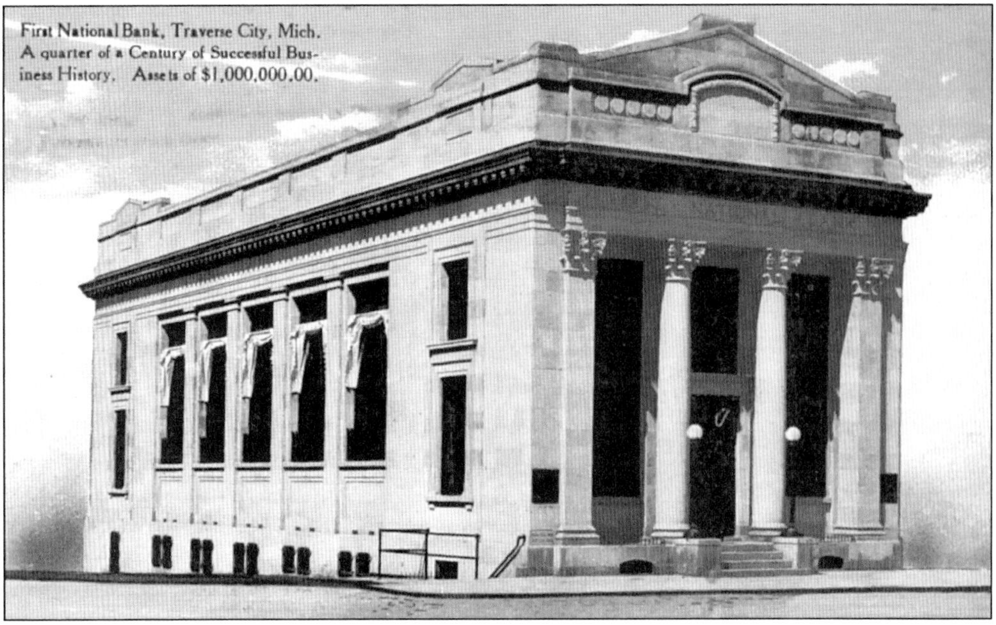

(*Above*) The First National Bank, once a prominent fixture on Front Street in downtown Traverse City, was built in 1908. During the early years of the twentieth century, the bank was a prosperous financial institution. In fact, after only a quarter of a century, First National Bank boasted assets of over $1,000,000, a substantial sum even by modern standards. Like so many other financial institutions of its day, First National Bank has become nothing more than a distant memory, although the number of financial institutions in the Traverse City area has grown considerably.

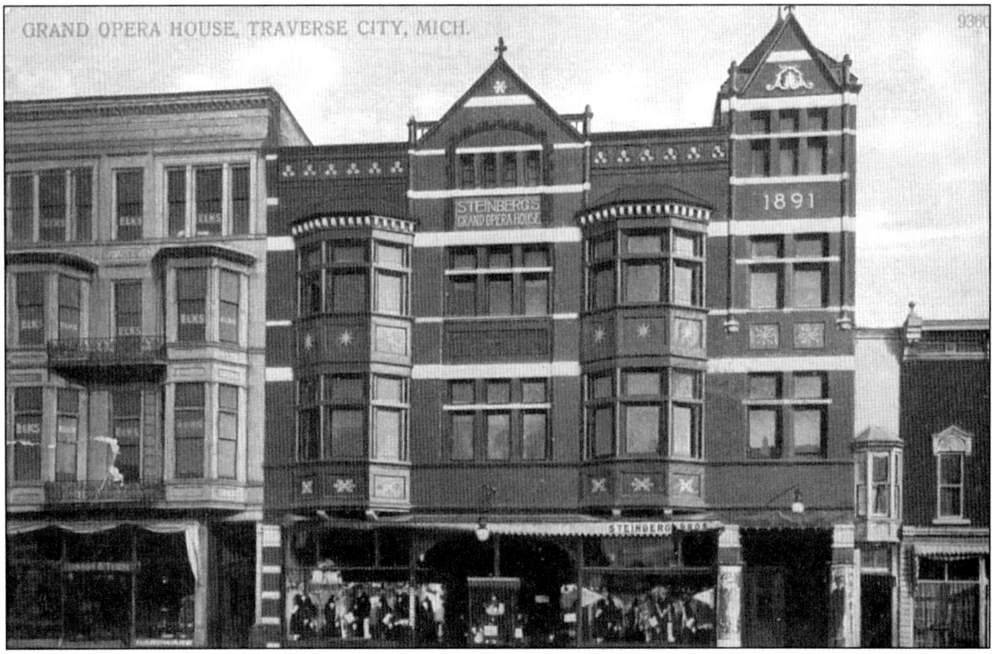

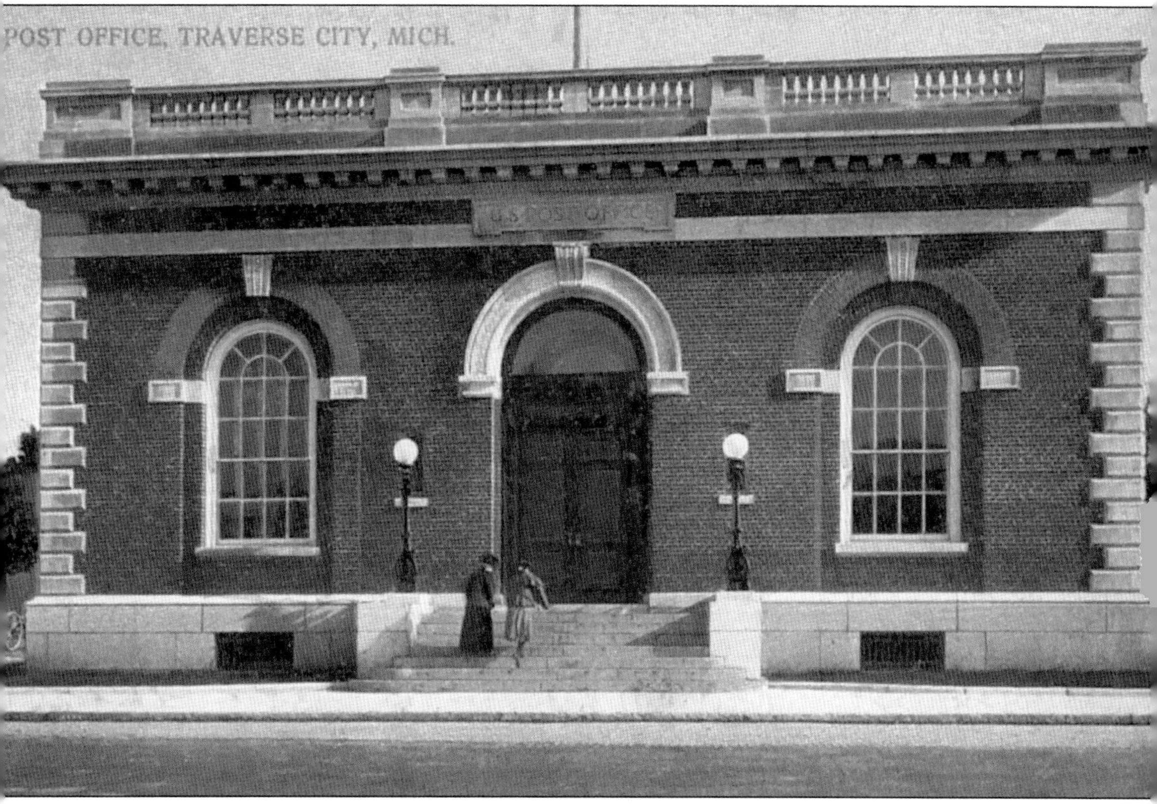

On February 7, 1854, Tracy Lay, a partner in the Hannah & Lay Lumber Mill, secured a post office for Traverse City. The first postmaster, Dr. David C. Goodale, processed incoming and outgoing mail from his home. It was not until 1904 that Traverse City built its first post office, on the corner of Cass and State Street. In the early days, mail straggled in by messenger, rail, and ship, and due to the distance involved, rural areas such as Old Mission had their own post office. The first postmaster at Old Mission, W.R. Stone was appointed in 1851 and supposedly kept the mail in a raisin box nailed to the wall of the log house where he lived with his family.

(*Opposite, bottom*) In an attempt to bring a bit more culture to Traverse City, Julius Steinberg, a local retailer, built Steinberg's Opera House in 1894. The opera house, located almost directly across the street from Hannah & Lay Mercantile, hosted Gilbert and Sullivan's *Mikado* the same year. Over the years, Steinberg, an amateur actor himself, brought a number of other acts to Traverse City, including the world's leading hypnotist, Professor Boone, and the infamous Dr. Jekyll and Mr. Hyde. The size of the eighth grade class in 1899—all of 94 students—required that they use the opera house for graduation exercises. In addition, cartoons, comedies, and movie reels were shown at Steinberg's Opera House, most of which were accompanied by music. Currently, the opera house is undergoing restoration.

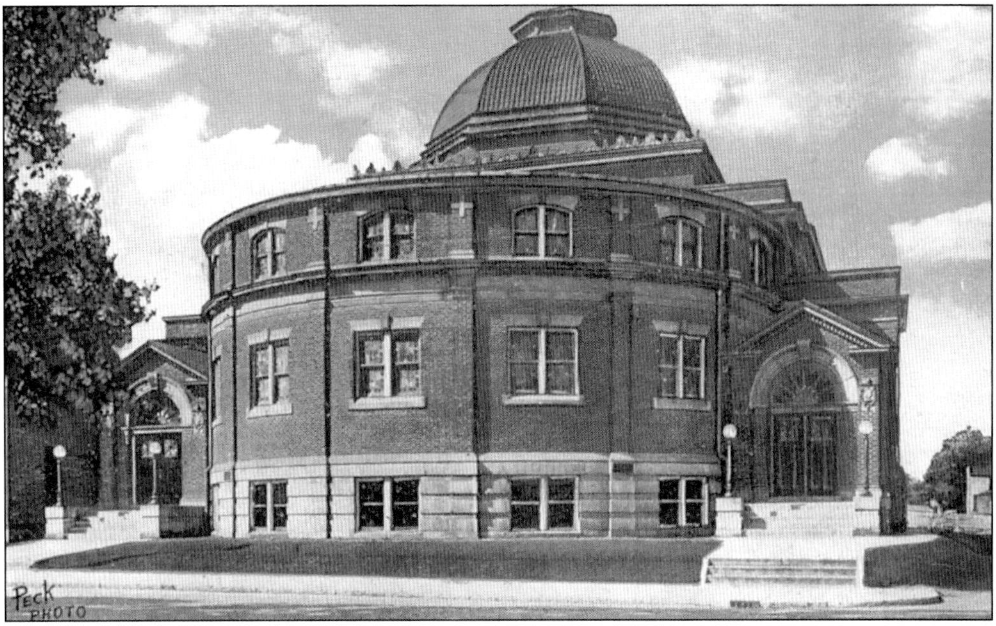

(*Above*) At the point where Washington Street dead-ends into Cass Street is an architectural feast for the eyes: the Central Methodist Church. The church is a two-storied, domed brick structure, and its cornerstone was laid in 1912. Since then, this house of worship has been a source of activity and strength for Traverse City residents and has provided numerous programs for parishioners. Today, as in the past, the congregation remains active in the community by providing both senior- and youth-oriented activities. In the summer, the church holds services at various parks throughout the city.

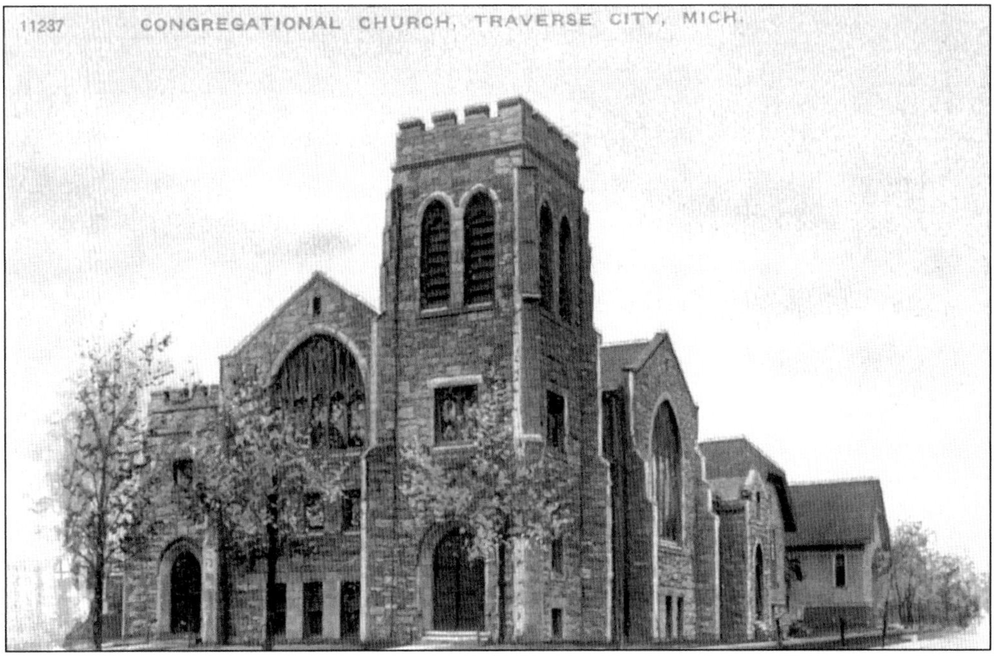

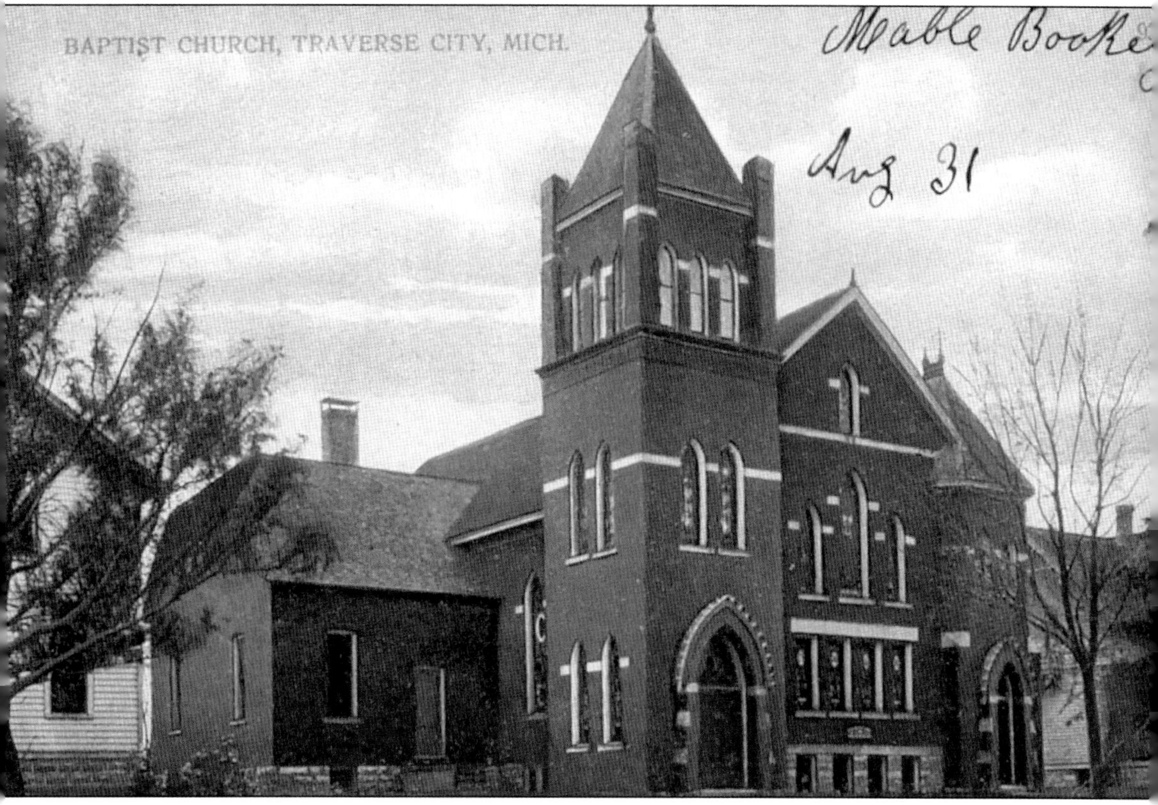

The First Baptist Church was built in downtown Traverse City in 1874 for a cost of slightly over $3,000. In the early days, members of the church were baptized in the Boardman River. The neighborhoods, schools, and churches were all a part of Perry Hannah's plan to create a model city for the future. To a great degree it worked, the schools and churches, such as the First Baptist Church, flourish to this day.

(*Opposite, bottom*)The former Congregational Church, located on Washington Street just to the west of the courthouse in downtown Traverse City, was purchased in 1959 by the congregation of the Bethany Baptist Church. A magnificent stone structure from around the turn of the century, the interior of the church was in dire need of restoration. Following the purchase of the building, the independent congregation restored the church, including the wooden chapel, to its original condition. The Bethany Baptist Church, which remains active in the community, holds services at the church every Sunday morning.

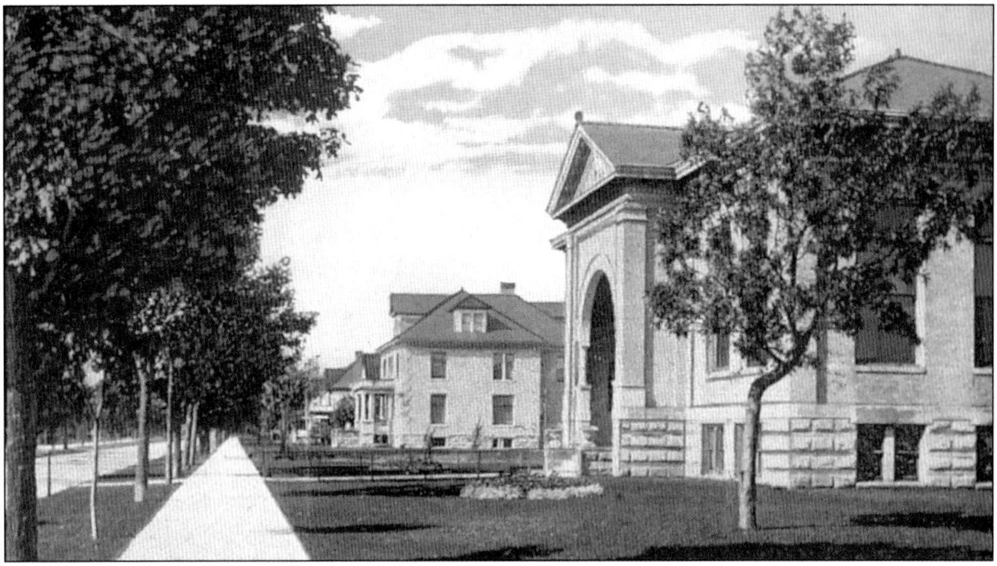

Looking down Sixth Street, the Carnegie Library and a number of homes dot the landscape of a carefully manicured historical district. While Perry Hannah seems to have had an influence on virtually everything in Traverse City's earlier days, nowhere is this truer than on Sixth Street. This was the cornerstone of what he envisioned as downtown Traverse City, a place where he could build his retirement home. The Carnegie Library, dedicated in 1905, was one of the jewels of Traverse City. Now, the former library serves as home to the Grand Traverse Heritage Center.

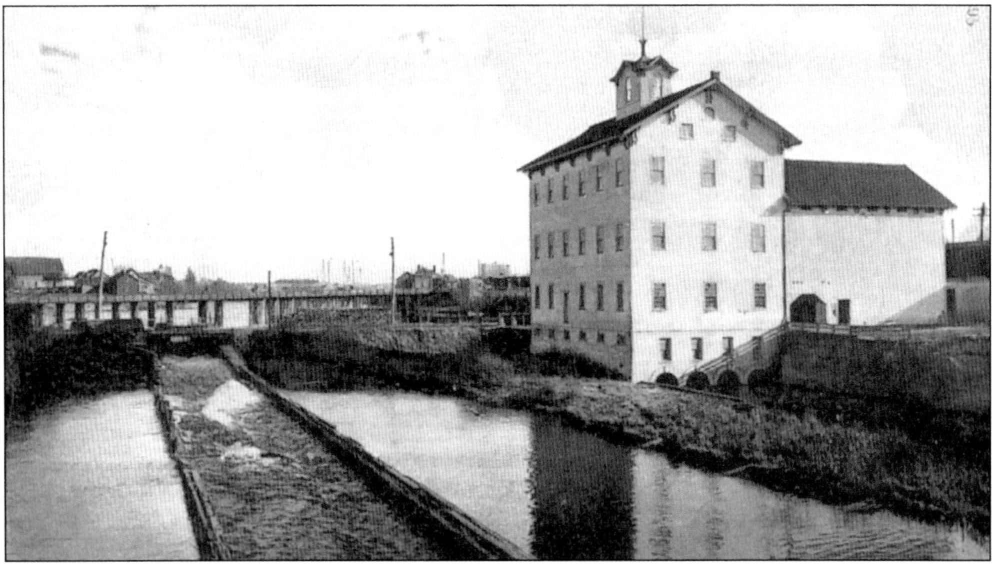

The old Grist Mill in Traverse City was one of the many enterprises in which founding fathers Perry Hannah and Tracy Lay were active participants. The mill was centrally located on the Boardman River in downtown Traverse City, so as to make it easier to send and receive shipments of goods by rail, as well as to utilize the existing water power as a source of energy. The mill, which sold its goods primarily at Hannah & Lay Mercantile, ground grains that were grown by local farmers.

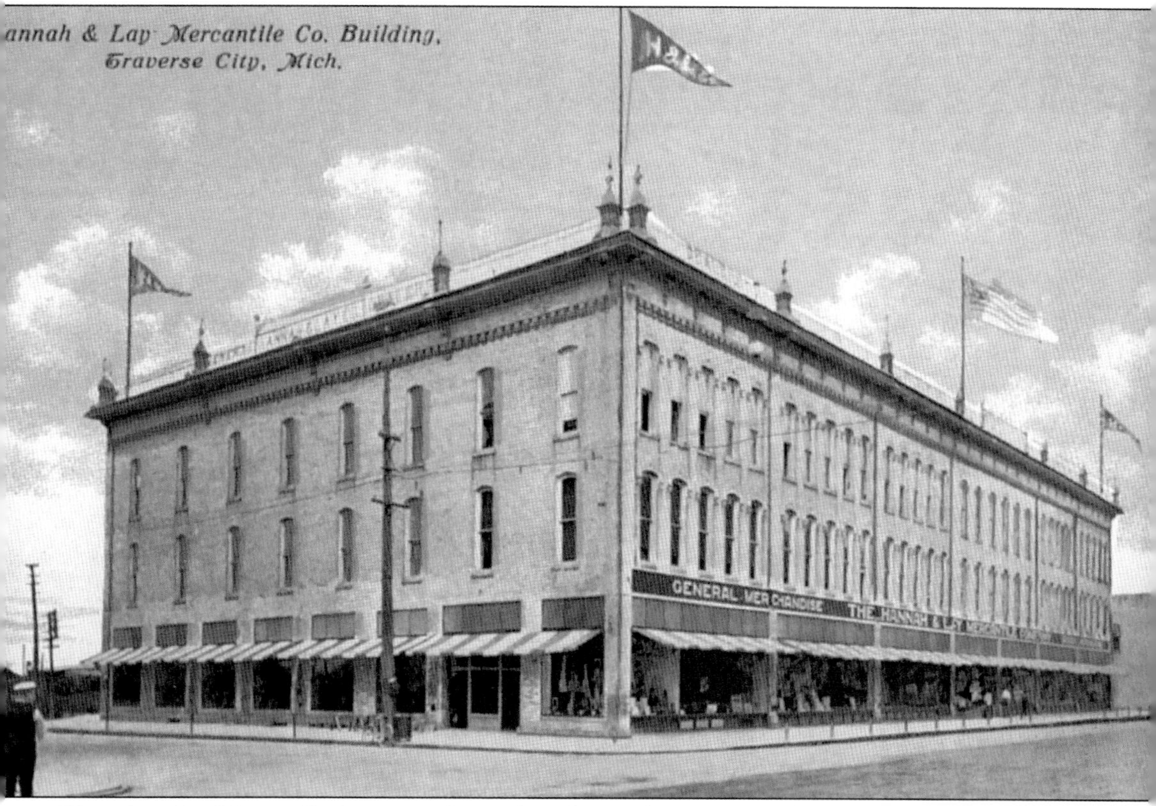

Hannah & Lay Mercantile Company, located on the northeast corner of Front and Union Streets in downtown Traverse City, was constructed in 1883. The building housed its own generator and had the only electricity in the downtown area. The Hannah & Lay store stocked everything from lace curtains and clothing to plumbing and hardware supplies. While only two-thirds of the original building stands today, it remains one of the largest buildings in downtown Traverse City.

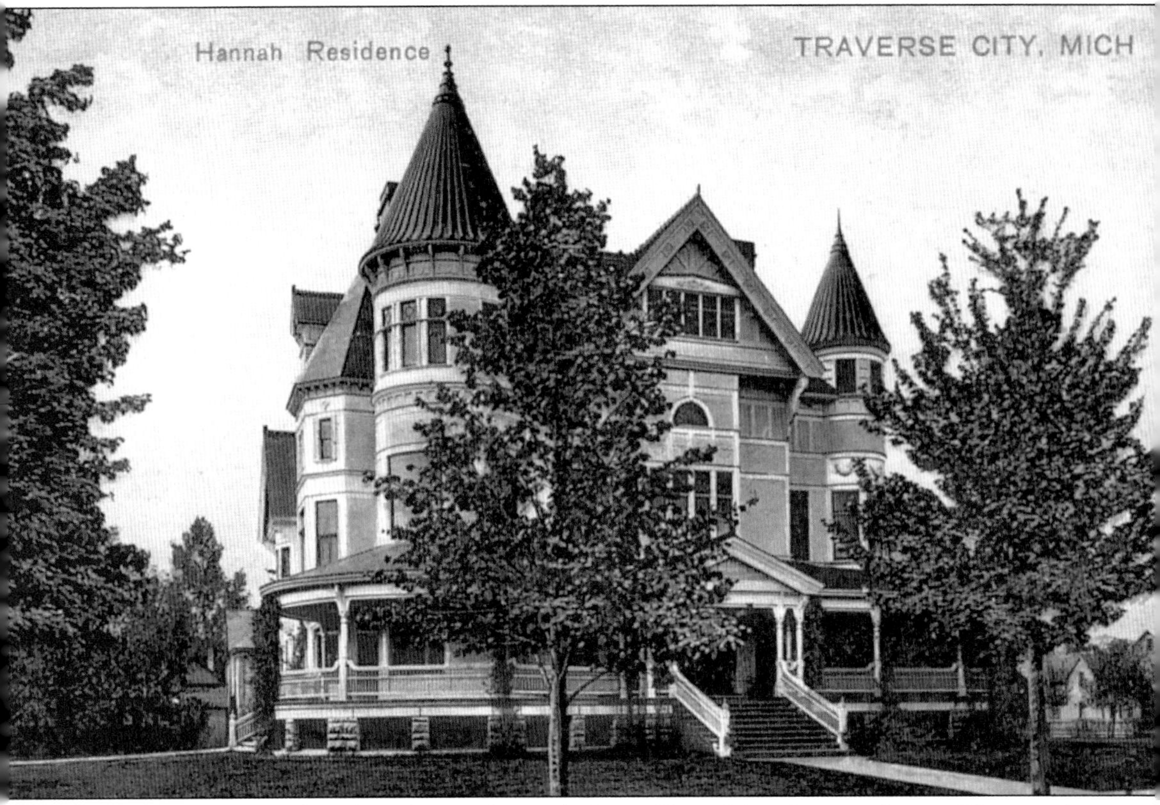

On the corner of Sixth and Pine Streets is Perry Hannah's retirement home. The mansion, a 14,000-square-foot Queen Anne style building complete with towers and gabled windows, is unlike any other home in Traverse City. Appointed with copper-clad ceilings, zinc glass, and hand-cut crystal chandeliers, and featuring an attic ballroom, this home remains virtually unchanged from the days when Perry Hannah roamed the halls. Nestled in what is now a historic neighborhood on the National Registry District, this home overlooks not only Hannah Park, which is situated on the Boardman River, but also the former Traverse City Public Library for which Hannah donated the land.

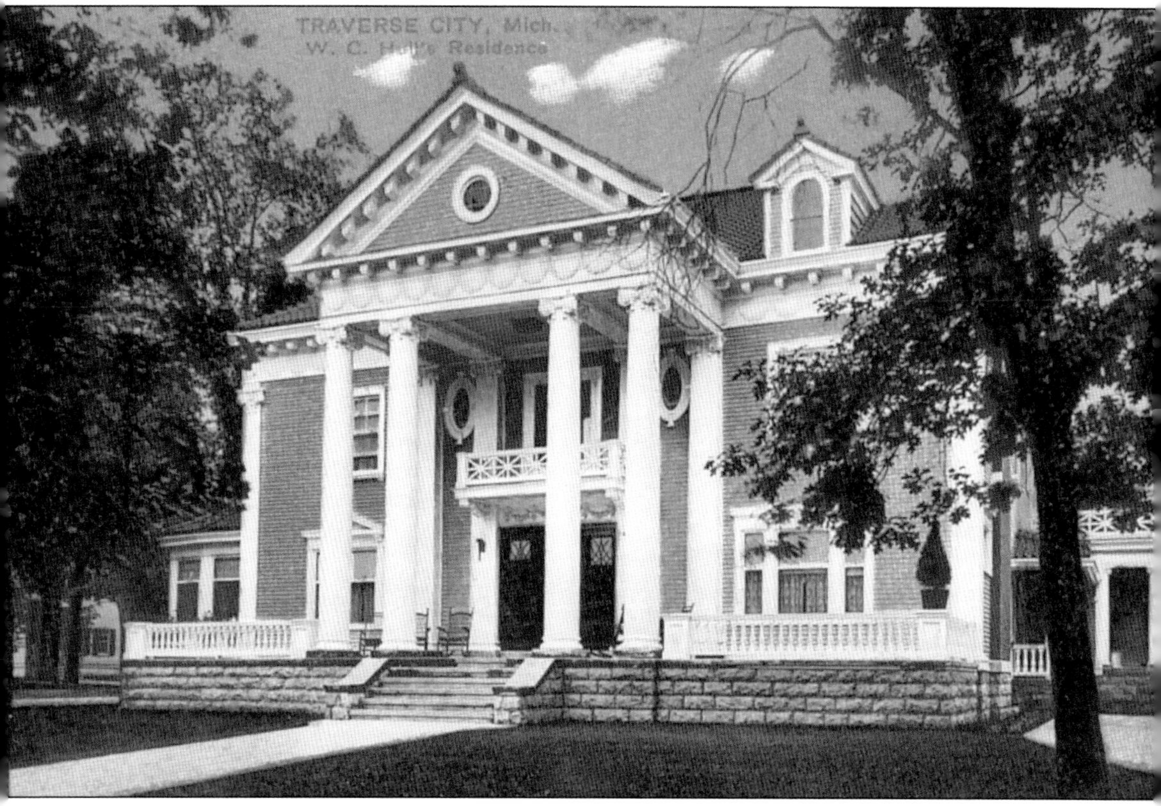

Now known as the Wellington Inn Bed & Breakfast, the W.C. Hull home located at the northwest corner of Washington and Wellington Streets has been through some rough times. Construction on the 10,000-square-foot home began in 1905 and was eventually finished in 1908. William Carey Hull, original owner of the home, was the son of the owner of the Oval Wood Dish Company. Interestingly, his father built the mansion directly across the street from his own residence. The mansion has been through several owners, as well as renters, since its construction in 1908. Following extensive renovation, its current owners have decided to turn it into a bed and breakfast. One of Traverse City's most opulent homes, the Hull mansion is in the heart of one of town's several historical districts.

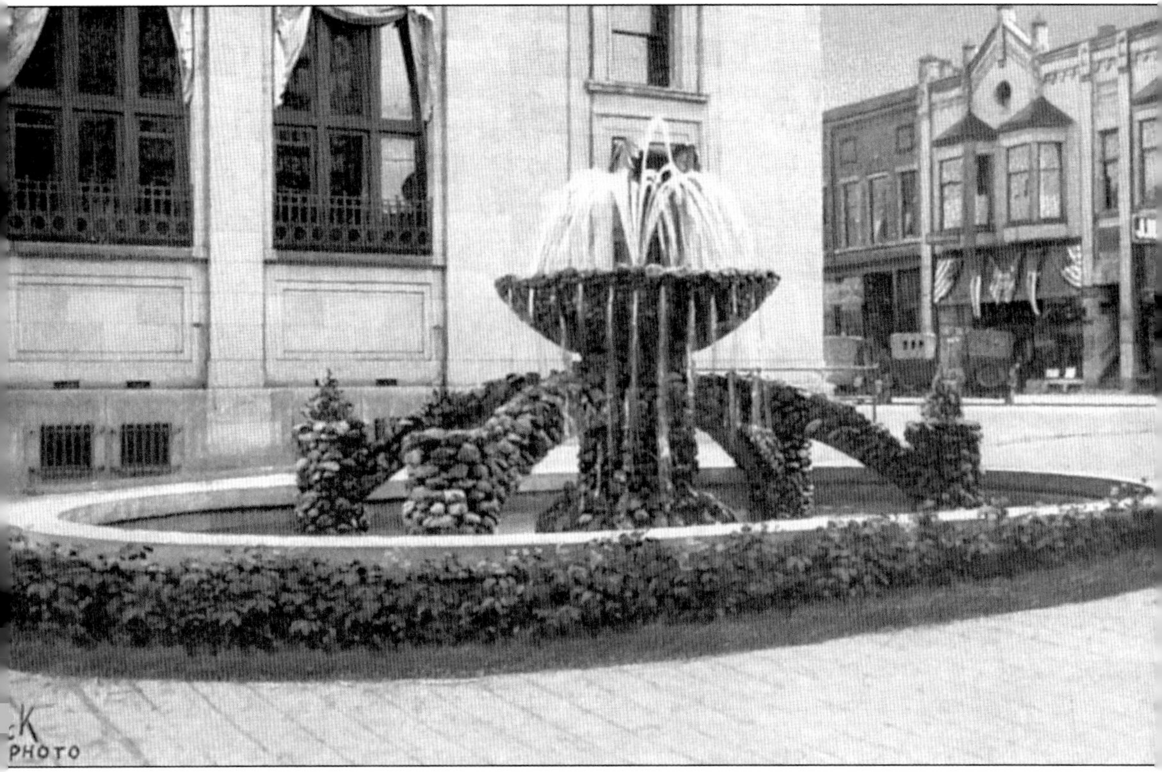

An enormous water fountain was constructed on Cass Street, just to the north of Front Street, in 1926. The fountain served as not only a monument to the economic success that Traverse City was experiencing, but also as a gateway to Clinch Park. Eventually, increased traffic and growth made it necessary to relocate Clinch Park to the waterfront and tear down the fountain, opening up Cass Street. In 1953, the Grandview Parkway was built, which allowed for cars to bypass downtown Traverse City by following the shoreline of Grand Traverse Bay. In order to facilitate the flow of traffic on Cass Street from Front Street to the Grandview Parkway, the fountain was razed in 1954.

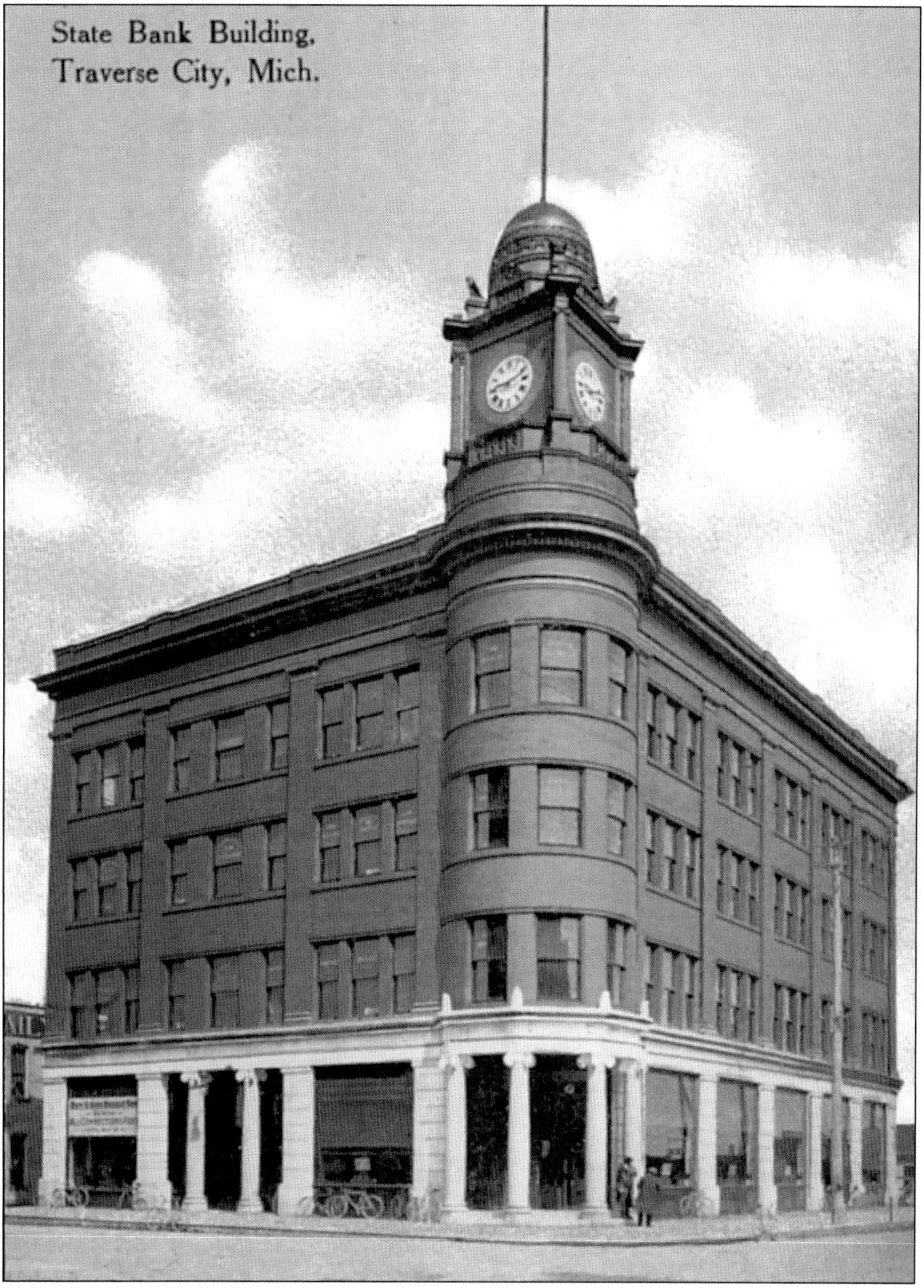

The Traverse City State Bank, an architectural landmark, has been essential to Traverse City's economic success. An impressive building, complete with marble columns at both the side and front entrances, the bank served as a financial catalyst to the booming lumber and agricultural economy in Traverse City's early days. The building, completed in 1903, is located on the northwest corner of Front and Union Streets in downtown Traverse City.

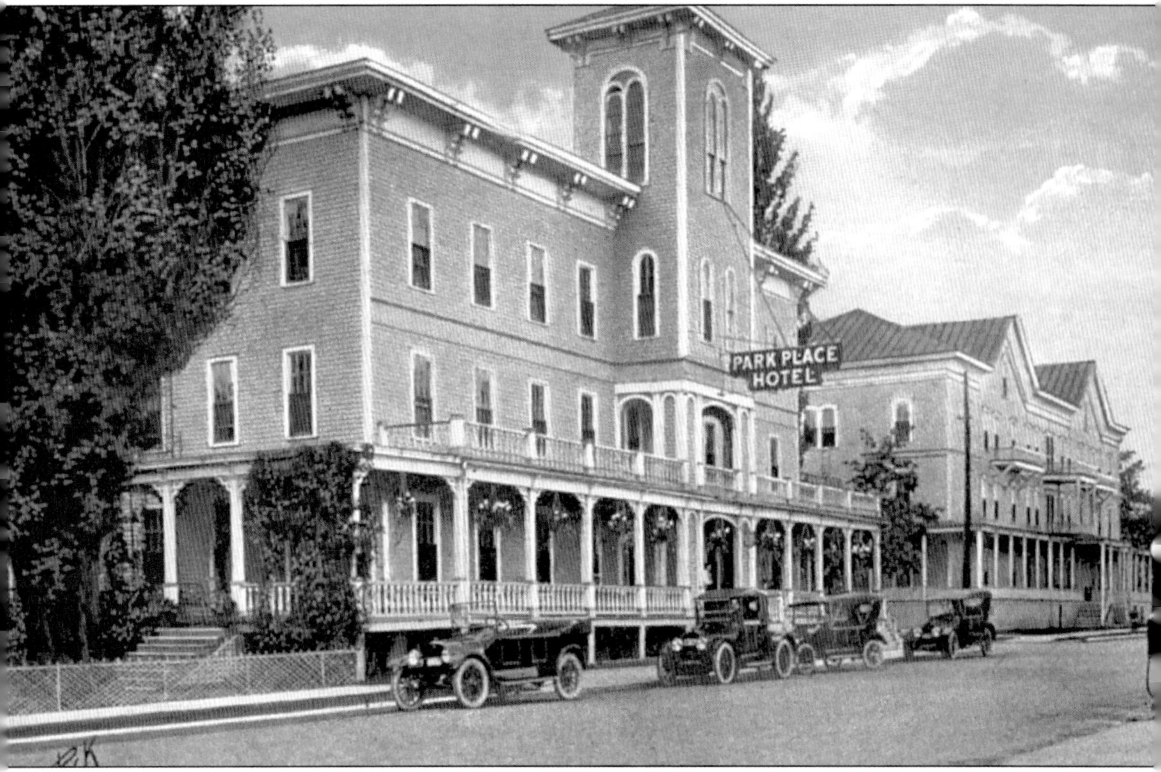

Henry D. Campbell purchased a parcel of park property from the city in 1873 so that he might build a hotel. In time the Campbell House, as it was known, was sold to Perry Hannah and Tracy Lay, Traverse City's lumber barons. Following the sale in 1878, the Campbell House was renamed the Park Place Hotel, and Hannah, Lay & Company set about creating an elegant establishment that would rival any world-class hotel. Construction began on revamping the Park Place Hotel, and it was not until 1930 that it was completed. The new hotel ended up being 10 stories high, making it Traverse City's tallest building. The Park Place Hotel, located at the end of Park Street, has undergone numerous changes over the years, yet the vision of a world-class hotel has endured.

(*Opposite, bottom*) Just off of Union Street, around the corner from Old Town, is Sixth Street. This is the street where Perry Hannah oversaw development, approved of specific residents, and determined the types of houses that were built. The street, lined with maple trees and houses set back off the street, was home to some of Traverse City's early movers and shakers. Cuyler Germaine, the father of "Wild Bill" Germaine, lived just down the street, as did "Vinegar" John Morgan, owner of Traverse City's first fruit canning company, and "The Man with the Million Dollar Smile," J.R. Santo. Each home on Sixth Street is an architectural gem in and of itself; most of them also have a story.

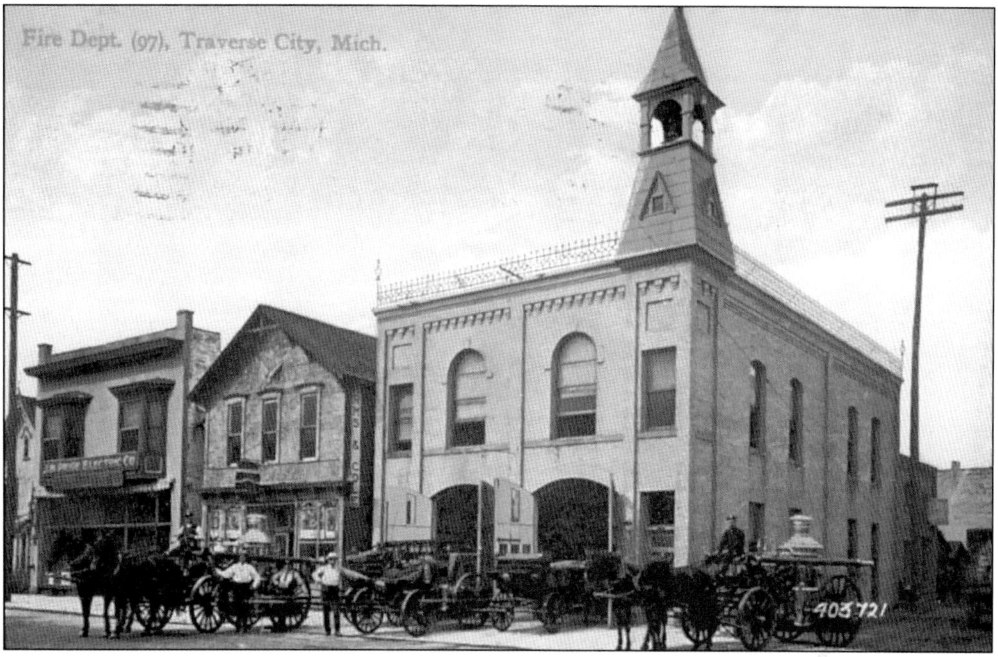

(*Above*) The initial home for the Traverse City Fire Department was built in 1878 on the corner of Union Street and Seventh Street, although a booming population made it necessary to relocate the fire station. For many years, the station was centrally located on Cass Street just south of Front Street. The hand pumps and horse-drawn wagons have gone by the wayside for obvious reasons, although the Traverse City Fire Department still prides itself on its heritage and record of service to the community. A surge in population growth and the need for more extensive services required that the fire department once again move in the early 1970s. Today, Traverse City's Fire Department, located on the west end of Front Street, provides fire attack and suppression, advanced life support, hazardous material services, and other emergency services, as well as public education, code enforcement, and non-emergency services to the citizens of Traverse City.

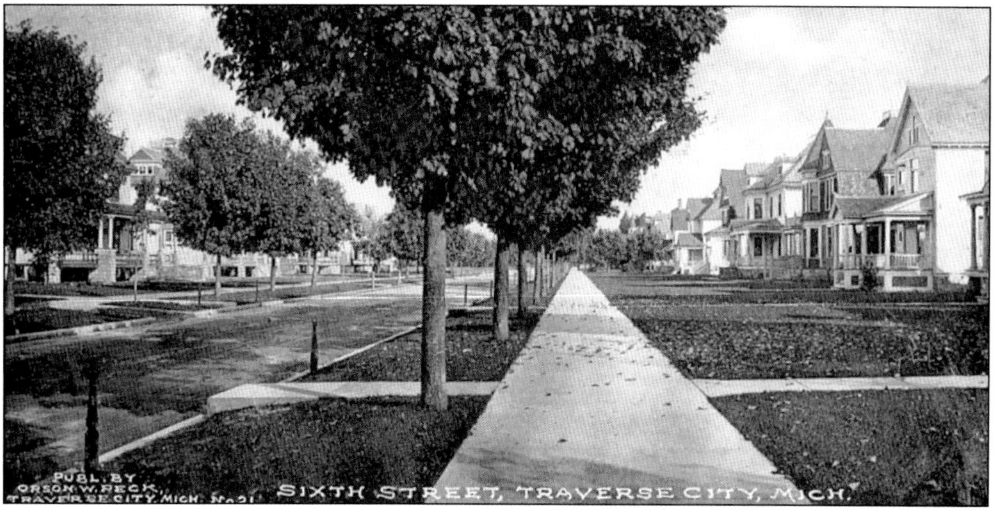

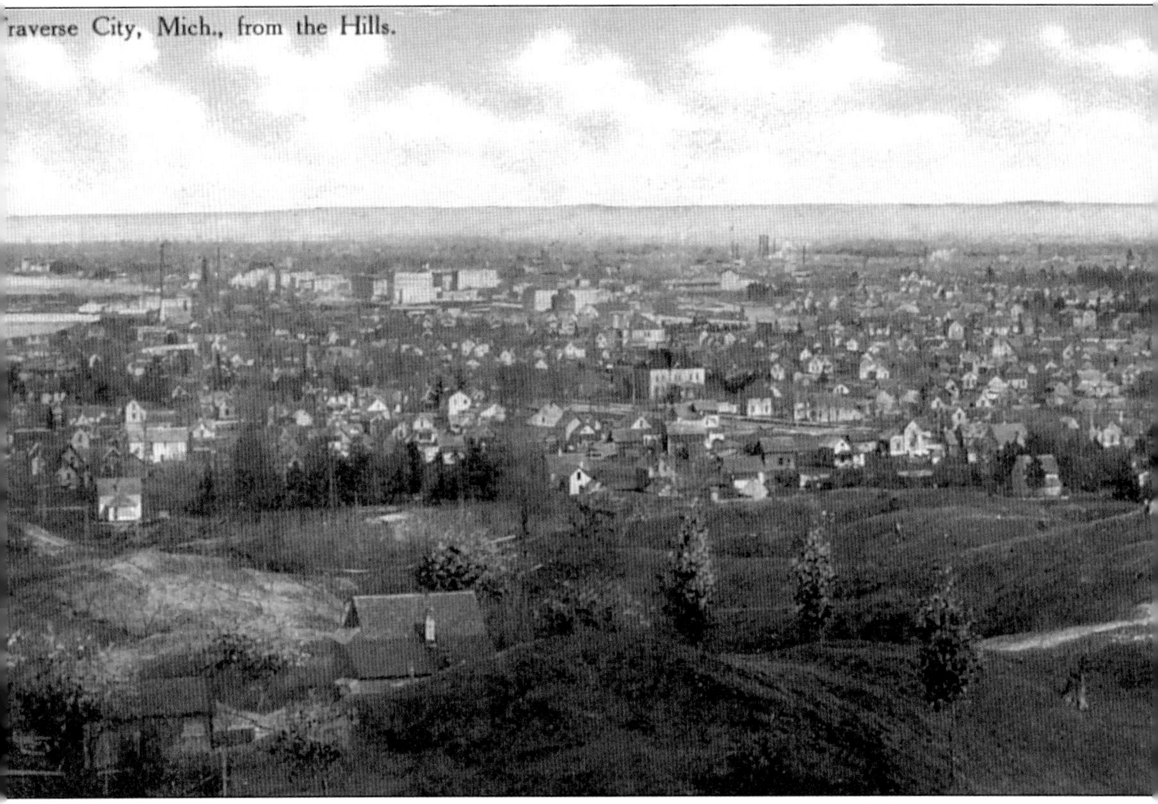

This bird's eye view of Traverse City looking east from the hills is from 1909. While providing a panoramic view of numerous homes and businesses, it is obvious that Traverse City was still a town very much reliant upon manufacturing for its economic base. Even though the Traverse City State Bank was completed in 1903, it is difficult to distinguish in this picture, as is the Park Place Hotel, which remained under construction until 1930. This was a time when lumber was still king in Traverse City and throughout Northern Michigan. A town growing by leaps and bounds, Traverse City was well on its way to fulfilling Perry Hannah's vision for its future.

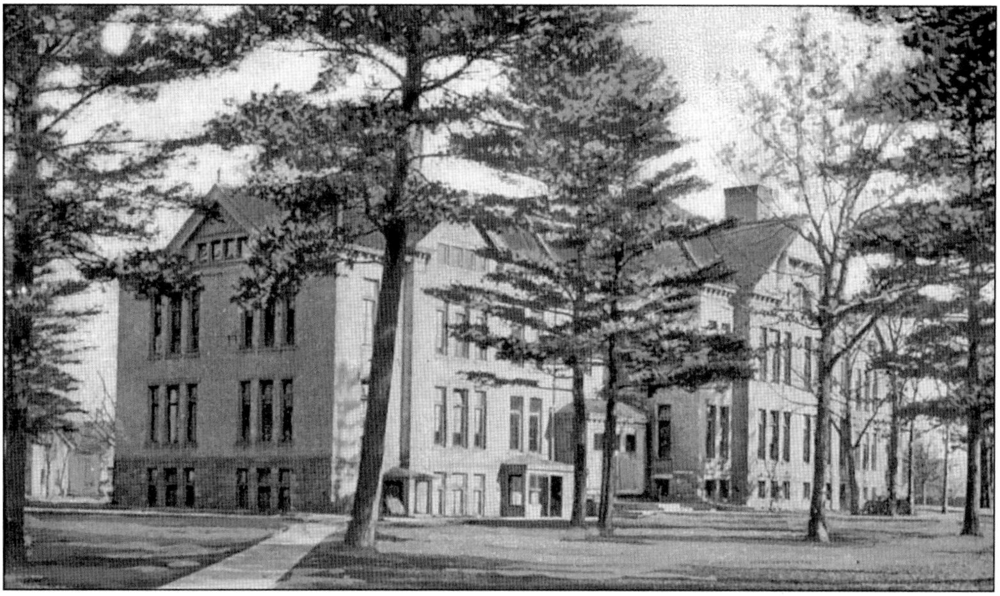

Aside from the parochial education offered at St. Francis, Traverse City Central High School was the only high school in Traverse City. In 1899, there was not enough room to hold graduation exercises for its 94 eighth grade students, and commencement was held at Steinberg's Opera House. Located on Seventh Street just west of Union Street, the original high school burned in 1934 and was subsequently replaced by a more modern brick building. A growing population made it necessary to build newer and larger junior and senior high schools, although Traverse City Central is still in operation as an elementary school.

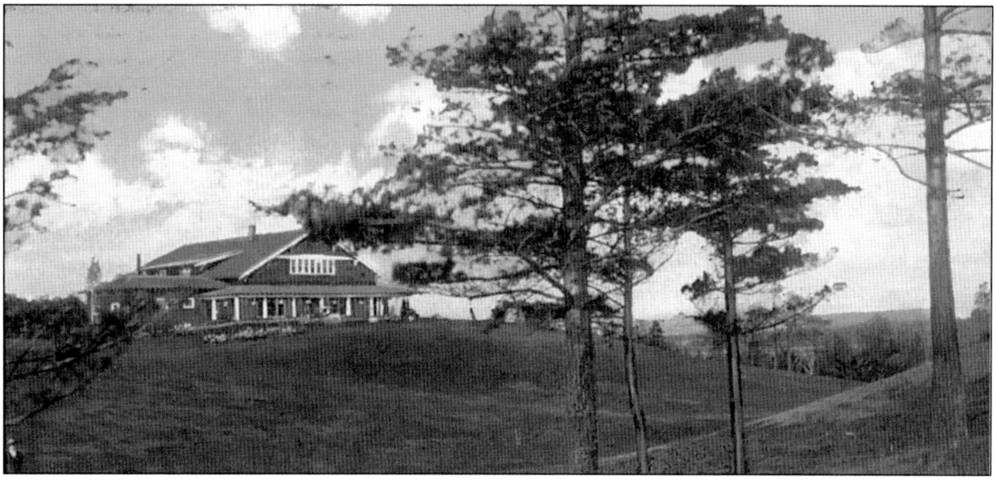

Perry Hannah donated the land just west of the old St. Francis Church to be developed as Traverse City's first golf course. Soon afterward, a number of Traverse City area residents formed the Traverse City Golf and Country Club, located on the top of the hill at the South end of Union Street. "The Club," as it is often called, offers dining, recreational, and social activities for its members. The original clubhouse burned down and a new one was built in the 1950s. While the Traverse City Golf and Country Club has a select membership, it has served as a catalyst for making the Traverse City area one of the nation's top golf destinations. At the present time, Grand Traverse County is home to more than a dozen golf courses.

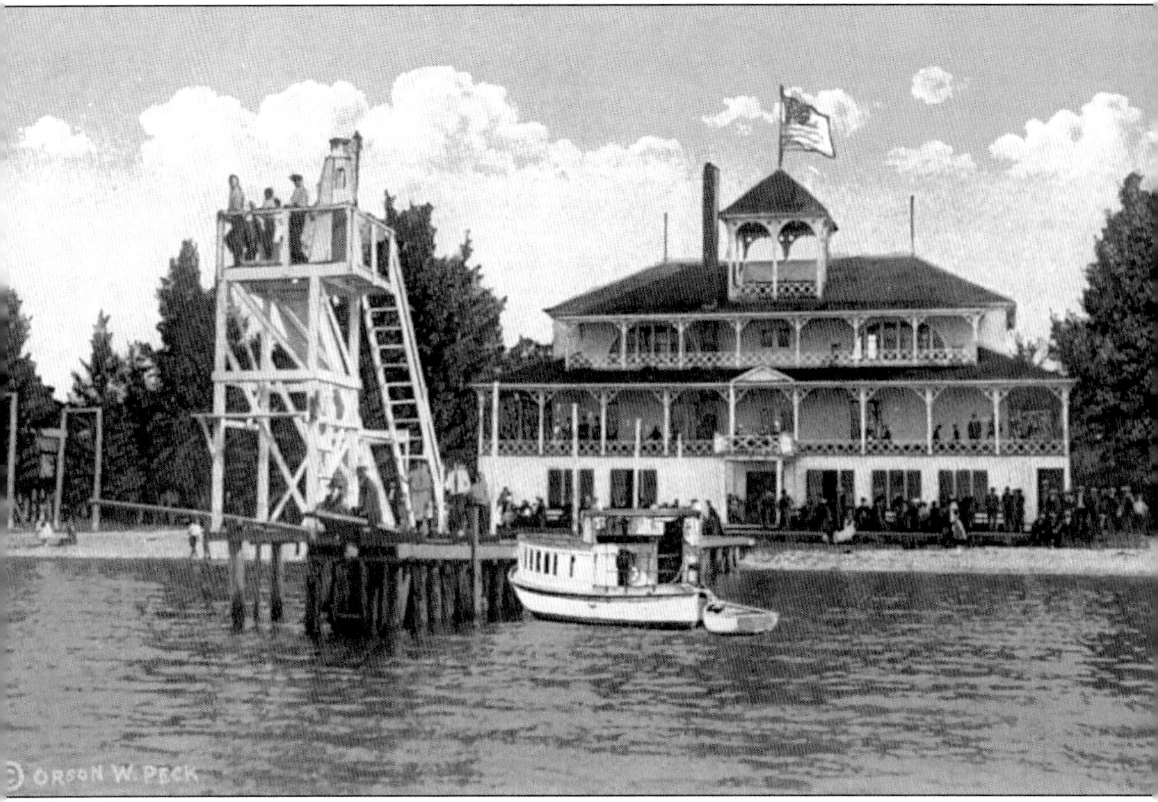

Located near the mouth of the Boardman River on the West Arm of Grand Traverse Bay, the Wequetong Club served as a social club for residents, as well as tourists. Both visitors and the local residents alike would stop by for a swim in the refreshing waters of West Bay, rent a boat, or enjoy a meal at the club's restaurant. In fact, Traverse City was originally known as Wequetong, or Head of the Bay, and back then what is now Grand Traverse County was known as Omena. That is, until Albert T. Lay, one of the proprietors of the Hannah, Lay & Company, secured a post office for the growing town in 1854.

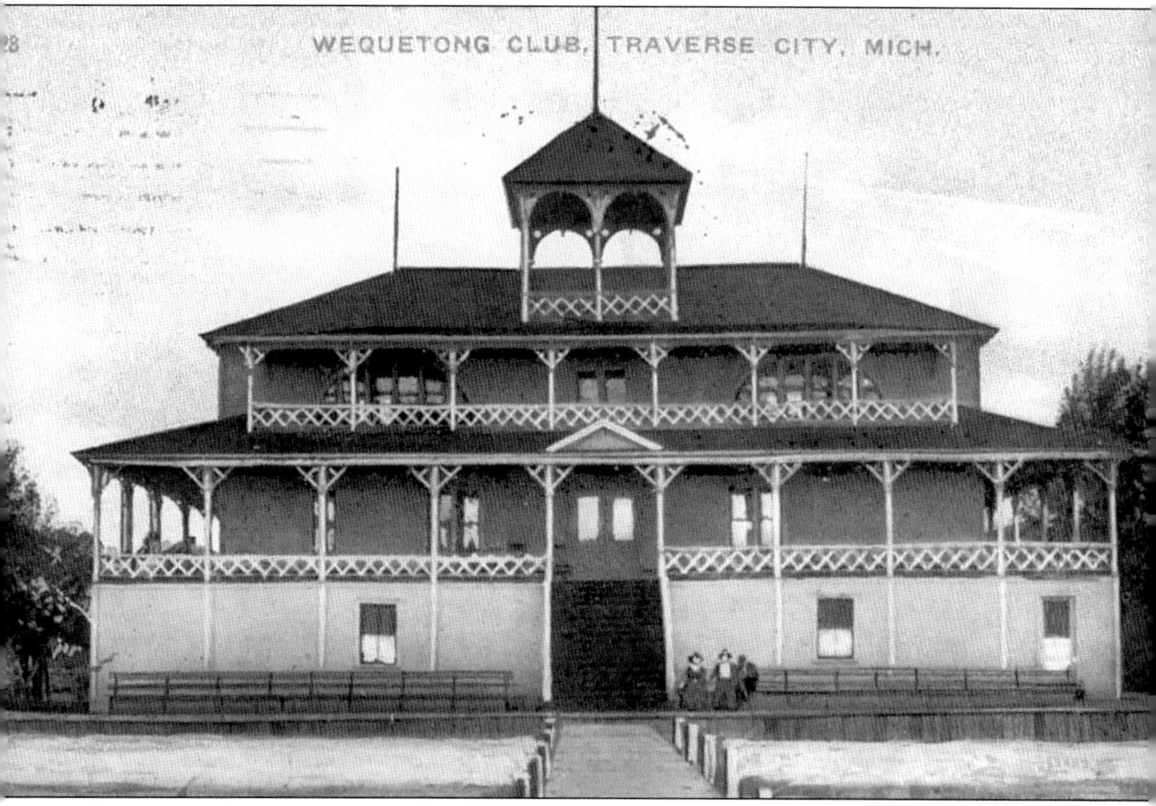

A forerunner of today's swim clubs, the Wequetong Club offered residents a chance to boat, swim, and dine, while at the same time hosting any one of a number of social events. The club, situated at the head of Grand Traverse Bay near the Boardman River, was extremely popular, in part due to its central location. While the Wequetong Club is no longer there, the public beaches in and around Traverse City swell with near-record amounts of boaters, sun worshippers, and swimmers each summer.

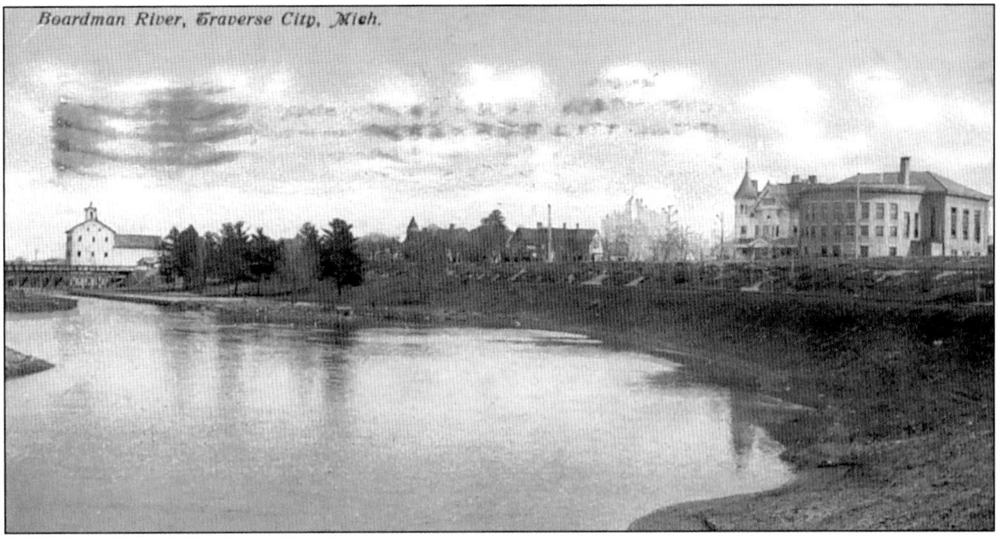

The Traverse City Library, or Carnegie Library, is located on the banks of the Boardman River, just off Sixth Street. The library was built in 1905, and its construction made possible by a donation of $20,000 from the Carnegie Foundation. While library service in the Traverse City area had begun as early as 1859, monies for the construction of a library did not become available until 1903. By 1966, there was a need for more space, and an addition was built onto the existing structure. In 1984, the Traverse Area District Library, which serves Traverse City and a number of outlying areas, was founded. A new library was built in 1999, and the Carnegie Library has taken on a new role as a cultural heritage museum.

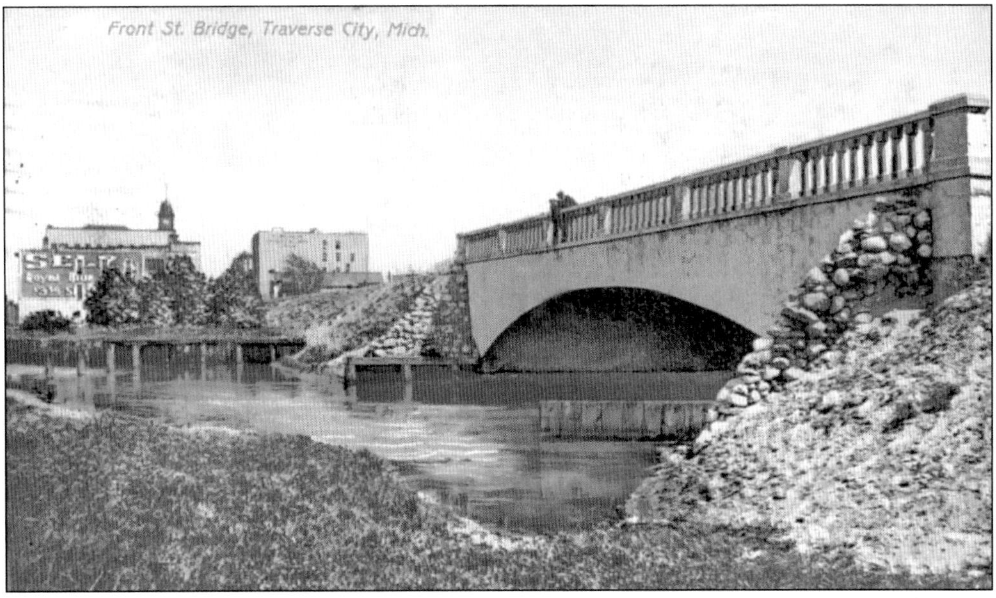

The Front Street Bridge, just to the west of State Street, provides both motorists and pedestrians passage across the Boardman River. The Boardman River meanders its way through Traverse City, eventually flowing into the West Arm of Grand Traverse Bay. In the background, the ever-present Traverse City State Bank, with its domed clock tower, rises above all of the other buildings.

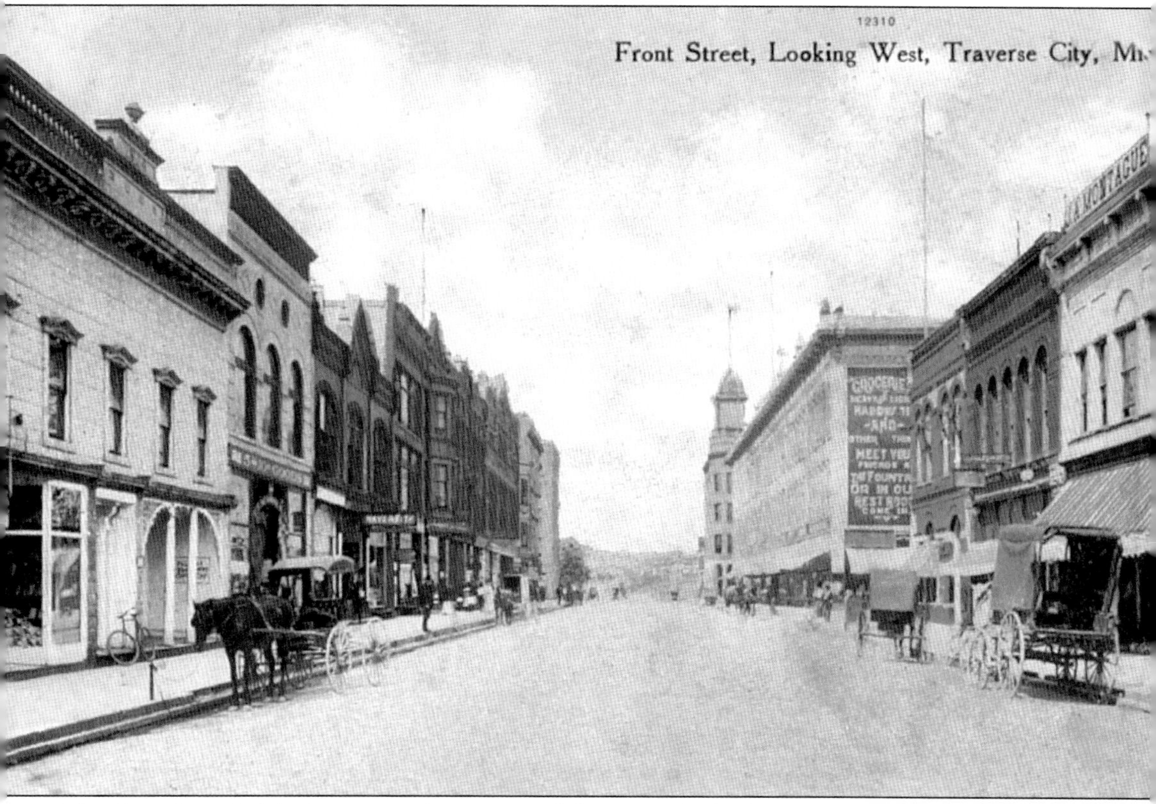

The domed roof of the Traverse City State Bank looms in the background of this 1913 view of Front Street in downtown Traverse City. The streets are unpaved and uncluttered, and hitching posts stand where parking meters are now. The Hannah & Lay Mercantile building—on the right side of Front Street, before the bank building—is a structure that, at one time, took up almost half of a city block. Across the street from Hannah & Lay and upstairs from Votruba's Leather Goods is the Steinberg Opera House, now known as the City Opera House. Very little has changed about downtown Traverse City over the past 90 years. While buggies are seldom seen anymore, and the street is paved, most of the buildings on Front Street look very much the same today as they did in 1913.

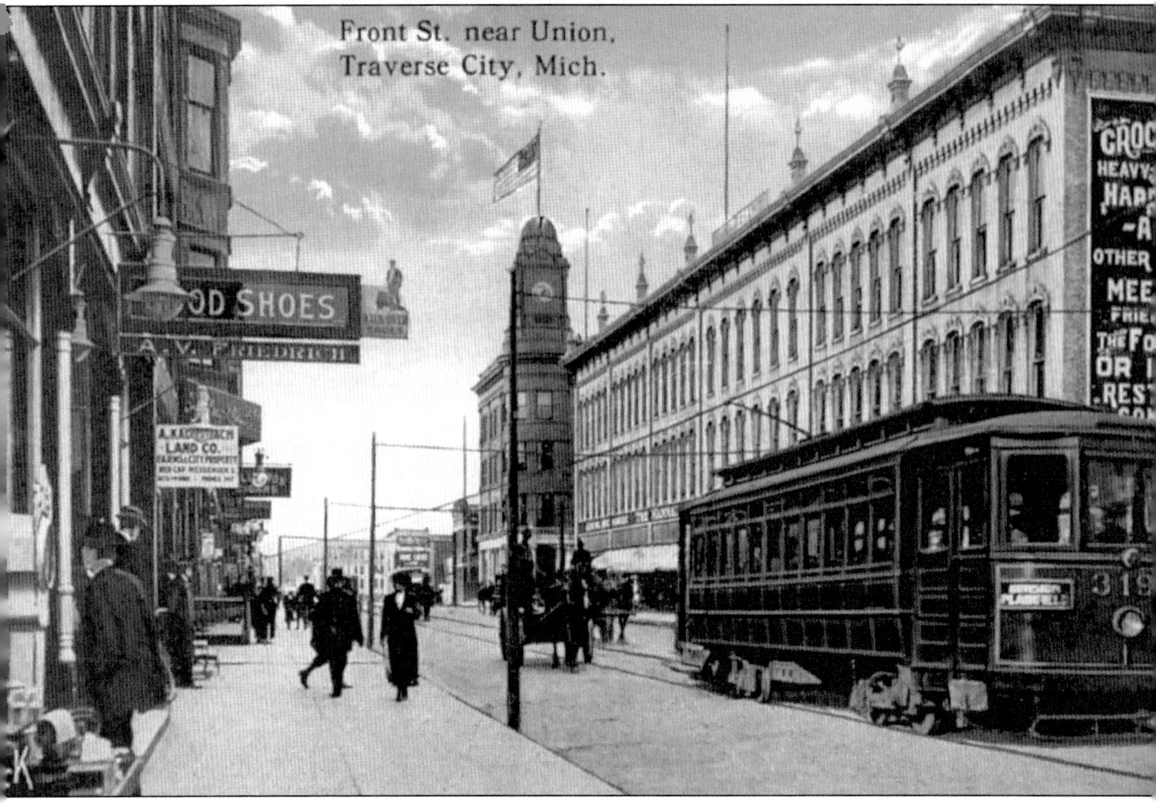

Looking as though it belongs in downtown Traverse City, this streetcar is nothing more than an artistic pipedream. While there was discussion in the town's early days as to how to provide efficient transportation, such a fanciful idea never came to pass. Given the fact that cities such as Chicago, Detroit, New York, and San Francisco all had their own streetcar systems, many residents felt that Traverse City should as well. Despite the fact that R.J. Cobb had driven an automobile down Front Street as early as 1899, the cost of purchasing a private motorized vehicle was prohibitive for most families.

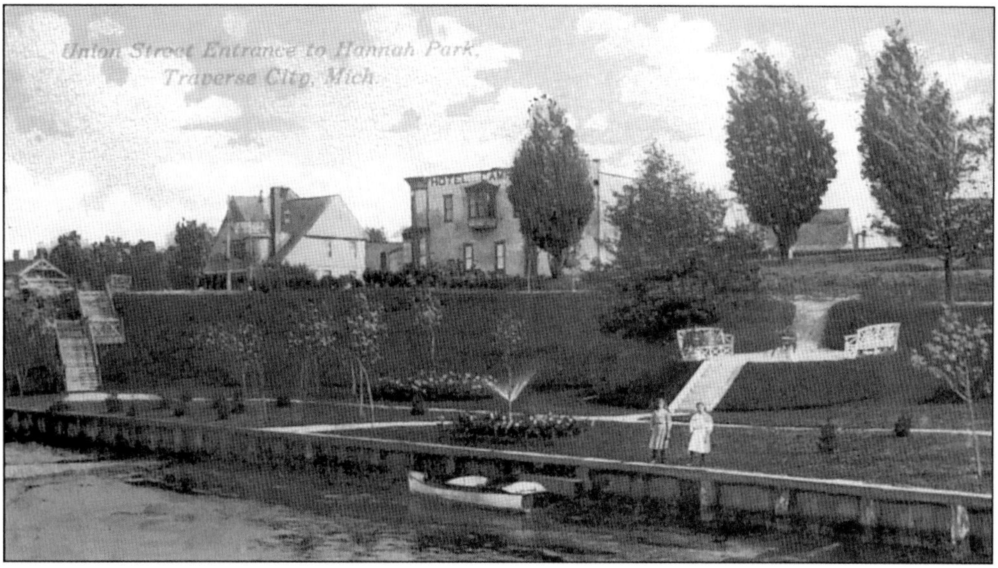

Hannah Park, on the Boardman River just off of the corner of Union and Sixth Street, was truly something to behold in its early days. The land for the park, donated by none other than lumber baron Perry Hannah, was complete with dockage, walkways, and a fountain. While the dockage and the fountain are no longer there, the walkways, flora, and fauna of this beautiful park, are still there for the enjoyment of all—kitty corner from the mansion that Hannah built on Sixth Street.

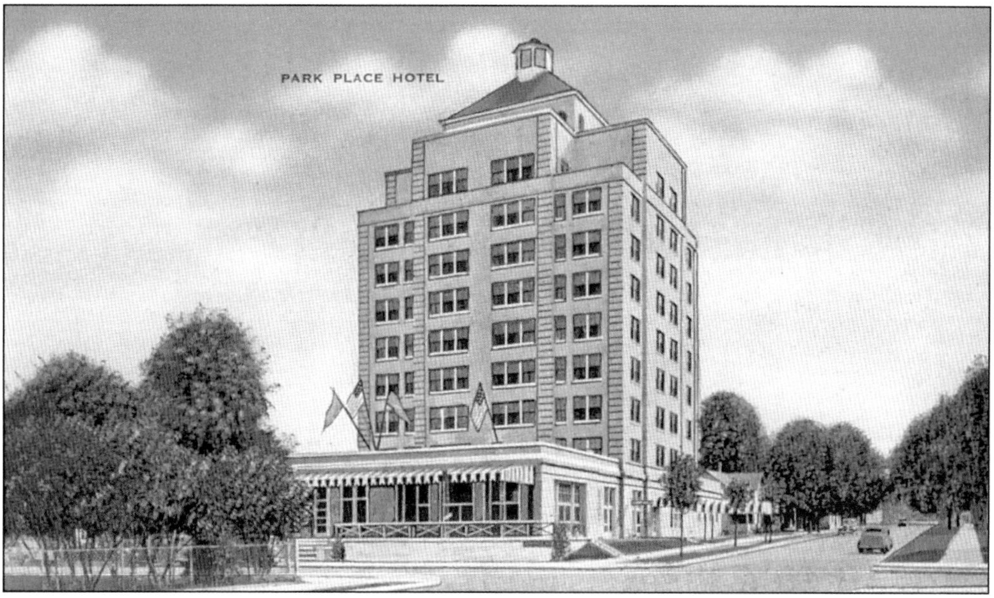

Purchasing a lot from the town council in 1873, Henry Campbell built a hotel known as Campbell House at the corner of Park and State Streets. In 1878, Hannah & Lay bought the hotel from Campbell and began to renovate it. The goal was to refurbish the hotel so that Traverse City would have a world-class hotel offering all of the amenities of the era. It was not until 1930 that the 10-story hotel, renamed the Park Place, would be completed. To this day, the Park Place Hotel is proud to offer some of the finest accommodations and dining in the Traverse City area.

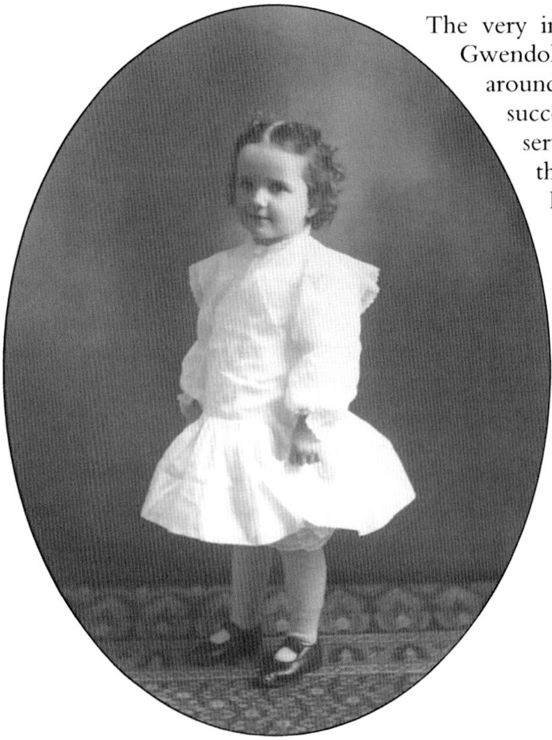

The very image of a prim and proper young lady, Gwendolyn Santo poses for this photograph, taken around 1904. Her father, John R. Santo, was a successful Traverse City area businessman who served as the town's mayor in 1903 and had the distinction of being the last Democratic Party candidate elected to state office from Grand Traverse County. Gwendolyn's dress and upbringing were not typical for the time period. Having grown up on Sixth Street, just down the block from Perry Hannah, young Gwendolyn went on to attend the University of Michigan in Ann Arbor.

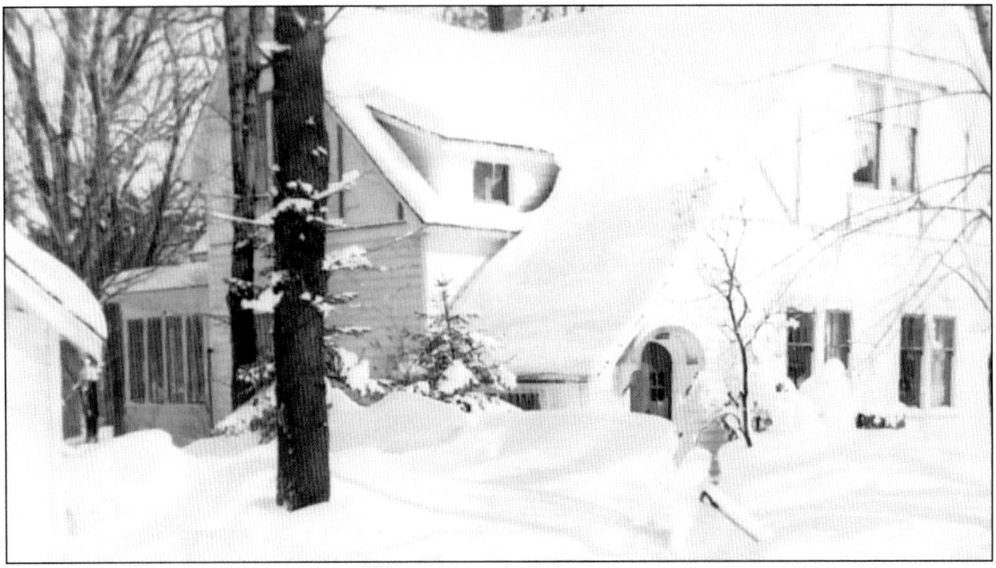

A heavy blanket of fresh fallen snow covers this house, located on West Grand Traverse Bay. Snowstorms, accompanied by gusts of wind, have always been a concern for those in the Traverse City area; especially those who choose to live on the water's edge. Fierce winds, ice damage, and higher heating bills are only some of the problems associated with living near the water. Yet, whether it is the dead of winter or midsummer, there is always something to do, especially if you live on Grand Traverse Bay. Given a home as large as this one, there appears to be a great deal of shoveling to be done.

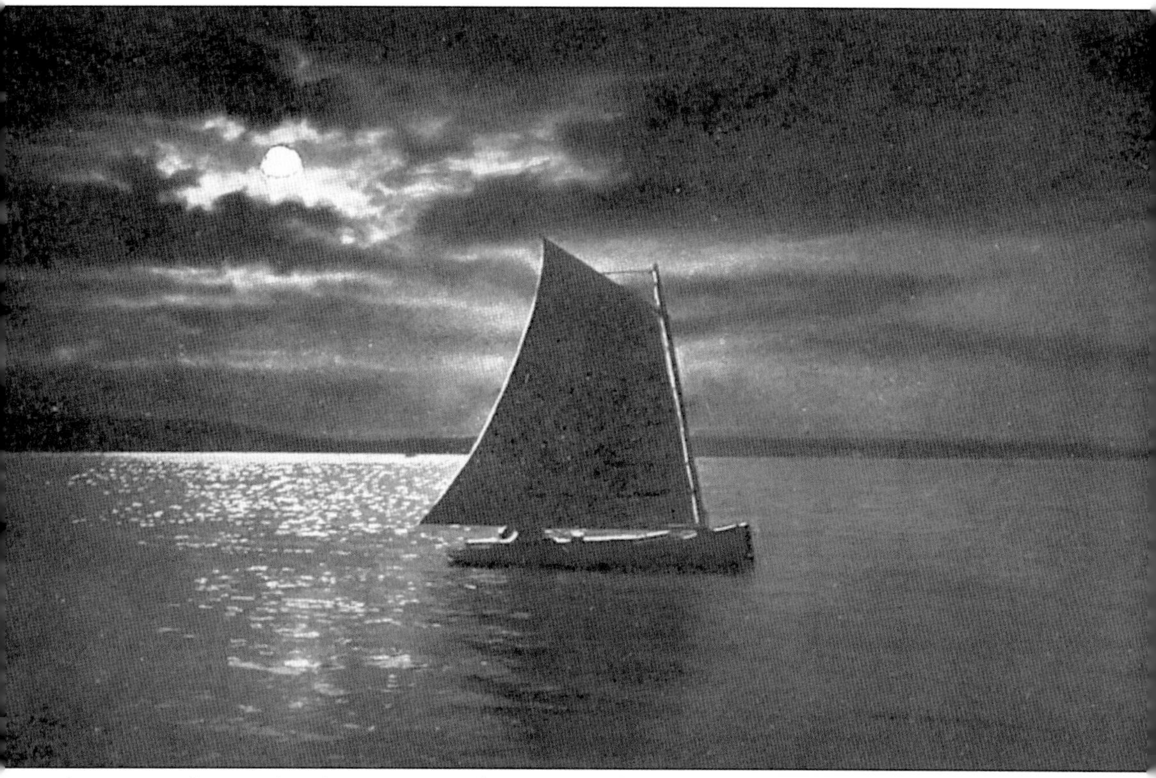

As serene and romantic as it may seem, sailing on Grand Traverse Bay or Lake Michigan at night is an activity that should be undertaken with caution. Calm waters and soft breezes all too easily lure unsuspecting sailors to the bay, and while for the most part it can be an enjoyable experience, there are always some people who lack respect for this powerful force. Grand Traverse Bay and Lake Michigan are both quite beautiful, yet while they may be calm one moment; a storm can sweep over the area in minutes creating gale force winds and whitecaps.

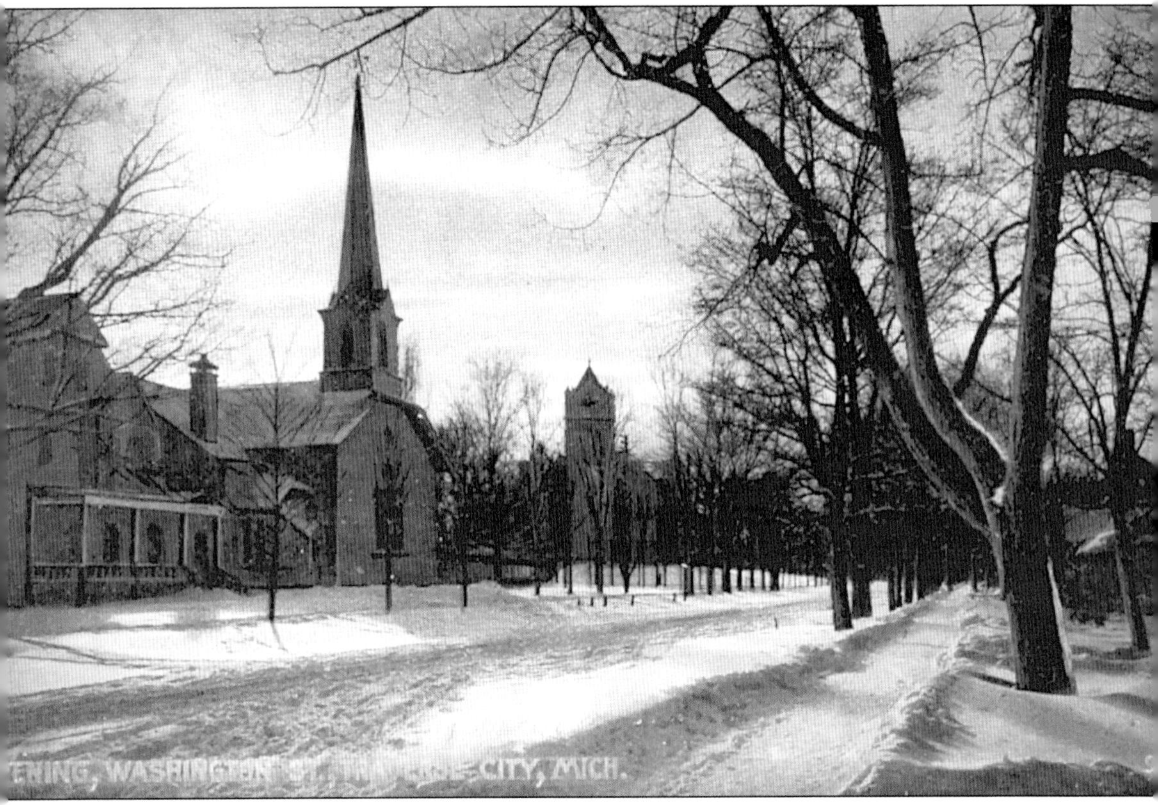

Dusk falls over Traverse City in winter, and the leafless trees, along with the church steeples and rooftops, make for ghostly silhouettes. The dark of night comes early in the winter, and at times there is little light except for that which is reflected off of the fresh snow. It took hardier souls to brave the winter months during Traverse City's early days. Many people worked outside, despite the freezing temperatures, and if the fire needed to be stoked, it was necessary for them to cut the wood. Northern Michigan in the late nineteenth century and early twentieth century was clearly not a place for frail individuals.

Tobacco was as popular in the early part of the twentieth century as it is unpopular today. Wilhelm, Bartak & Company of Traverse City had "Tony's Choice" manufactured expressly for them by another firm. In fact, as a courtesy to their customers, the majority of businesses allowed smoking on the premises. For those who preferred chewing tobacco there was usually a spittoon as well. The character featured on the front of the package leads the consumer to believe that they too can lead a relaxing life if they use this product.

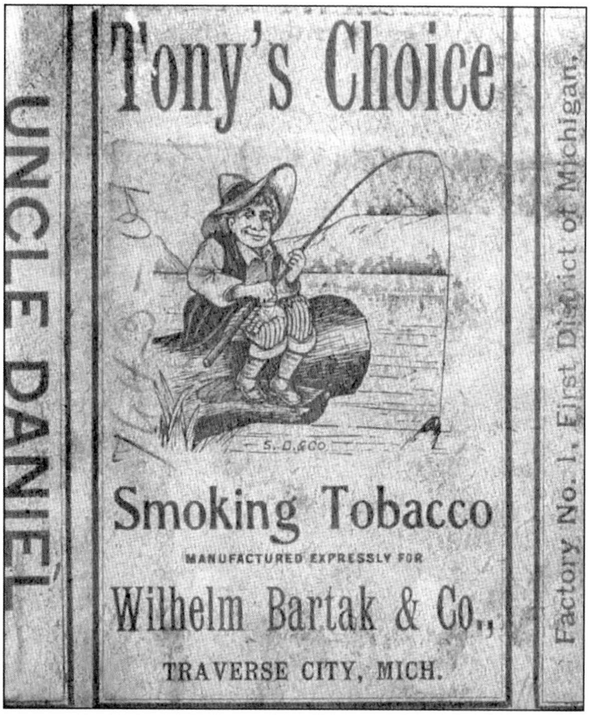

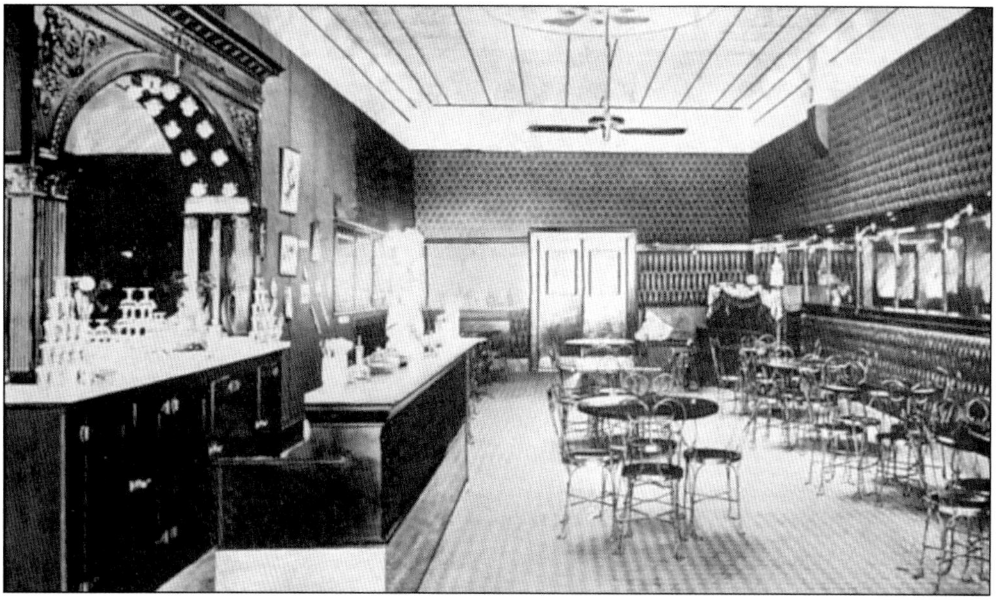

The Palace Ice Cream Parlor, located in the lobby of the Palace Theater at 128 East Front Street in downtown Traverse City, had something for everyone. There was no better way to draw people downtown than with an ice cream parlor, especially during the summer months. In the 1920s and 1930s, ice cream was one of the few commodities that everyone could afford. Whether vacationing in the area or merely on a shopping trip to downtown, there was always time for ice cream. While the Palace Ice Cream Parlor is now part of Traverse City's history, there are still a number of establishments that offer homemade ice cream.

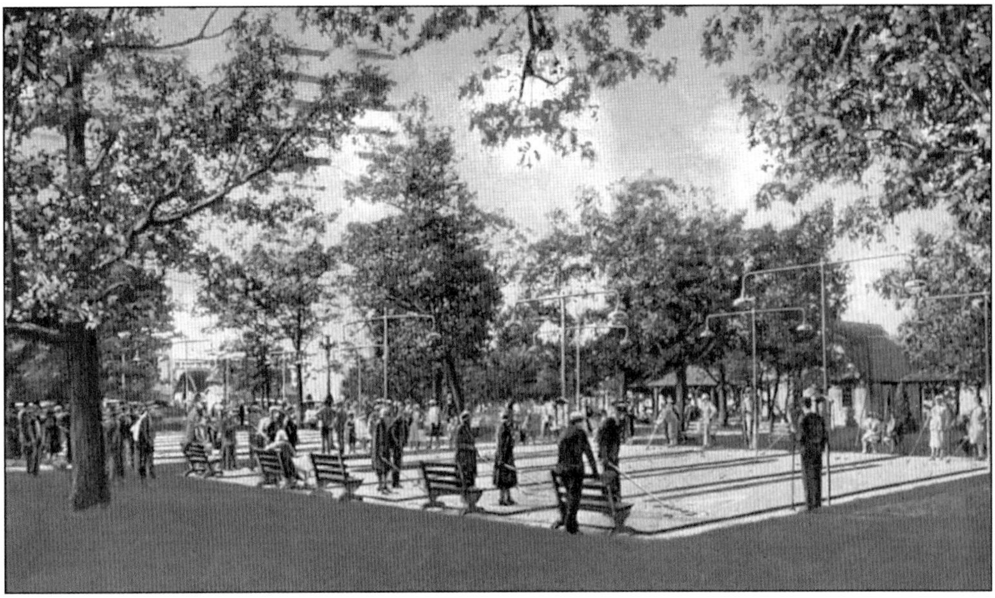

(*Above*) The shuffleboard court in Traverse City was once one of the largest of its kind in the nation. In fact, state and national tournaments have been held at the facility in the past. Currently, the shuffleboard court and its building are being used as the Traverse City Senior Center. Northwest Michigan Human Services Agency operates the Senior Nutrition Program at the site, serving lunches to senior citizens daily. The center also offers seniors educational and exercise programs. The programs are made possible through federal and state grants to the Area Agency on Aging of Northwest Michigan, the City of Traverse City, and the Michigan Office of Services to the Aging. Once each year, during the National Cherry Festival, a state sanctioned shuffleboard game is held at the Traverse City Senior Center, and for a brief moment, this old shuffleboard court is once again the center of attention.

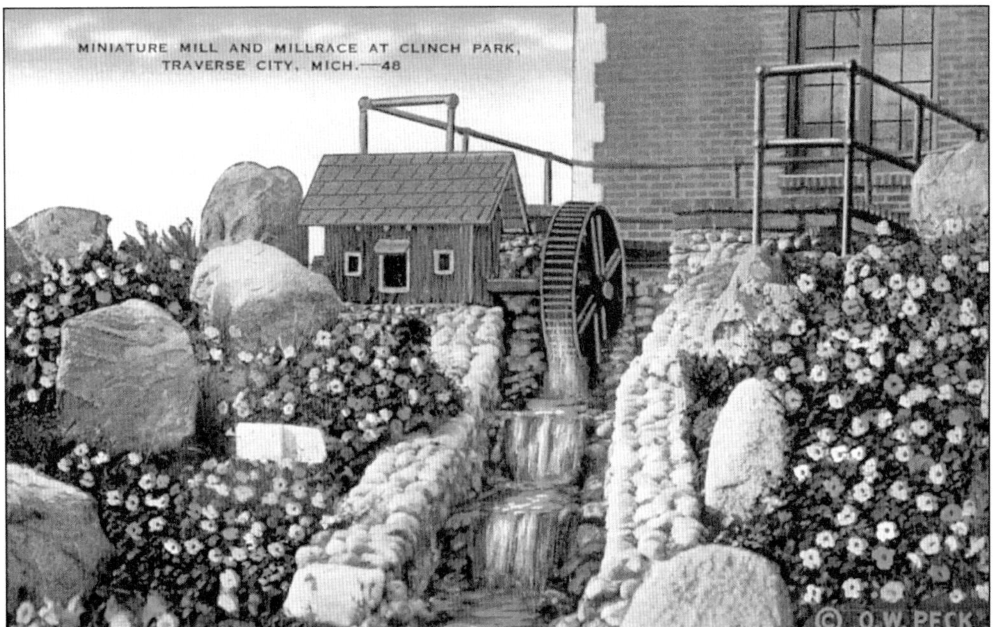

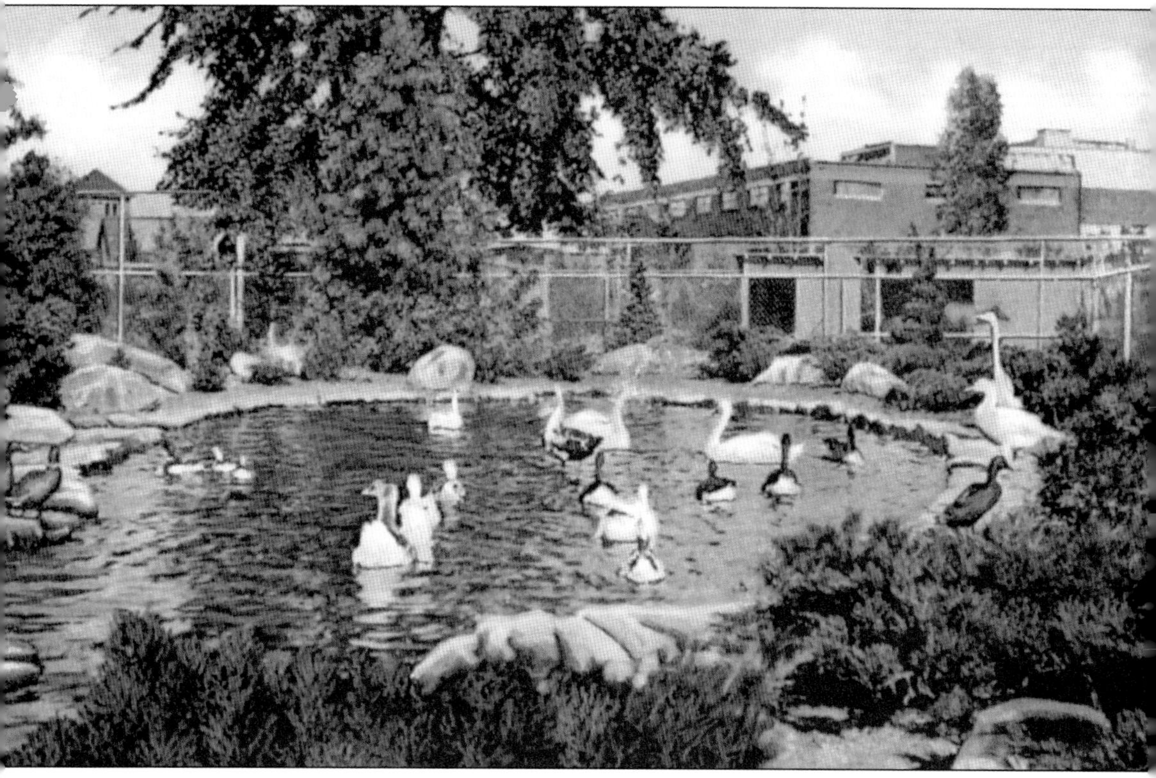

Swans and other indigenous waterfowl were always among the main attractions at the Clinch Park Zoo. While the birds are no longer on exhibit in the pond, there are an aquarium, an aviary, and numerous other animals at Clinch Park. The original zoo was located on the Boardman River, north of Front Street, although it was relocated to the water's edge when the Grandview Parkway was built in 1953. The Clinch Park Marina and Beach, as well as the Open Space project, surround the 3.5-acre zoo, located on the banks of the West Arm of Grand Traverse Bay.

(*Opposite, bottom*) The original design for the Clinch Park Zoo and Aquarium, as it was called, did not merely feature fish, wildlife, and birds swimming on a pond; rather it also focused on the cultural heritage of the area. In its earlier days, the park displayed a mill and millrace, remnants of Traverse City's lumber days. Over the years, the park has undergone significant changes and, as a result, some of these displays have been redesigned. Some of the smaller exhibits, such as those housed at the Con Foster Museum, have been relocated to the Grand Traverse Heritage Center on Sixth Street.

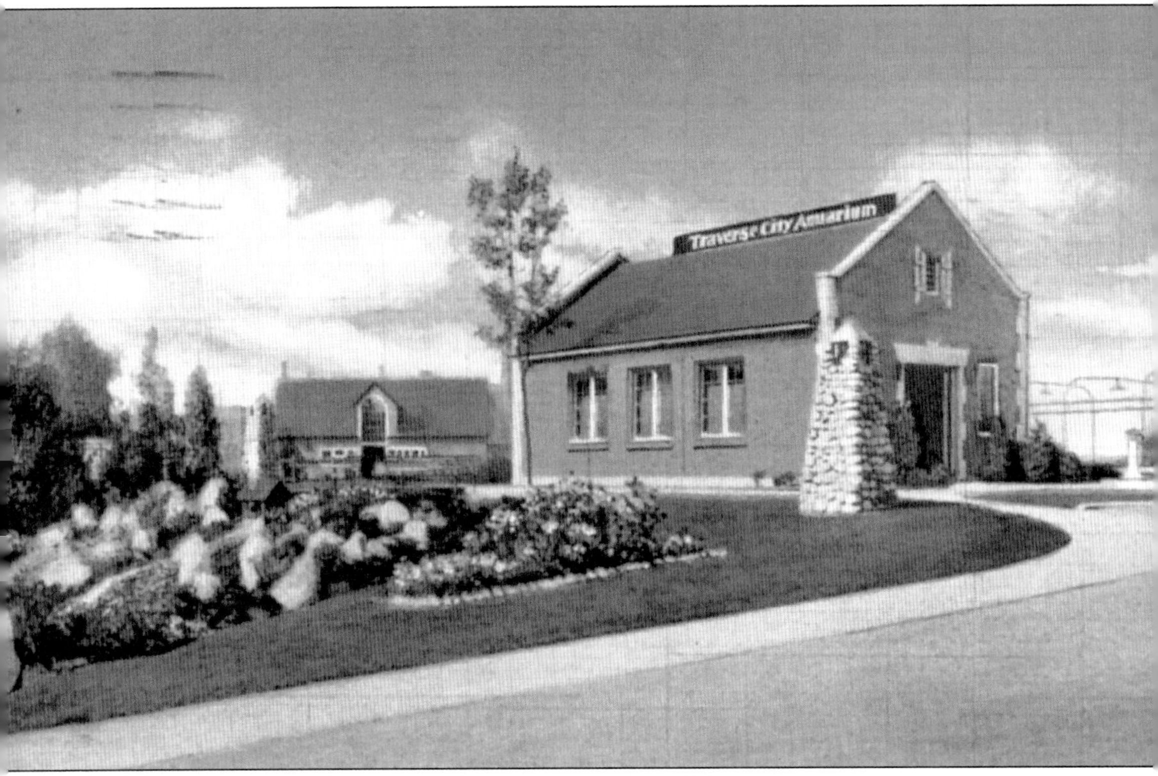

The Clinch Park Aquarium and Zoo was built in 1932 with the intention of exhibiting animals indigenous to Michigan. Occupying approximately 3.5 acres, Clinch Park Zoo is situated just off of Grandview Parkway in downtown Traverse City. Currently, the zoo is home to 31 mammals and 13 birds, including beavers, bears, deer, otters, and other forms of wildlife. Clinch Park Zoo is also home to the Con Foster Museum and is rated as one of the top 100 zoos in the United States.

(*Opposite, bottom*) A favorite of children and adults alike, the miniature city at Clinch Park featured a replica of what Traverse City looked like in 1931. On display at the zoo until the 1970s, the model featured over 100 buildings, from Wellington Street to Oak Street and from Grand Traverse Bay to Washington Street. Time and exposure to the elements took their toll, and eventually the miniature city was in need of restoration. Volunteers have been painstakingly restoring the miniature city to its original condition and, while it will not be displayed at Clinch Park, it may be viewed at the Music House starting in early 2004.

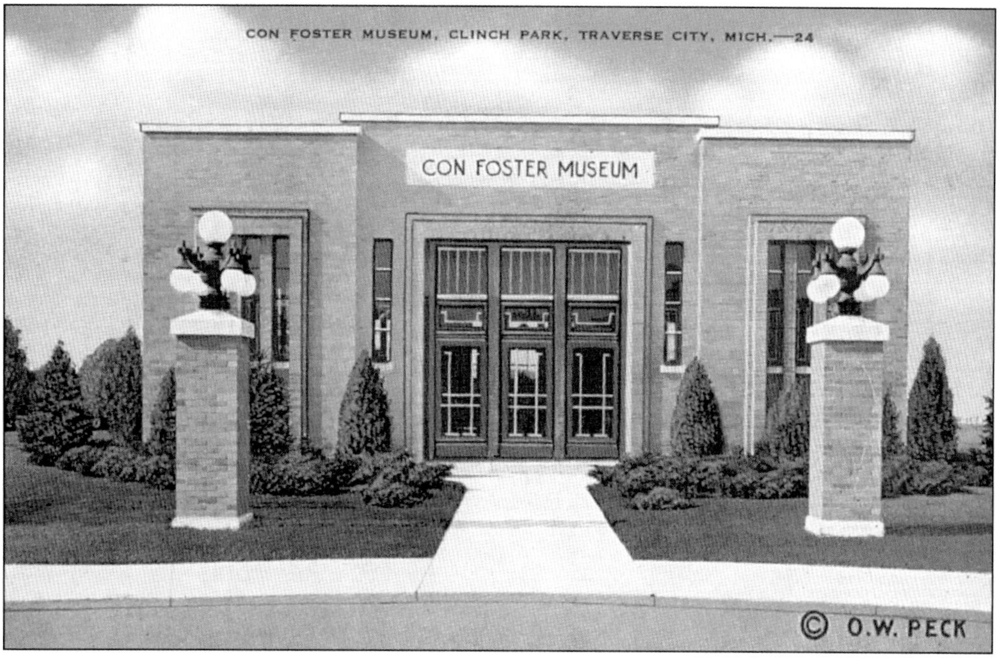

(*Above*) Founded in 1934, the mission of the Con Foster Museum, located at Clinch Park, has been to present exhibits concerning the cultural heritage of Grand Traverse area pioneers and Native Americans. The contents of the museum have recently been moved to the former Traverse City Public Library on Sixth Street, now known as the Grand Traverse Heritage Center. Initially, the museum holdings of over 8,000 items came from a collection of handcrafted Native American tools, as well as farming, logging, and railroad memorabilia, assembled by Conrad Foster. The former museum is currently in use as part of the Clinch Park Zoo.

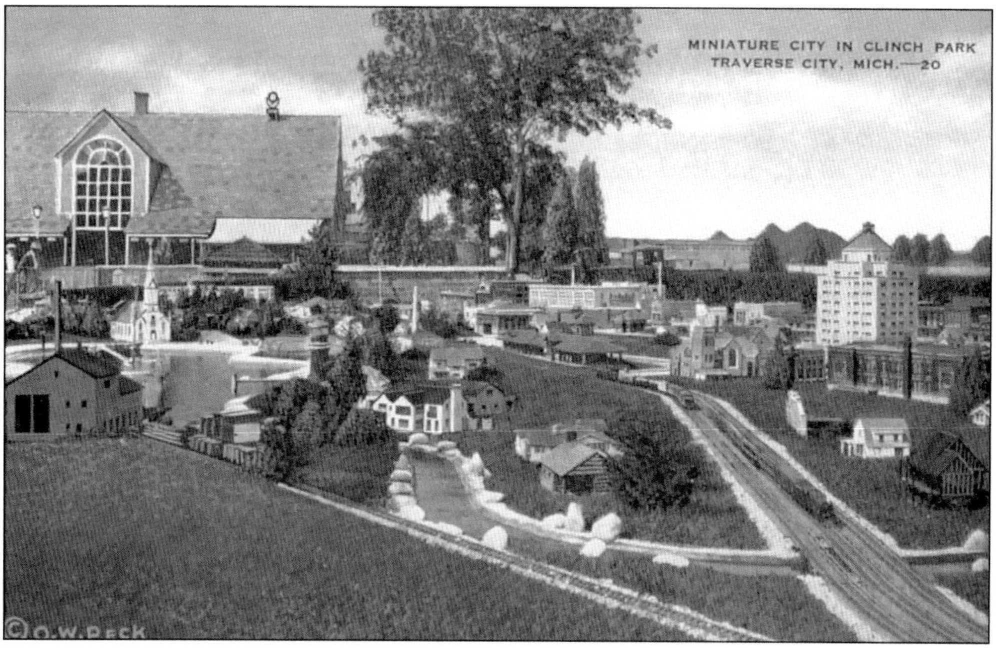

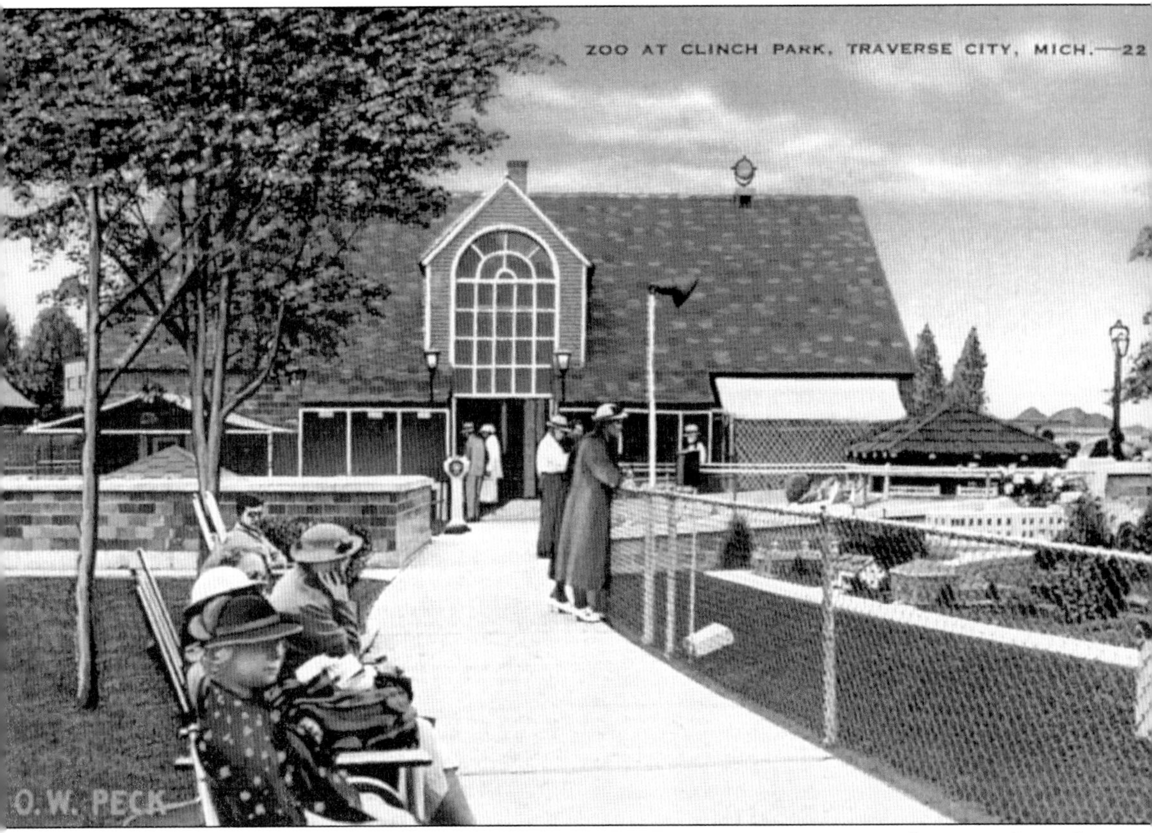

Clinch Park, long a popular tourist attraction in downtown Traverse City, has something for everyone. While the miniature city has been moved to the Music House in Acme, primarily to protect it from the elements, the zoo still abounds with a number of species of animals, fish, and birds. In addition, the Spirit of Traverse City, a miniature locomotive, offers rides around Clinch Park on a daily basis in the summer months. To the north of the park is the recently renovated Clinch Park Marina, located on West Grand Traverse Bay.

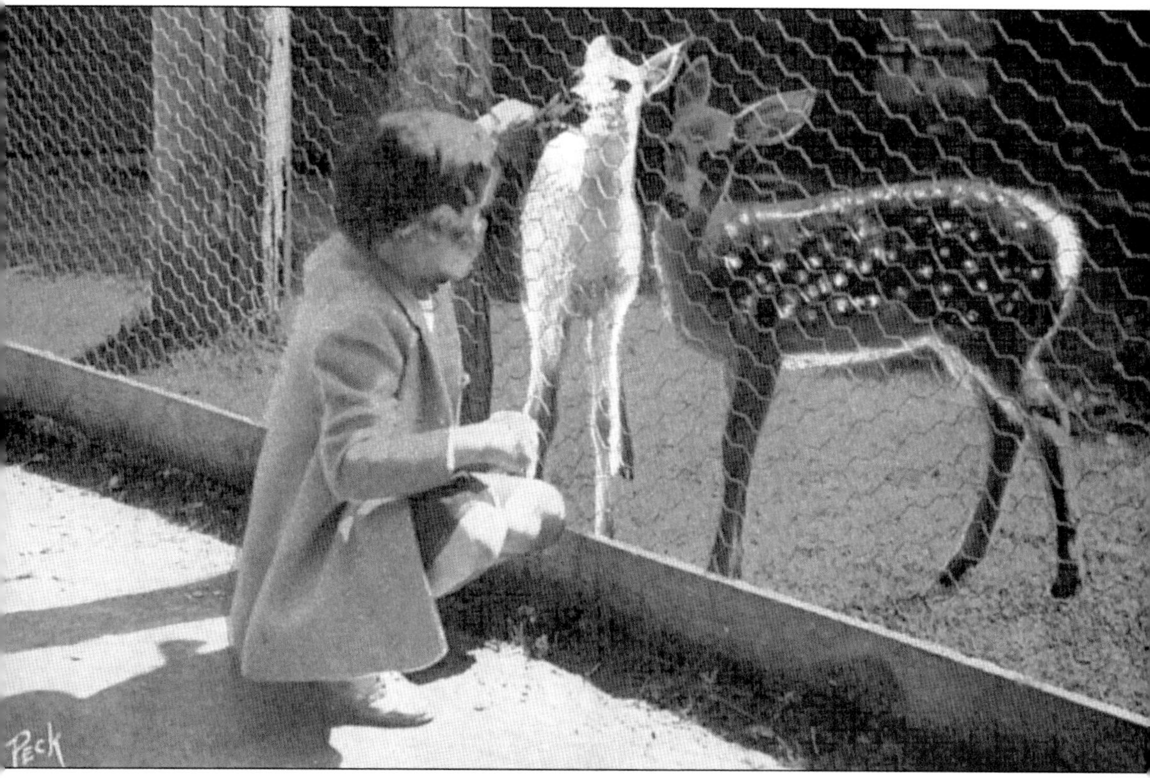

While feeding the animals, even the fawns, is not recommended at Clinch Park Zoo, there are times when children seem to do as they wish. The zoo is owned and operated by the City of Traverse City and is open daily from April 15th until November 1st. Clinch Park Zoo is Northern Michigan's only zoo, housing animals that are indigenous to the area. Recently, the Clinch Park Zoo renovated the otter exhibit; according to plans, the bear exhibit will be expanded and renovated in the near future. In addition, the former Con Foster Museum will soon become home to an all-new aquarium exhibit.

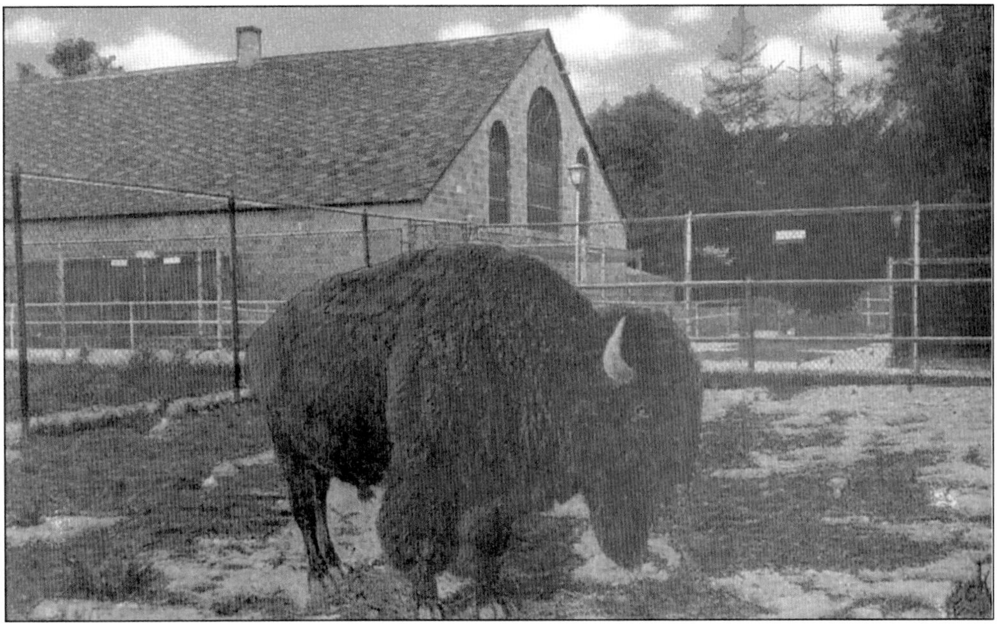

Buffalo play at Clinch Park, due in large part to the fact that the Oleson family of Traverse City owns the largest herd east of the Mississippi. The herd, owned by the Oleson Farms of Traverse City, totals approximately 750 bison, or buffalo as some people prefer to call them. Typically, buffalo weigh between 350 and 400 pounds; have a massive head and front quarters, dark, woolly brown hair, and short, sharp upturned horns. Native to North America, the buffalo were near extinction at the turn of the nineteenth century and as a result, are now found mostly in preserves and zoos.

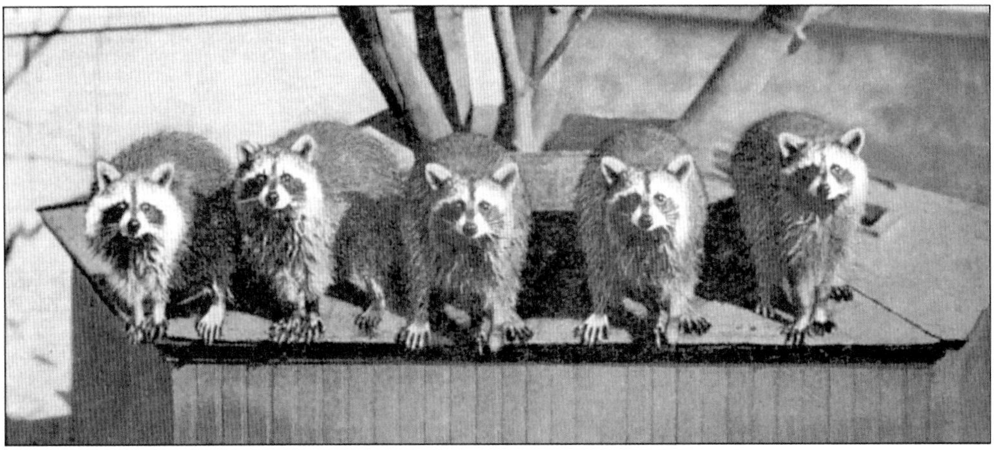

Raccoons, those pesky critters known as masked bandits—who always seem to be getting into everything from the garbage to camping supplies—are on exhibit at the Clinch Park Zoo in Traverse City. In fact, back in the 1920s, the zoo had the distinct privilege of being home to quintuplets. To most people, raccoons appear to be cute, although maybe a bit on the clumsy side. In fact, raccoons are actually quite sly and crafty animals and are quick and agile as well. Raccoons will eat just about anything, but do not feed them. The raccoons at the Clinch Park Zoo are on a special diet, and no matter how cute they might look, they are still wild animals.

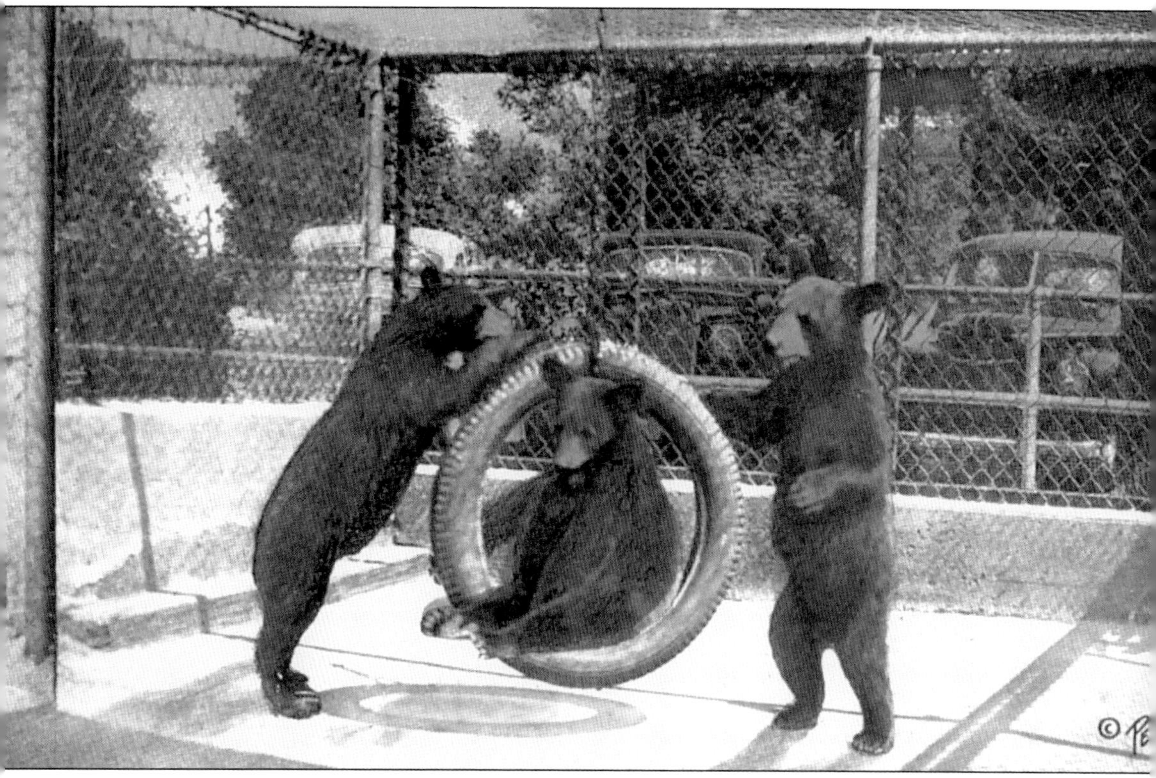

Bears, especially bear cubs, have always been a popular attraction at the Clinch Park Zoo. Indigenous to the area, the northern black bear is not the type of animal that will normally bother people, unless its habitat or cubs are disturbed. Cute and playful, at least as cubs, these bears will stand approximately four feet in height and weigh close to 500 pounds when mature. While visiting Clinch Park, officials admonish guests not to feed the bears, or any of the other animals, due to their strict dietary regimens.

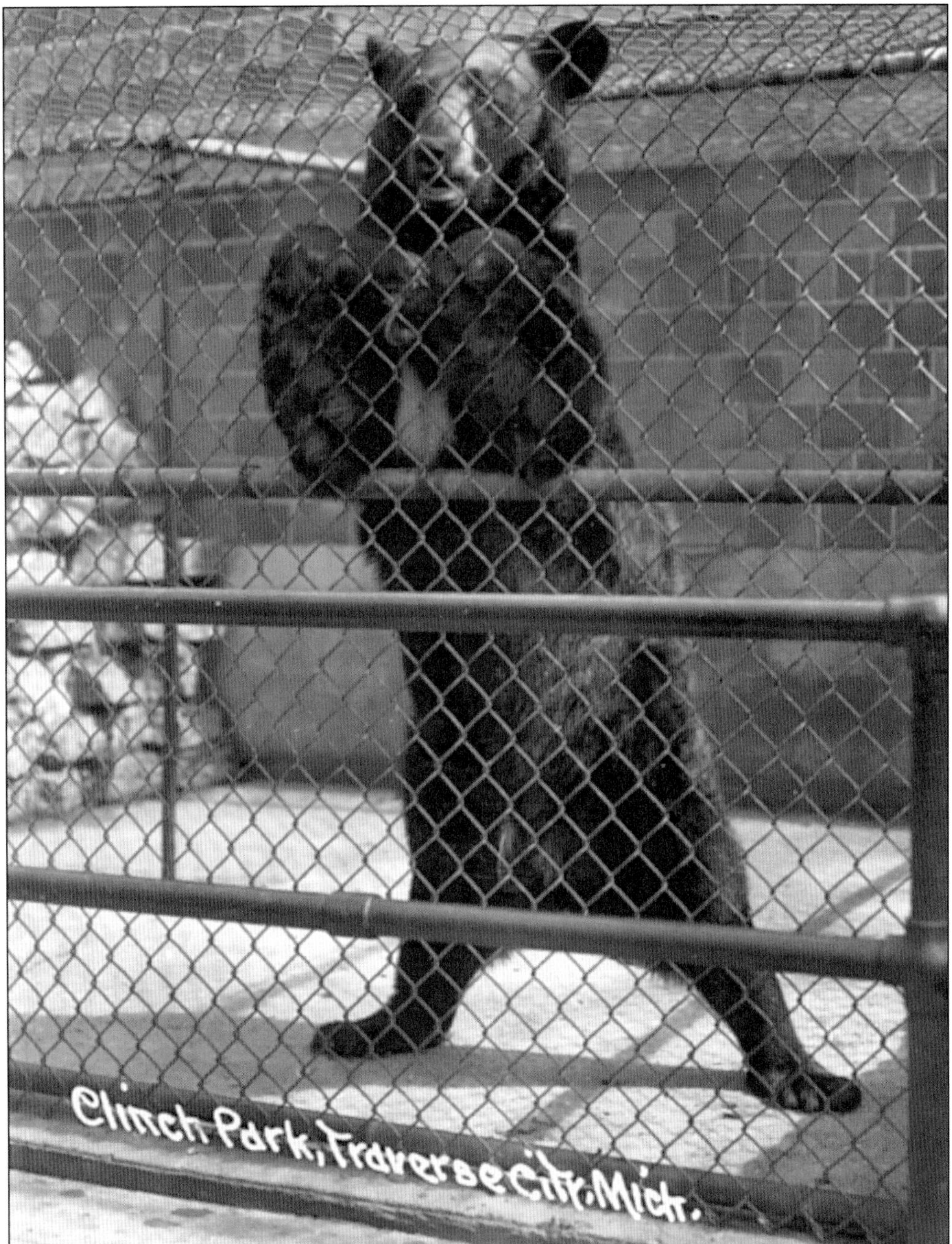

A full-grown male black bear, a resident of the Clinch Park Zoo in Traverse City, stands erect with his paws on the cage. This bear, like many of the animals at Clinch Park, was probably abandoned and subsequently adopted by the zoo. For the most part, the black bears indigenous to Michigan are not fierce animals, unless their cubs or habitat are disturbed. While these black bears are magnificent animals, and the cubs are quite cute, the best place to observe them is in a zoo. When visiting Clinch Park, or any other zoo, keep in mind that not only is it not safe to feed the animals, but it is unhealthy for them as well. Most zoo animals are on strict diets.

Three

TRANSPORTATION AND TOURISM

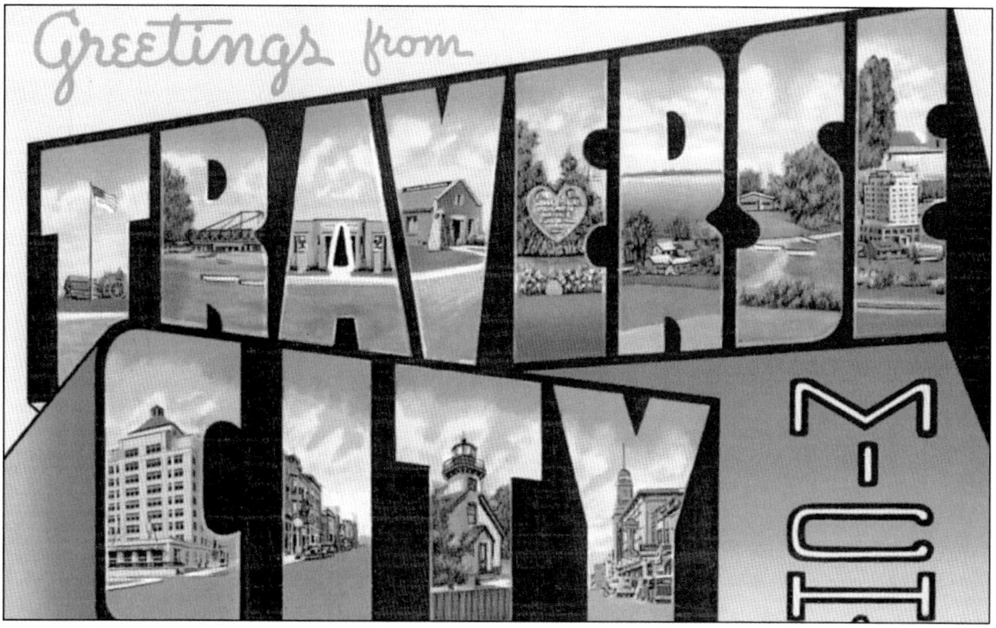

The underlying message of this greeting card tends to be more of an invitation to come and visit Traverse City. This conveys a friendly greeting and, at the same time, shows the reader just a few of the reasons to vacation in Traverse City. At the top left hand side is a picture of the American flag next to some old logging wheels, followed by one of the many bridges in the area. The Con Foster Museum, Clinch Park Zoo and Aquarium, as well as the Heart of Nature's Playground landscape are also shown. A view of Grand Traverse Bay and a picture of the Boardman River are next, followed by Munson Medical Center. On the bottom left is a picture of the completed Park Place Hotel, a view of the south side of Front Street, the Old Mission Lighthouse, and the north side of Front Street with the Traverse City State Bank in the background.

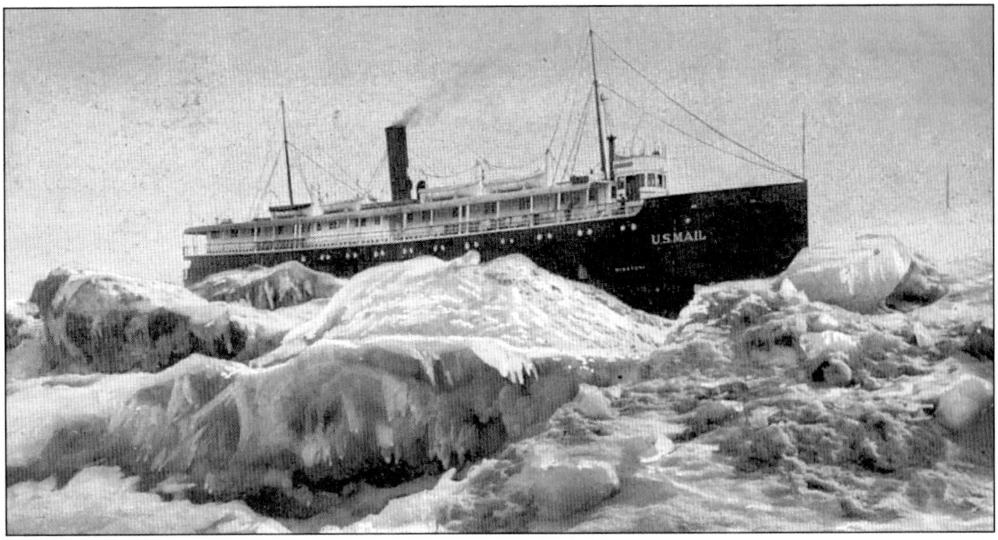

In the early part of the twentieth century, one of the few reliable ways in which to transport goods or mail to the Traverse City area was by ship. During this time, the S.S. *Missouri* was one of a number of ships to sail the Great Lakes performing such services. Owned by the Northern Michigan Transportation Company from 1904 until 1918, this was a ship built to cut through the ice. Built by the Chicago Ship Building Company in 1904, the *Missouri* boasted a length of 225 feet, was 40 feet wide, was nearly 25 feet in height, and could carry almost 2,500 gross tons. After going through several owners, the S.S. *Missouri* was scrapped in August of 1947. Still, there are few sights as majestic as watching a ship crash through the waves or cut its way through ice.

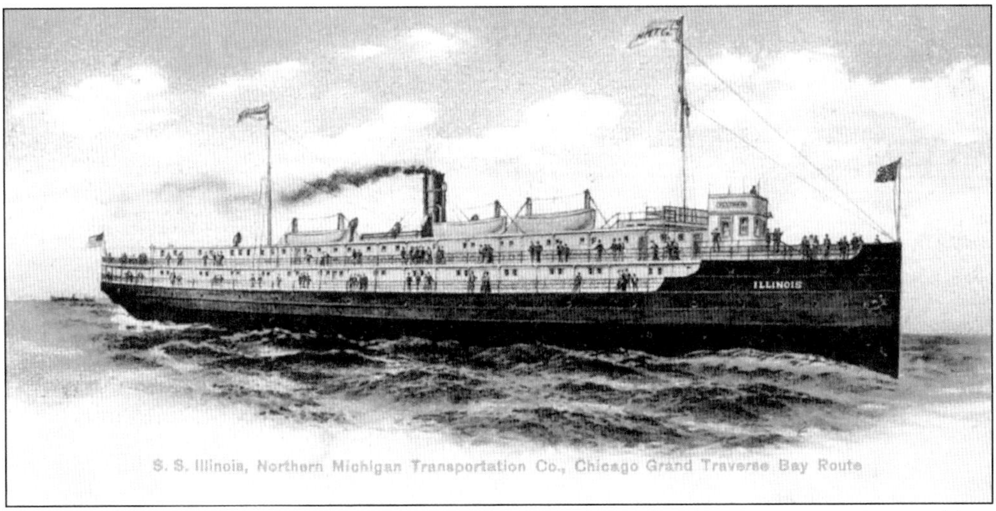

A sister ship to the S.S. *Missouri,* the S.S. *Illinois* was also built by the Chicago Ship Building Company. The S.S. *Illinois* was finished in 1899 and began service that very same year. Also owned by the Northern Michigan Transportation Company, the *Illinois* was primarily a mail ship, but was known to carry passengers from time to time. Built of steel, the dimensions of the S.S. *Illinois* are virtually the same as the S.S. *Missouri*. During her tenure on the Great Lakes, no less than seven different companies owned the *Illinois*, traversing the lakes from 1899 until 1947. In July of 1947, the S.S. *Illinois* was towed down past Detroit by the tugs *Helena* and *McQueen* and scrapped by the Steel Company of Canada, Ltd. of Hamilton, Ontario.

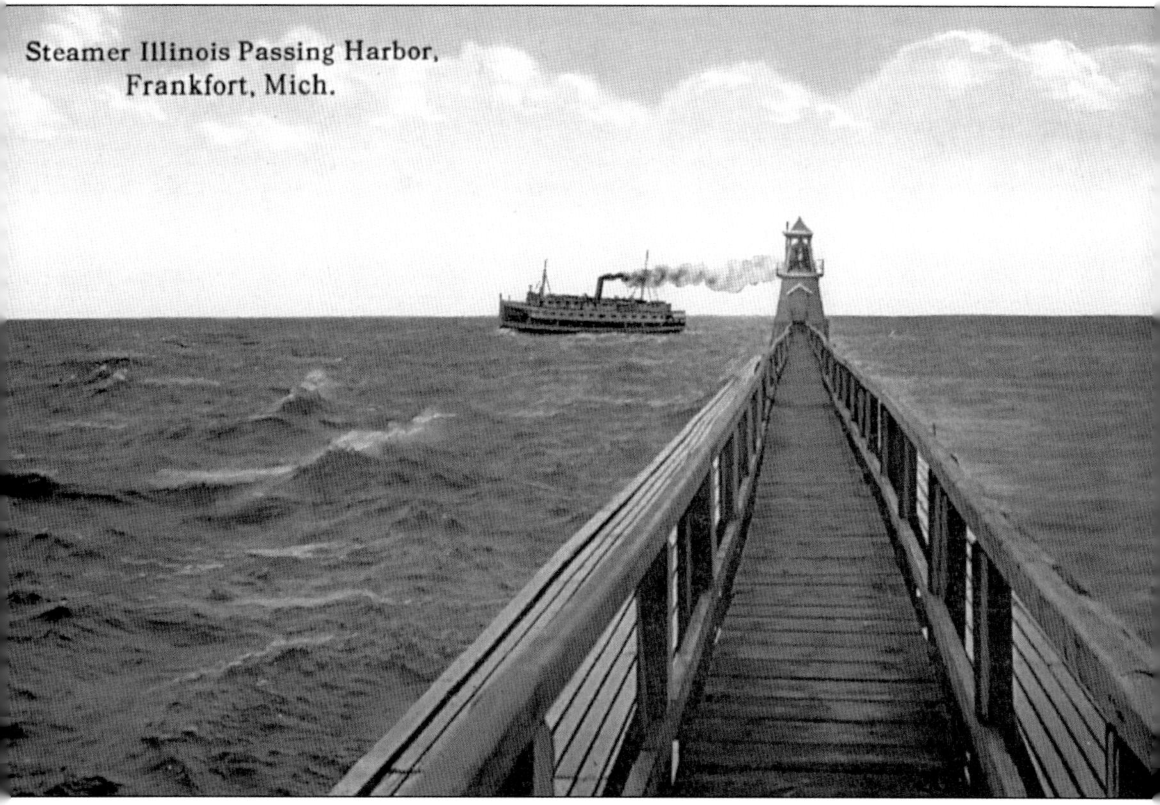

The southbound steamer U.S.S. *Illinois* passes the pier at the Frankfort Harbor. For the most part, the days of the passenger boats have all but disappeared. The advent of interstate highways has contributed to their demise, although there was a day not too long ago when the number of passenger ships on Lake Michigan equaled the number of freighters. Traverse City, Frankfort, Charlevoix, Mackinac, Petoskey, and Ludington were all at one time popular ports, and residents awaited the arrival of ships with great anticipation. After all, if tourists were not arriving by rail, they were most likely aboard one of the many steamers that sailed the Great Lakes.

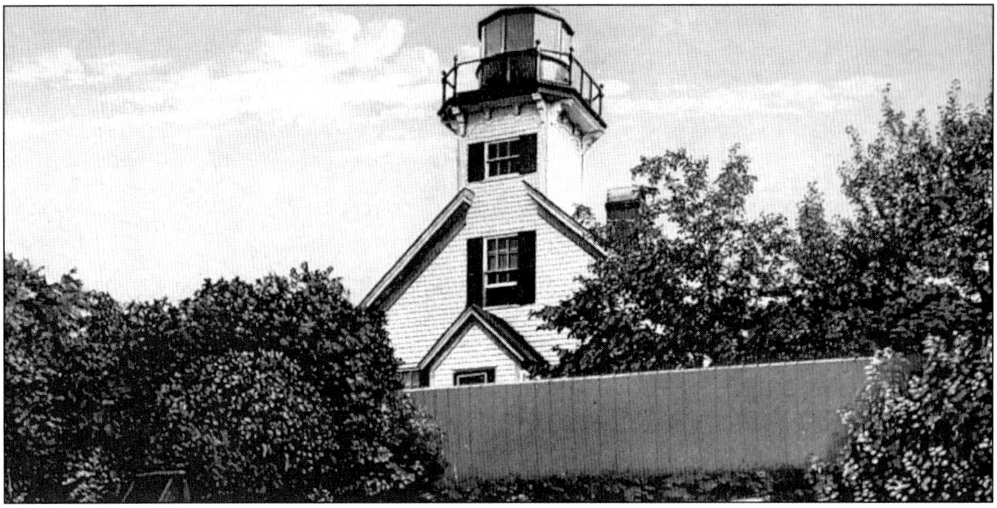

The Old Mission Lighthouse is on the tip of the Old Mission Peninsula, about 18 miles north of Traverse City. Approved by the federal government in 1865, the lighthouse was not built until 1870, primarily due to a lack of manpower. A duplicate of the Mama Juda lighthouse built on the Detroit River in 1866, the wooden house is painted in white with black trim and has a small 309-foot tower at the roofline with a black parapet, which once housed the lighthouse lantern. In 1933, the lighthouse was decommissioned and now serves as the residence of the manager of the Old Mission Park. The lighthouse is located on the 45th parallel, halfway between the Equator and the North Pole, at Old Mission Point.

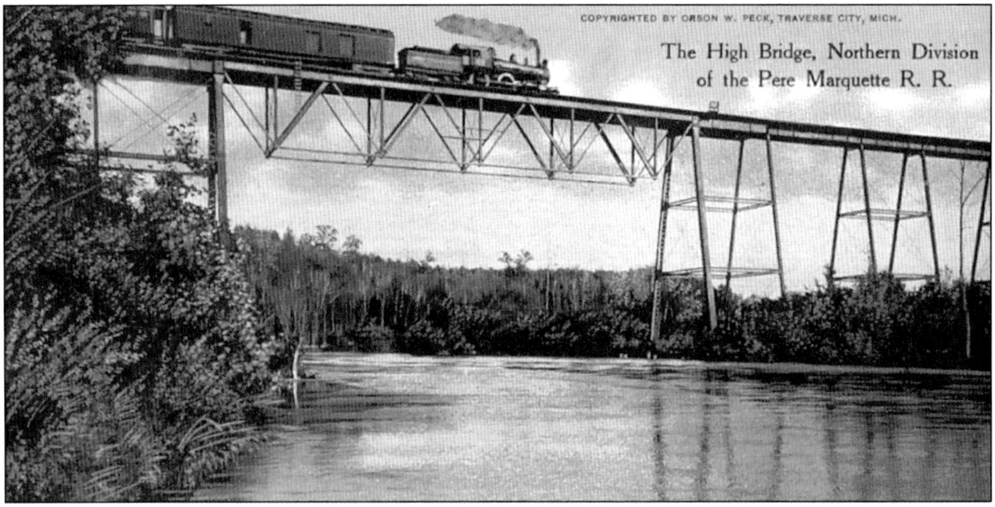

Transportation in the early years, especially if one was to travel a significant distance, was preferably done in the comfort and elegance of a railway car. The Pere Marquette Railroad, which for many years served the Traverse City area, was an outgrowth of several mergers and acquisitions that took place in the early 1900s. Providing luxury accommodations to travelers who were visiting the Traverse City area and to local residents headed to Chicago, Detroit, or Grand Rapids, was initially secondary in importance. First and foremost, the railroad transported lumber and other products to market and also provided residents with some of the more refined goods not available locally. Many of those rails still wind through Traverse City, following the shoreline of Boardman Lake and the course of the Boardman River.

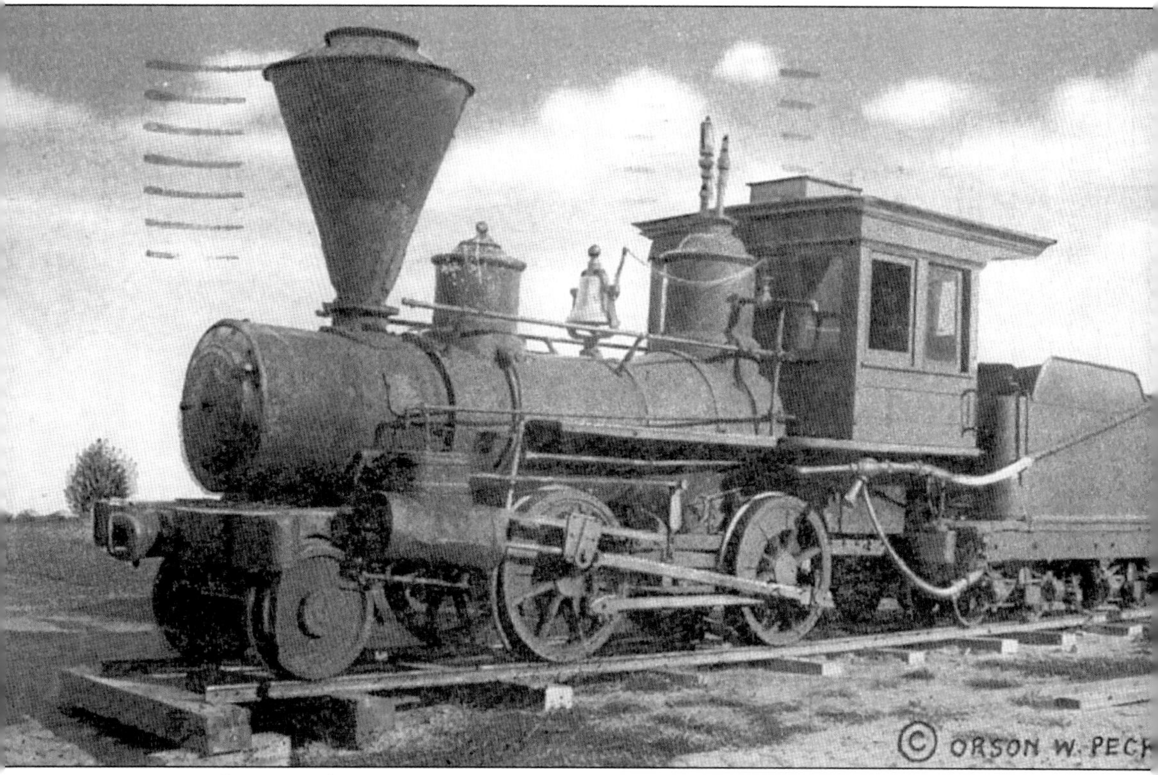

Logging, a vital aspect of Traverse City's economy in the early days, relied heavily upon the railroads to transport lumber to market and to bring in much-needed goods and refineries to the area. Locomotives such as this one, which at one time was on display at Clinch Park in downtown Traverse City, were crucial not only to the growth of Traverse City, but to all of Northern Michigan. The Pere Marquette, which over the years became a conglomeration of a number of railroads, and the Manistee & Northeastern were the primary rail companies serving the Grand Traverse area. The Manistee & Northeastern depended more upon lumber and produce shipments, taking on few passengers, while the Pere Marquette transported both passengers and goods on a regular basis.

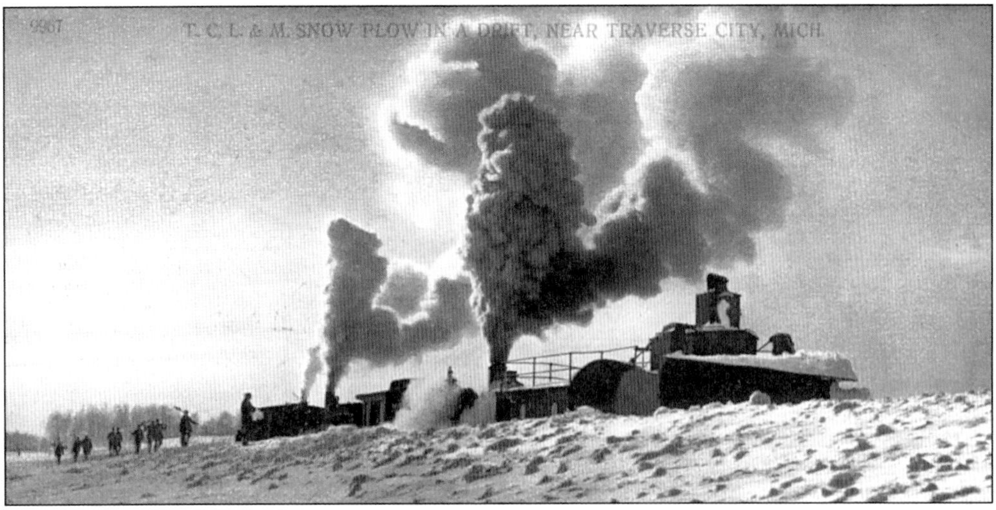

Winter storms are a part of life in Northern Michigan and of course, Traverse City is no exception. While paved streets and highways have, to a great extent, made traveling easier, it was not so long ago that cars, trucks, and yes, even railroad trains had a great deal of difficulty moving through the ice and snow. It was necessary to clear railroad tracks of any and all obstructions, and during the winter months, the crew of a snowplow such as the TCL & M, would do their best to ensure that the trains ran on time. In its infancy, the railroad was crucial to the economic and social well-being of not only Traverse City, but also the entire region.

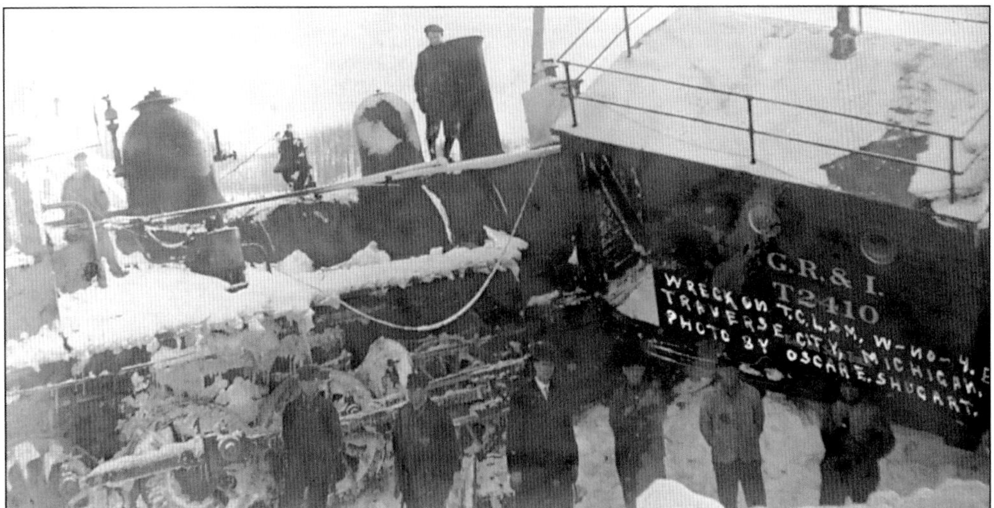

In April of 1925, during what might be termed a late season snowstorm, the Traverse City, Leelanau & Manistique Railroad suffered a wreck near Summit City. The TCL & M was a subsidiary of the Manistique & Northwestern Railroad Company, a line associated with the Grand Rapids & Indiana Railroad. While not a cause for undue concern, ice and snow build-up on the railroad tracks led engineers to proceed with caution. Incorporated in 1901, the Traverse City, Leelanau & Manistique initially ran between Manistique and Northport, with stops in Traverse City and some of the neighboring towns. Acquired by the Manistique, Marquette & Northern Railroad Company in 1902, the line eventually became part of the Pere Marquette Line, changing hands numerous times prior to its demise in 1968.

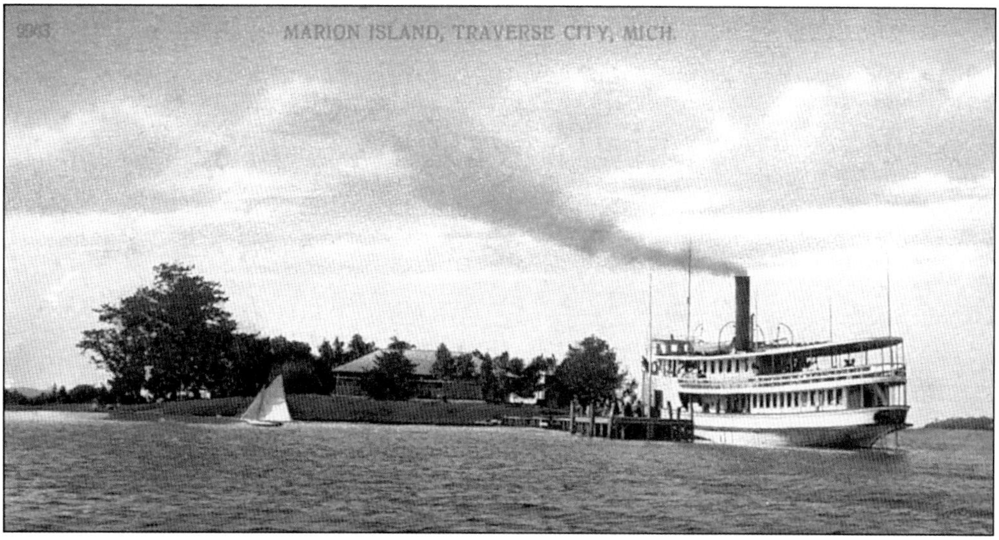

Bassett Island, which is actually connected to Power Island during low water levels, is located at the northeastern tip of the island. Dockage on Power Island, or Marion Island as it was called in 1906, allowed small ships such as the *Columbia* to portage passengers from the mainland to the island. In the early 1900s there was a 50-foot by 100-foot dance hall located on Bassett Island. For those adventurous types seeking an evening of socializing, the dance hall provided just such an outlet. The dance hall is long gone, although there are numerous hiking paths and even a few camping spots on the island. Oddly enough, it is one of the few places in Northern Michigan where there are no deer, squirrels, or chipmunks.

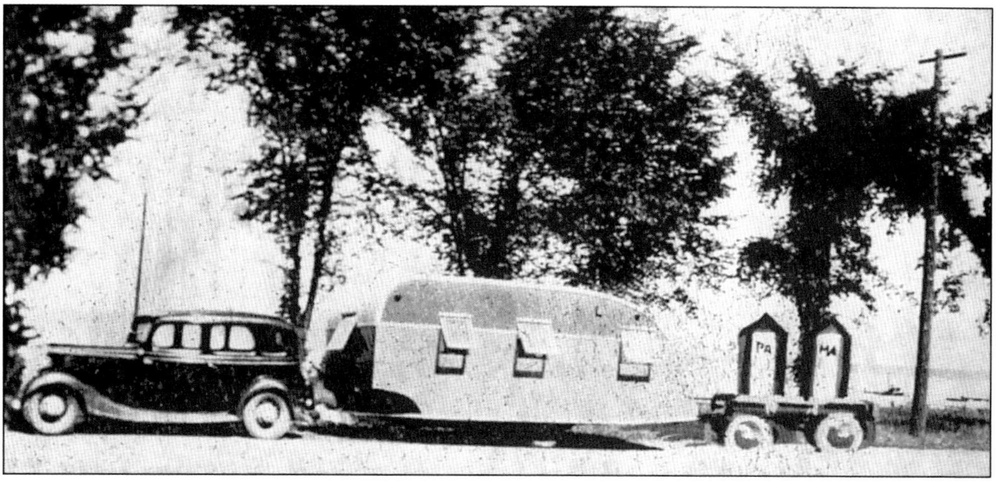

The mass production of the automobile gave Americans a great deal of mobility, and that meant the freedom to travel. With the advent of the automobile and the construction of state and interstate highways, people were no longer limited by the destinations of the rail and shipping lines. An automobile, a camper, and an outhouse or two had all the makings of an all American family vacation. For many Michigan residents, as well as a number of others, there was no question of where to spend a vacation. Their destination was Traverse City, with its quaint downtown, swimming for the kids on East and West Grand Traverse Bay, and more fish than people could hope to catch in most other vacation spots. The city offered all this and more, especially if visits took place in the month of July, during the National Cherry Festival.

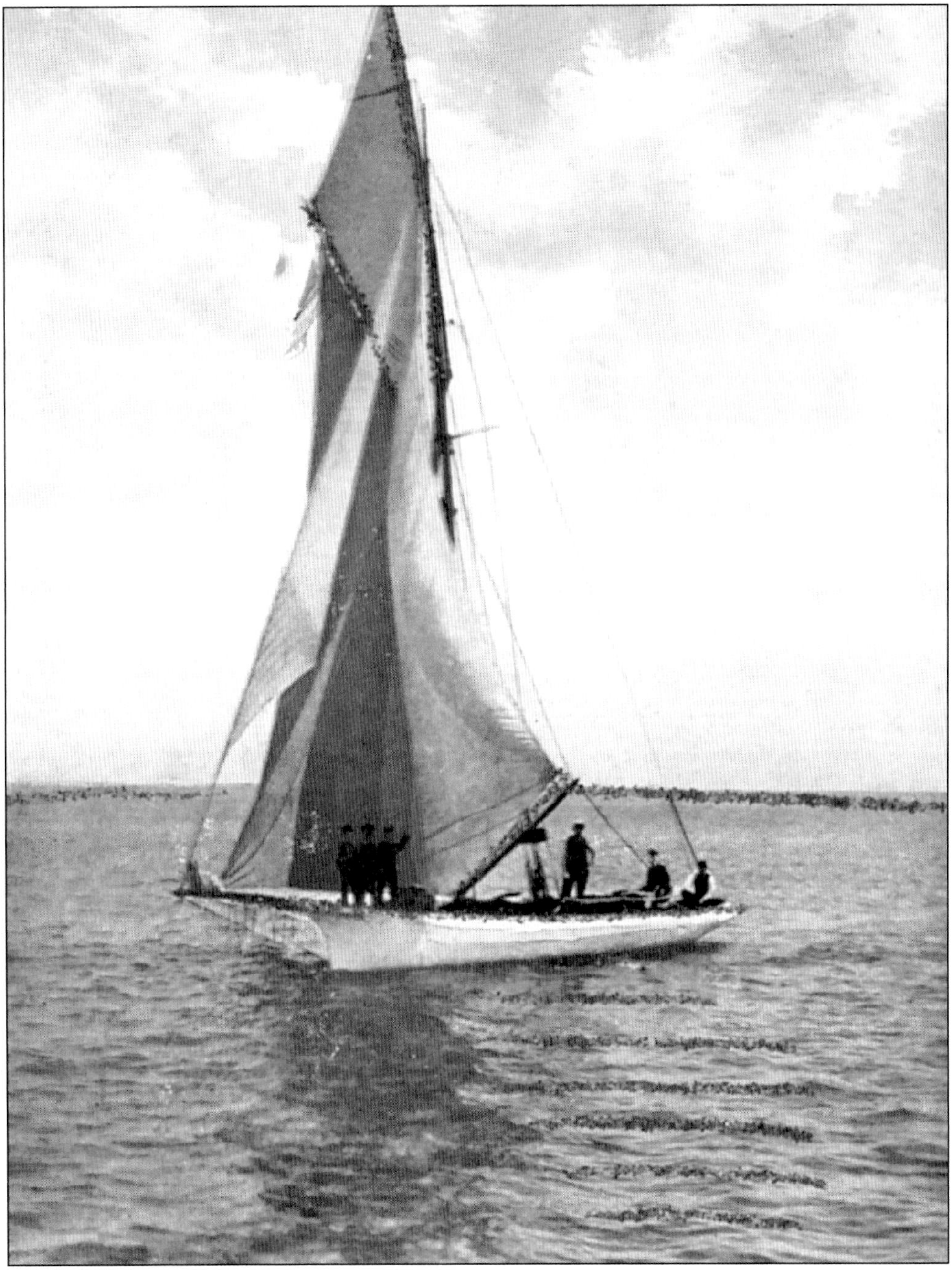

Yachting on Grand Traverse Bay has always been a peaceful, relaxing way to spend a day or even a weekend for that matter. From the days of homemade sailboats to the sleek, refined yachts of today, Grand Traverse Bay has been and remains a favorite among the boating crowd. The days of two-masted schooners delivering goods to the area and hauling locally-made goods to market is a distant reminder of Traverse City's past, replaced to a great degree by the railroads that began servicing the area early in the twentieth century. Today, sunrises and sunsets on the tranquil waters of Grand Traverse Bay are solely at the behest of the sailor and sportsman.

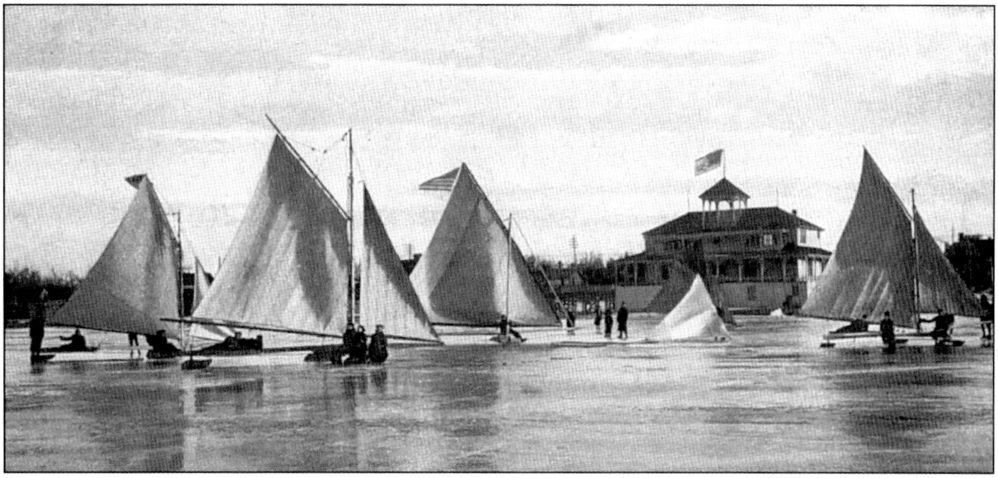

During the winter months, there are several popular sports in the Traverse City area, and iceboating is definitely one of them. These iceboats, from around 1910, are sailing on Grand Traverse Bay in front of the Wequetong Club. The reasons for owning an iceboat are quite similar to those for any other type of watercraft: pleasure and racing. The Grand Traverse Ice Yacht Club holds races in the Traverse City area, such as the Annual Fun Regatta in March, attracting approximately 50 entrants and seven different types of iceboats. In addition, there are some iceboaters on hand to merely give rides and share in the iceboating experience. Iceboats such as the ones pictured here are called stern-steerers and have a steering rudder mounted at the tail end of the boat.

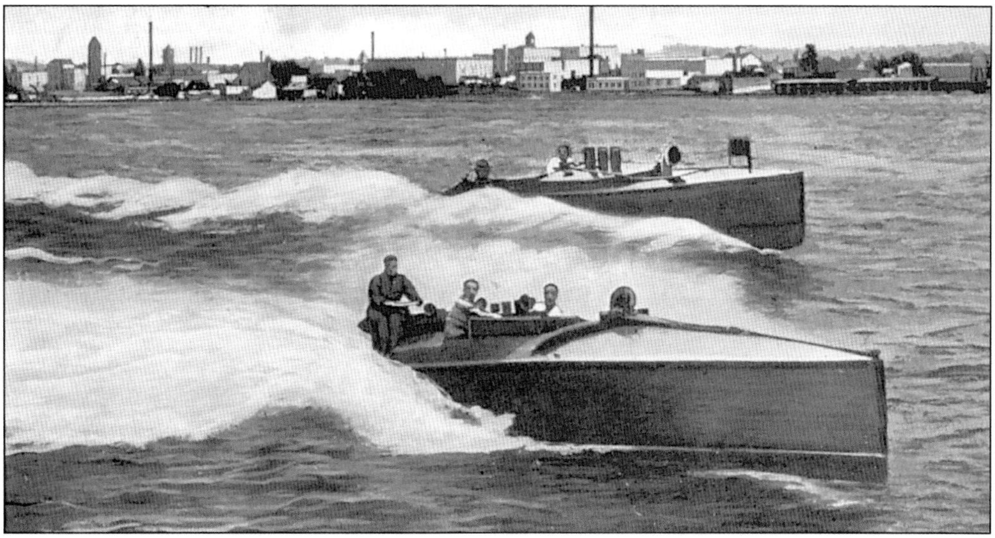

Speedboat races, such as the one depicted in this postcard, are a common sight on Grand Traverse Bay, especially West Bay—although the days of Chris-Craft, Garwood, Thompson, and other wooden vessels are for the most part history and nautical legend. Each summer, both East Bay and West Bay are deluged with boats of every type, size, variety, and color. Families on their way to a picnic on the island, sport fishermen trying to catch that elusive walleye or lake trout, water-skiers, and yes, even the occasional speedboat race, are not uncommon sights. And while boat races have been and probably always will be a welcome sight on Grand Traverse Bay, this depiction is most probably the creation of a fanciful imagination.

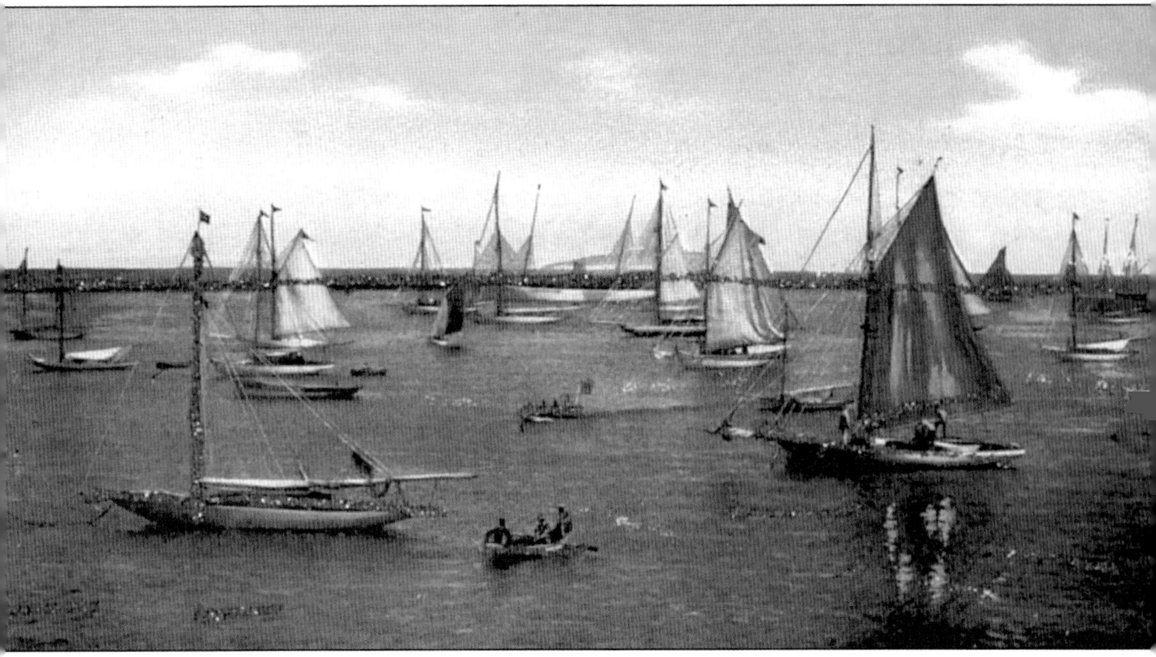

All forms of boating are extremely popular in the Traverse City area and most probably have been since the beginning of time. While the idea of boating may produce visions of a serene afternoon on Grand Traverse Bay, the fact of the matter is that there are sure to be quite a few other people with the same notion. Canoes, kayaks, skiffs, schooners, rowboats, cabin cruisers, and speedboats all share the waters of Grand Traverse Bay and, other than the occurrence of the occasional storm, everyone seems to have a good time.

(*Opposite, bottom*) Obviously proud of the accomplishment, an angler displays the day's catch for everyone to view. Northern Michigan, in particular the Traverse City area, is well-known for its sport fishing. Bass, bluegill, perch, pike, trout, and walleye are among a few of the varieties of fish found in the lakes, rivers, and streams around the Traverse City area. Arbutus Lake, Bass Lake, the Boardman River, Long Lake, and Silver Lake, as well as the East and West Arms of Grand Traverse Bay, have always provided the sport fisherman with a number of places to drop a line, sit back, and enjoy the day.

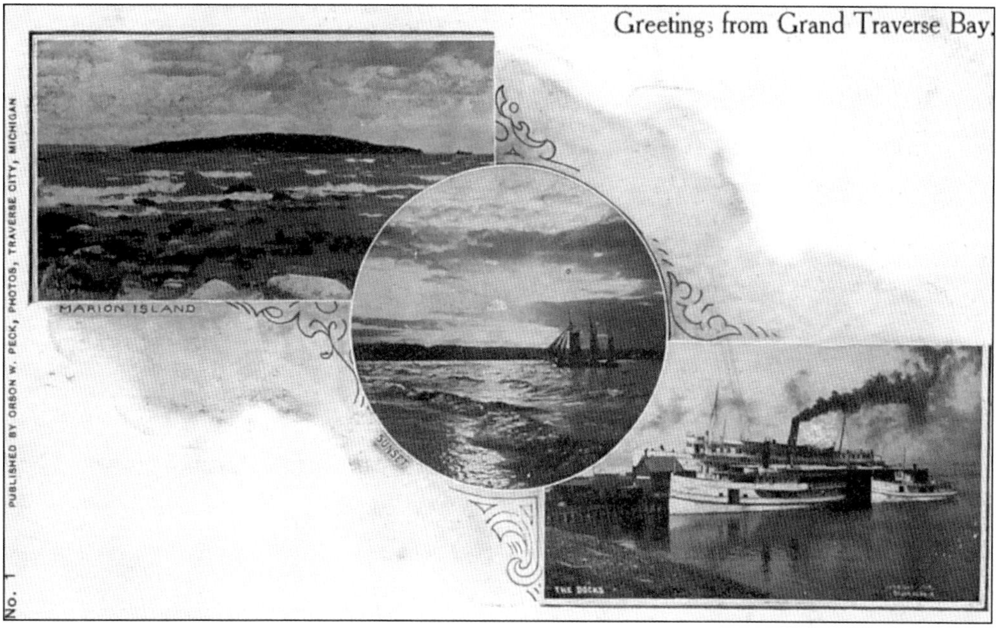

(*Above*) At the far upper left is a picture of Power Island, an island that has had many monikers beginning with its original owner who named it after his daughter, Marion; then Henry Ford owned the island from 1917 until 1944, and for a time it was known as Ford Island. The island was then sold to the Rennie family of Traverse City and came to be called Rennie Island; the most recent owner was a man by the name of Power, who donated the island to Grand Traverse County. In the center is a picture of a four-masted schooner making its way across the bay at sunset, and in the lower right corner several ships are shown arriving at the coal docks just off of West Bay Shore Road.

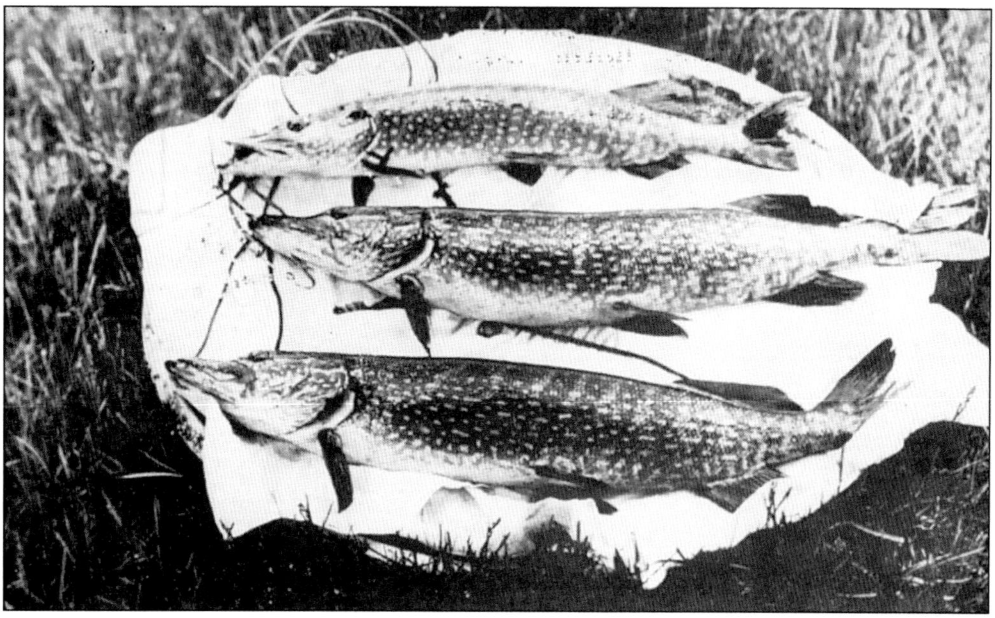

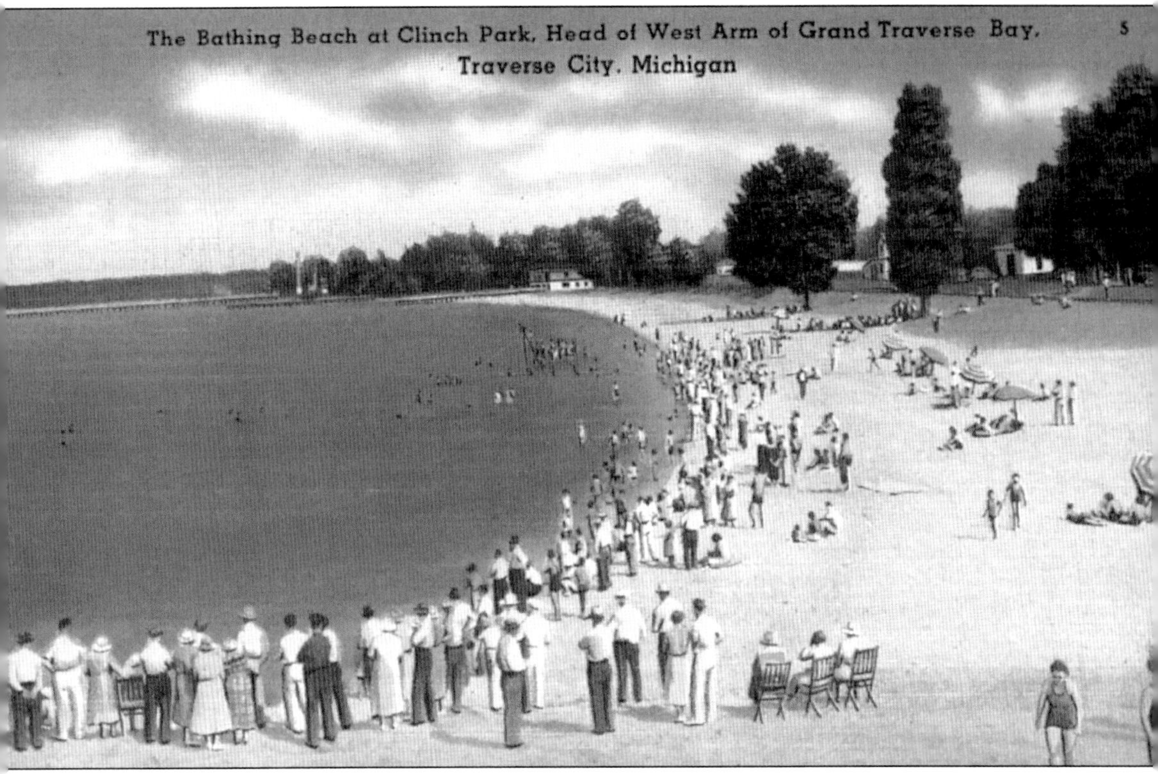

Clinch Park Beach has always been one of the most popular beaches in the Traverse City area. The park is located just to the east of the recently remodeled Clinch Park Zoo and Marina, at the head of the West Arm of Grand Traverse Bay. In the past, Clinch Park has been home to numerous events held annually in July during the National Cherry Festival, including the milk boat regatta and sailboat and speedboat races. From Traverse City's earliest beginnings to the present day, people have flocked to the sandy beach of Clinch Park to picnic, sunbathe, and swim.

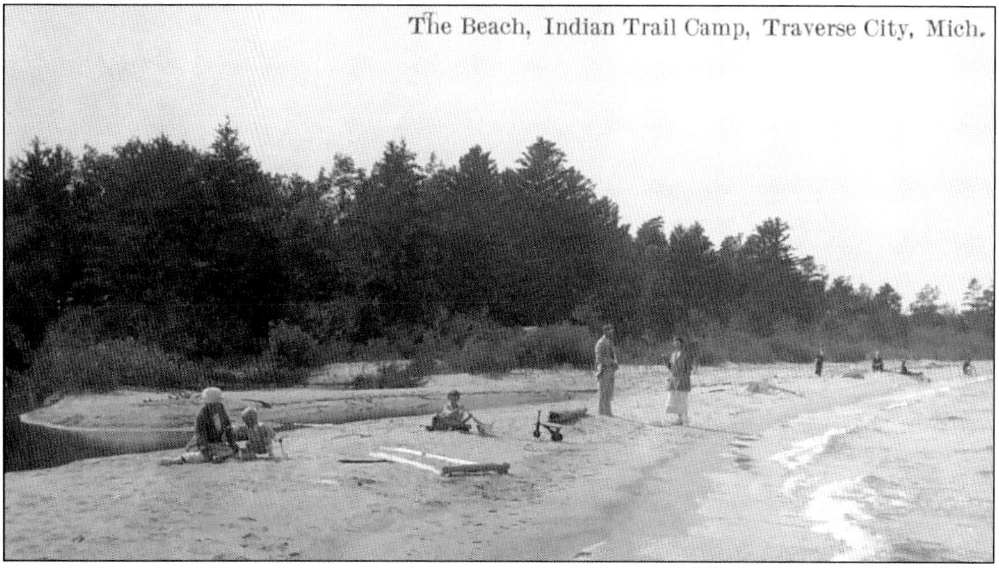

The beach at Indian Trail Camp, now known as Traverse City State Park, is located approximately three-quarters of a mile east of Traverse City. The shallow waters of East Grand Traverse Bay make the Traverse City State Park a favorite among locals, as well as visitors, many of whom return annually for a family vacation. It is here that the mouth of Mitchell Creek, at the far west of the beach, empties into East Bay. During the summer months, the beach is teeming with people and—for those who intend on finding a spot on the beach to sun themselves—it is always best to arrive early.

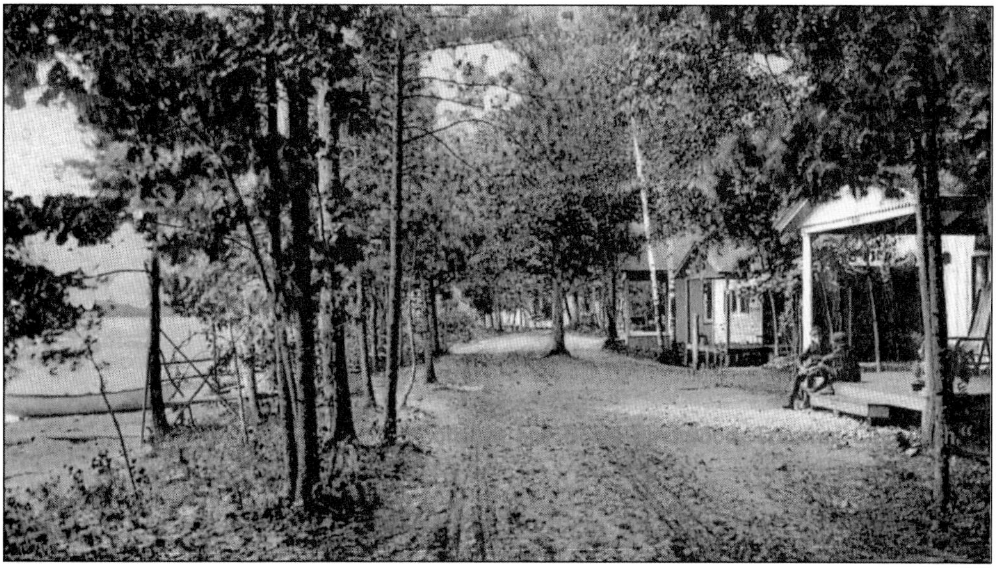

The cottages at Birchwood, while somewhat rustic, afforded a good number of people the opportunity to leave their troubles behind and enjoy the peace and solitude of Grand Traverse Bay. Similar to many resorts of its day, Birchwood did not offer a great number of amenities; rather it simply gave people the chance to get away from the hustle and bustle of the daily grind. Long since gone, the cottages at Birchwood were located on the west shore of East Grand Traverse Bay.

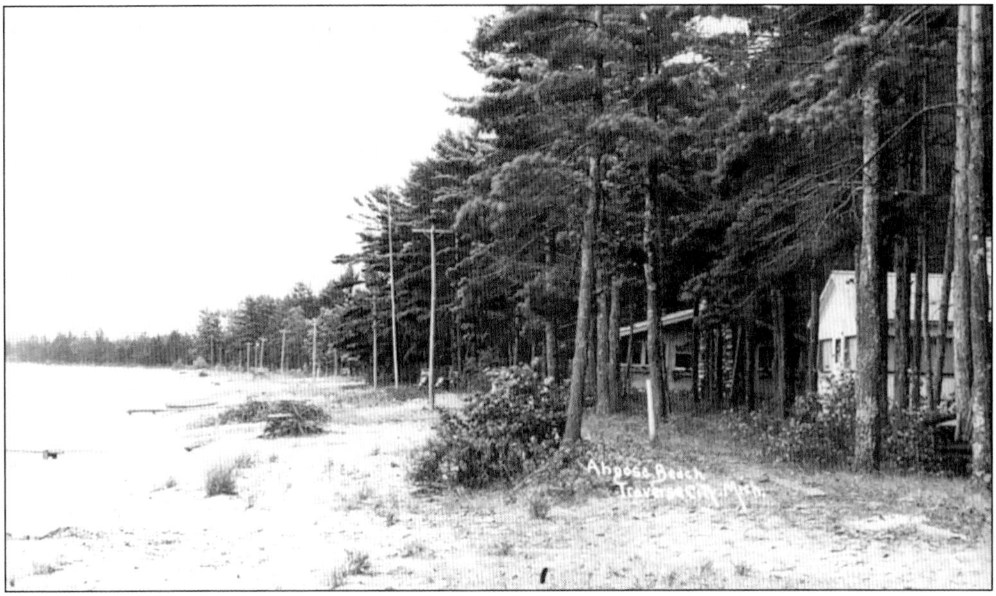

Aghosa Trail, at the headwaters of the East Arm of Grand Traverse Bay, is home to a collection of residences, both summer and year round, that are a throwback to earlier times. Located in the heart of Traverse City, just off of Eighth Street and Munson Avenue, Aghosa Trail is more a conclave of beachfront homes than a trail. Named for Chief Aghosa, the Ottawa Indian Chieftain who refused to sell land on the Old Mission Peninsula, this area has it all, with its sandy beaches and sweeping vistas of East Grand Traverse Bay.

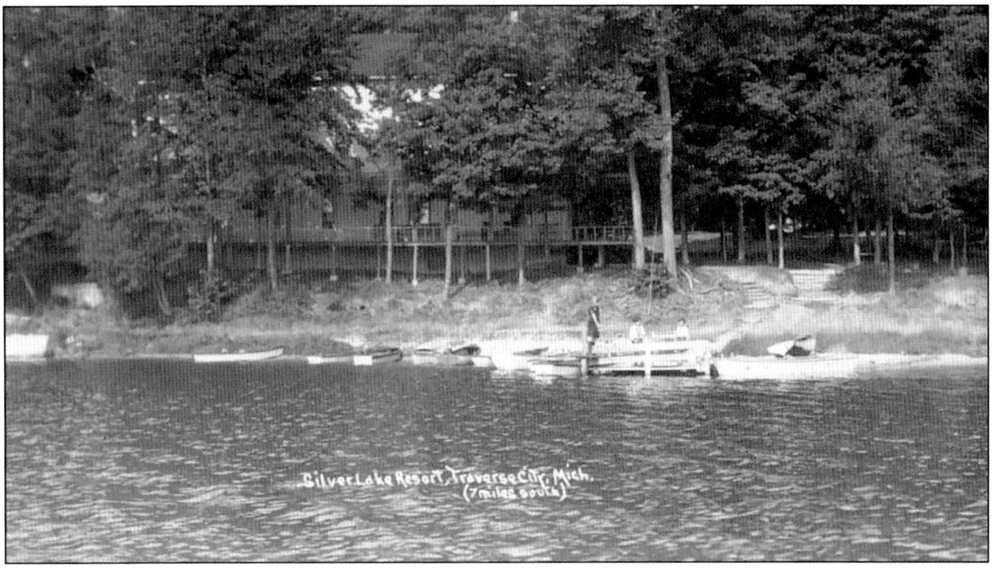

The Silver Lake Resort, located on Silver Lake about seven miles southwest of Traverse City, was a sprawling ranch-like resort. In fact, in the 1920s it was part of a new generation of resorts being built in the Grand Traverse area. Most of these resorts were, in fact, what we would now consider bed and breakfasts. Little has changed on Silver Lake over the years; some of the older resorts are no longer there, although there are cabins and a couple of newer lodgings to take its place. To top it off, the fishing on Silver Lake is just as good now as it was in the early part of the century.

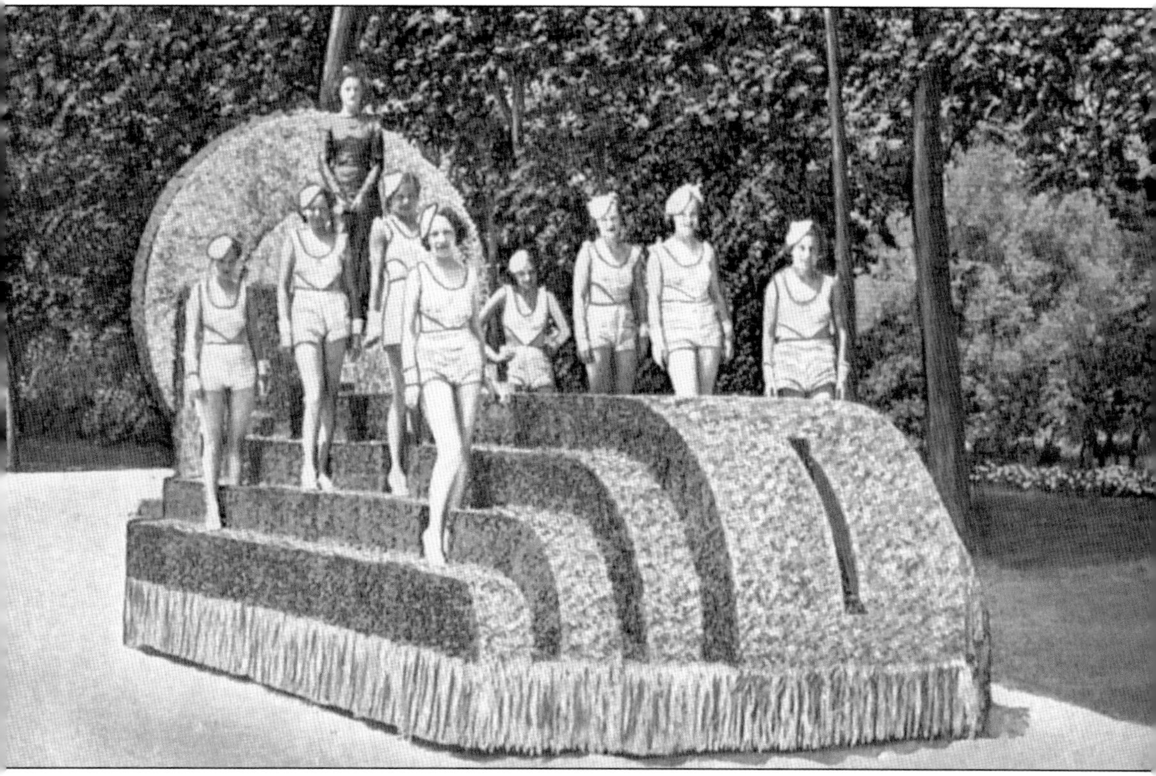

In 1934, these young women were among many who took part in the National Cherry Festival. The first cherry harvest celebration, the Blessing of the Blossoms, which takes place to this day on the Old Mission Peninsula, attracted 3,000 people in 1924. This was the beginning of what was soon to become the National Cherry Festival; an event that during one week each summer draws over 500,000 people from around the world. The festival, which today features over 150 events, annually brings in approximately $20,000,000 to the area. A local tradition, the festival is intended to promote the cherry industry, tourism, and community involvement, as well as cultivate the business, entertainment, and cultural aspects of the region.

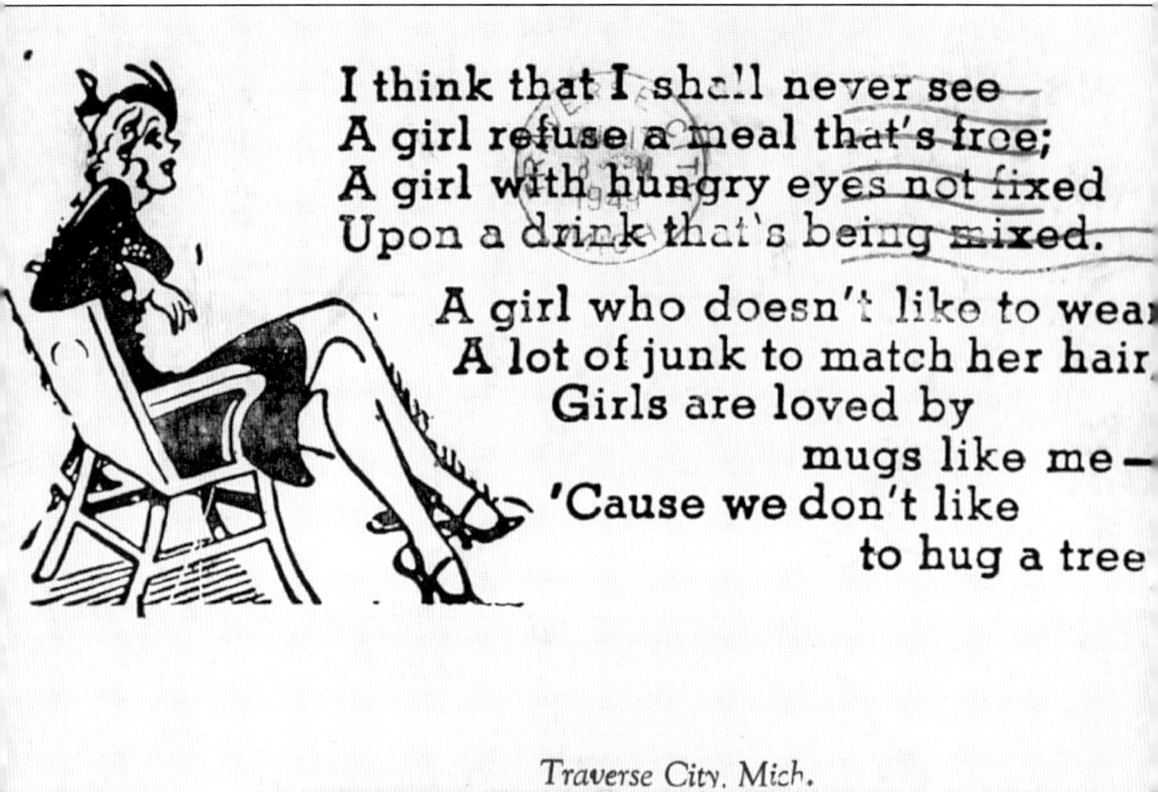

Sensibilities, at least with regard to sexism, were quite different back in the years preceding World War II. To a great degree, Traverse City was a microcosm of American society, and especially during the early part of the century, men were considered the dominant force and women were still treated as objects. As in this case, flirtatious and fun-loving as it may seem, the dapper gents of the day were very objectifying towards women. All in all, the message is rather unusual, suggesting that women do not care for environmentalists.

(*Opposite, bottom*) There was a time not very long ago—and not just in Traverse City, but throughout the country—when taking care of the children was seen as woman's work. While this cartoon, actually mailed from Buckley (20 miles south of Traverse City), takes a lighthearted view of the situation, it was hardly anything to laugh about. Back in 1914, when this card was sent, sayings such as, "spare the rod and spoil the child" were seen more as truths than fiction.

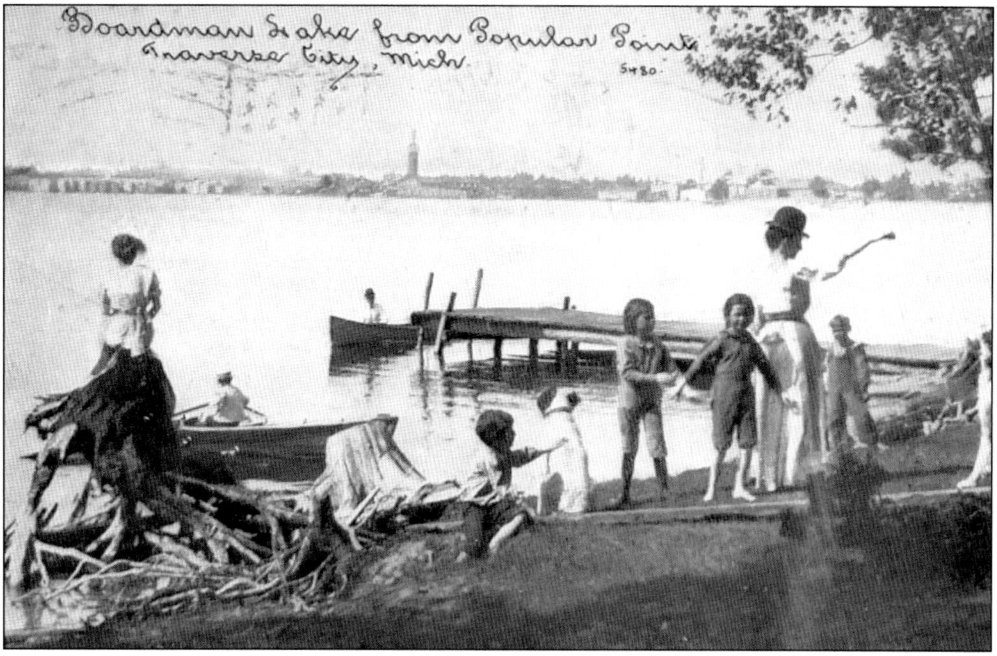

(*Above*) The banks of Boardman Lake were at one time quite popular with swimmers, and even though that might surprise some people, it was one of the most visited areas in the entire Grand Traverse region. To a great degree, Boardman Lake is thought of as scenic and is still a favorite among fishermen, but the fact remains that most local residents would not think of going swimming in it because Boardman Lake and the Boardman River have suffered from an ecological standpoint. Recently, the Boardman River Project has begun a campaign focused on restoring the waterway and raising public awareness with regard to the need for a healthy watershed.

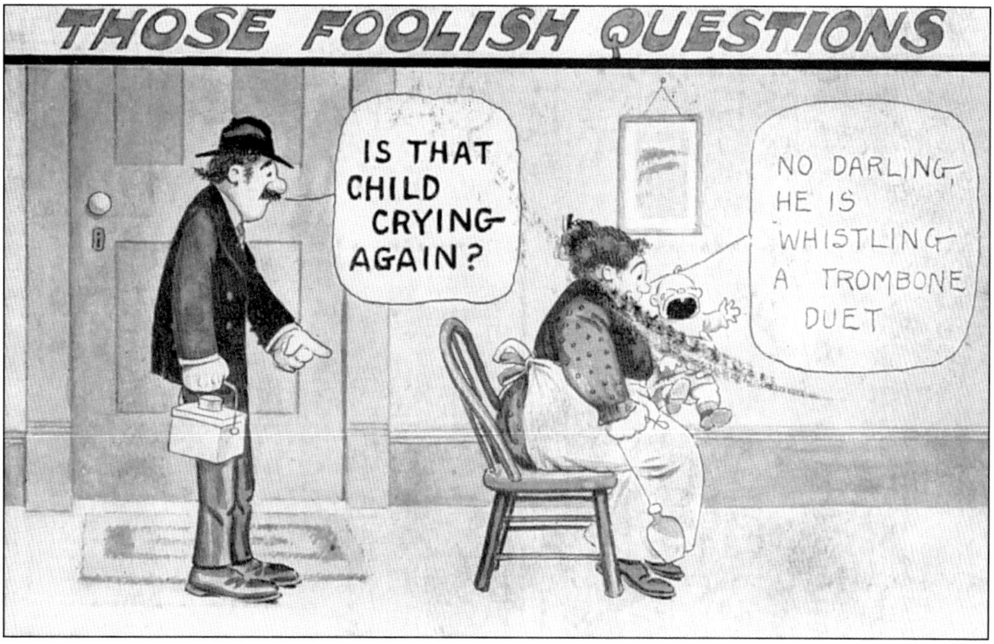

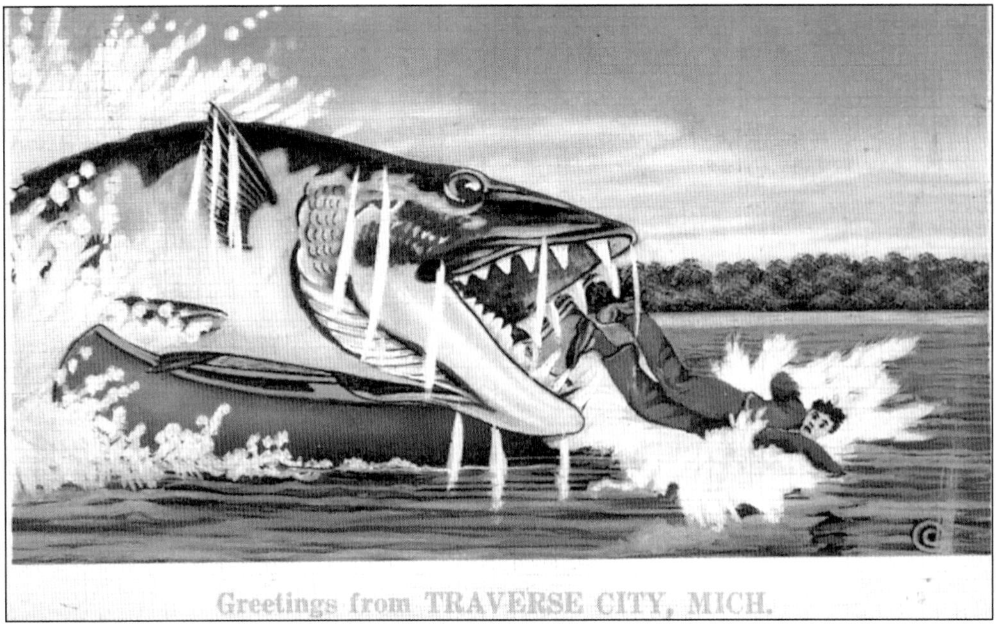

Sport fishing has always been popular in Traverse City and, while it is not unheard of to catch your limit, it is the size of the fish that is usually in question. The area is still known for its sport fishing, although at one time there were also a number of commercial fishermen operating out of both Grand Traverse and Leelanau Counties. Grand Traverse Bay, as well as the numerous inland lakes, provide an outlet for anglers seeking to catch the big one and are as popular today as they were 100 years ago.

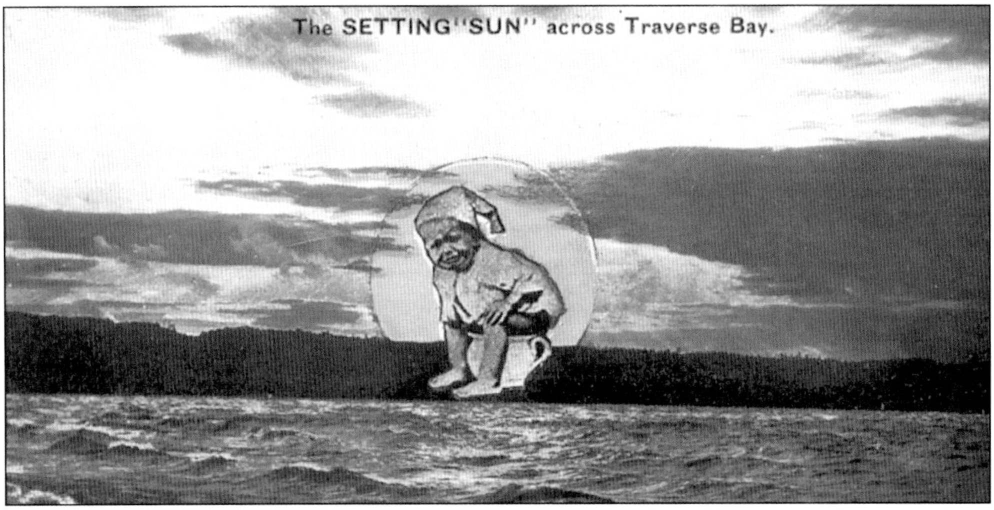

Orson Peck may have catalogued much of Northern Michigan's history, although he also had a sense of humor, one in keeping with the times. As the sun sets in Grand Traverse Bay, he offers up a vision of a "sitting son" to coincide with the magnificent Traverse City sunset. This toddler, posed on a chamber pot, appears prepared to set himself down as the sun sets in the west. The humor of not only Mr. Peck, but in general of the people in the Grand Traverse region should not be underestimated. After all, given the circumstances, the residents need a way to make it from season to season.

Four

A Scenic Drive

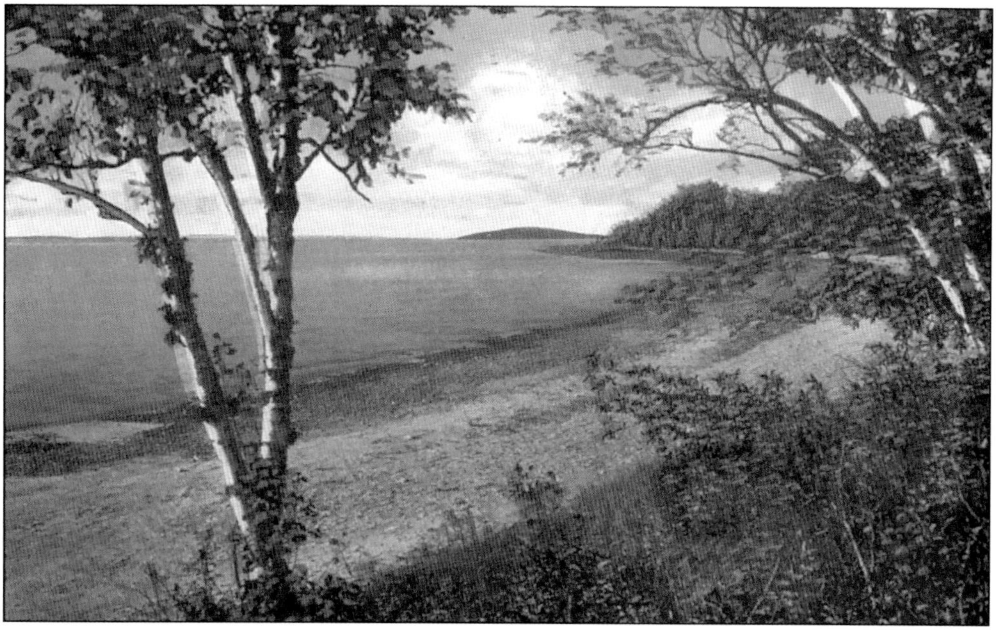

There are numerous turnouts on the Old Mission Peninsula that provide a glimpse of Grand Traverse Bay. This particular view is of the West Arm of Grand Traverse Bay, with what was then Ford Island in the distance. Most of the turnouts are well-hidden, two tracks with an overgrowth of trees and bushes leading down to the beach. Perfect for a family picnic, sunbathing, or swimming, finding a stretch of beach that is uninhabited during the summer is quite rare. If nothing else, a short walk down to one of the many beaches on the Old Mission Peninsula inspires many people, who are astounded by the natural beauty of the area.

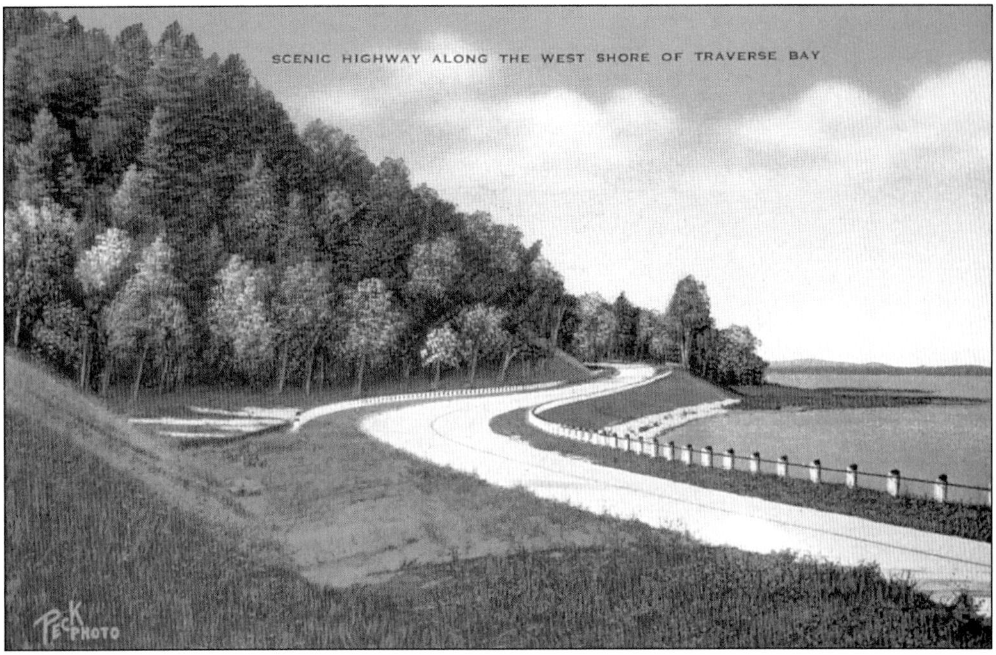

(*Above*) A day trip out of Traverse City, on West Bay Shore Road, is a leisurely one with spectacular views of Grand Traverse Bay. Following the Grandview Parkway in a westward direction, travelers soon find themselves in Leelanau County. West Bay Shore Road, or M-22, leads the way to Suttons Bay, Omena, and Northport, on the tip of the Leelanau Peninsula. The journey and the turnouts along the way are half of the fun. Glancing back at Traverse City in the distance, or looking straight across the bay to Power Island, makes the trip worthwhile. The villages on the Leelanau Peninsula, each with their own character, are quite unique and quaint.

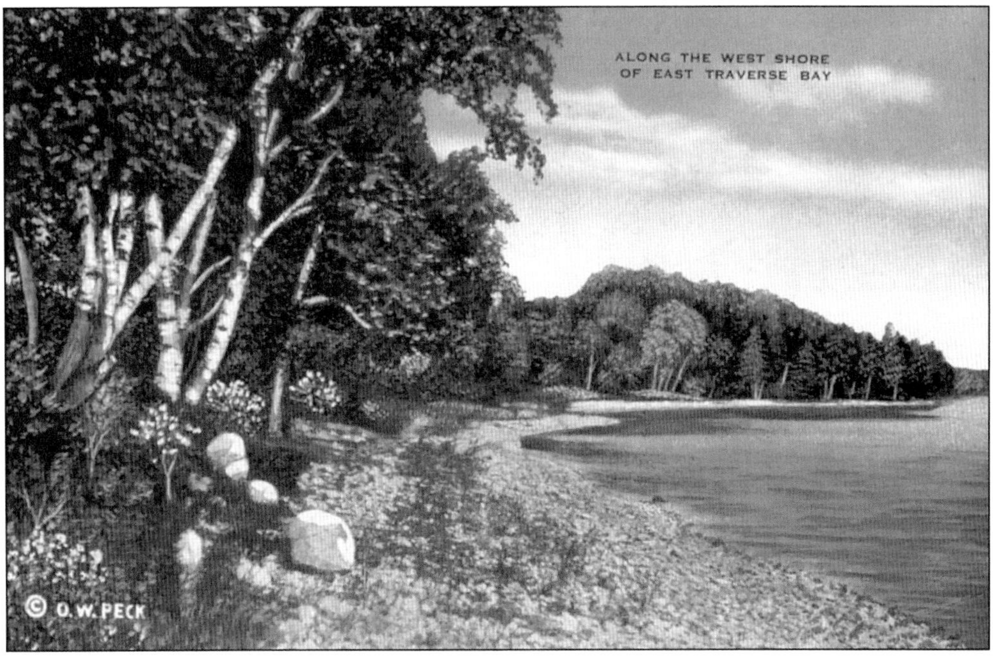

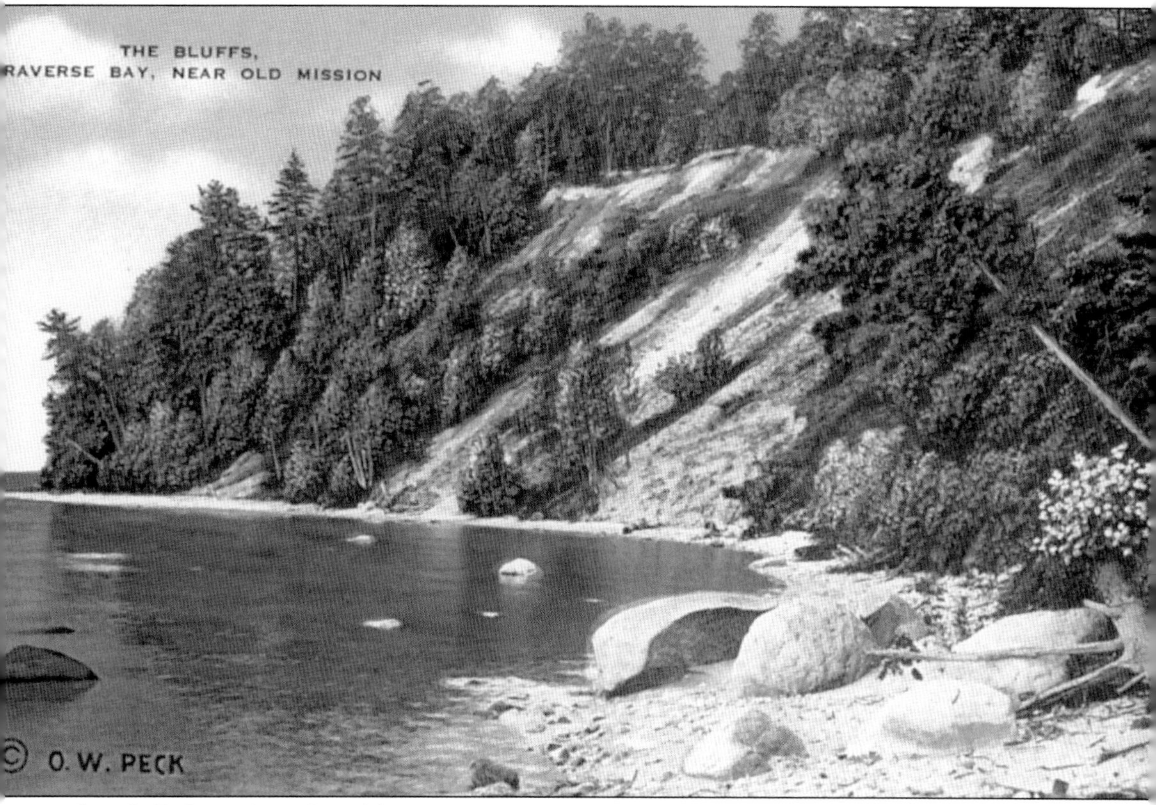

The Bluffs, located on the Old Mission Peninsula, are miniscule compared to the sand dunes at Sleeping Bear National Lakeshore, although their geological history is very similar. Formed by the glaciers that also created the Great Lakes, The Bluffs are situated on the west side of East Grand Traverse Bay and, on a clear day, it is possible to see them from the opposite shoreline. Turning off of Center Road, a few miles after it intersects with East Bay Shore Road, is Bluff Road, home to some of the oldest cherry orchards in Grand Traverse County. Bluff Road follows the shoreline of East Grand Traverse Bay and, with a short jog onto Beersaw Road and Smokey Hollow Road, Haserot Beach and the Old Mission Public Access are in sight.

(*Opposite, bottom*) While the West Arm of West Grand Traverse Bay extends out onto the Leelanau Peninsula, East Bay Shore Road follows the shoreline out the Old Mission Peninsula. The West Arm of East Grand Traverse Bay provides a view of the Grand Traverse Resort, its tower seemingly rising out of nowhere to greet visitors. This is cherry country, and once East Bay Shore Road meets Center Road, there is little else to be seen other than cherry farms and the occasional vineyard. At the end of the Old Mission Peninsula, the road dead-ends at Old Mission Point and Lighthouse Park.

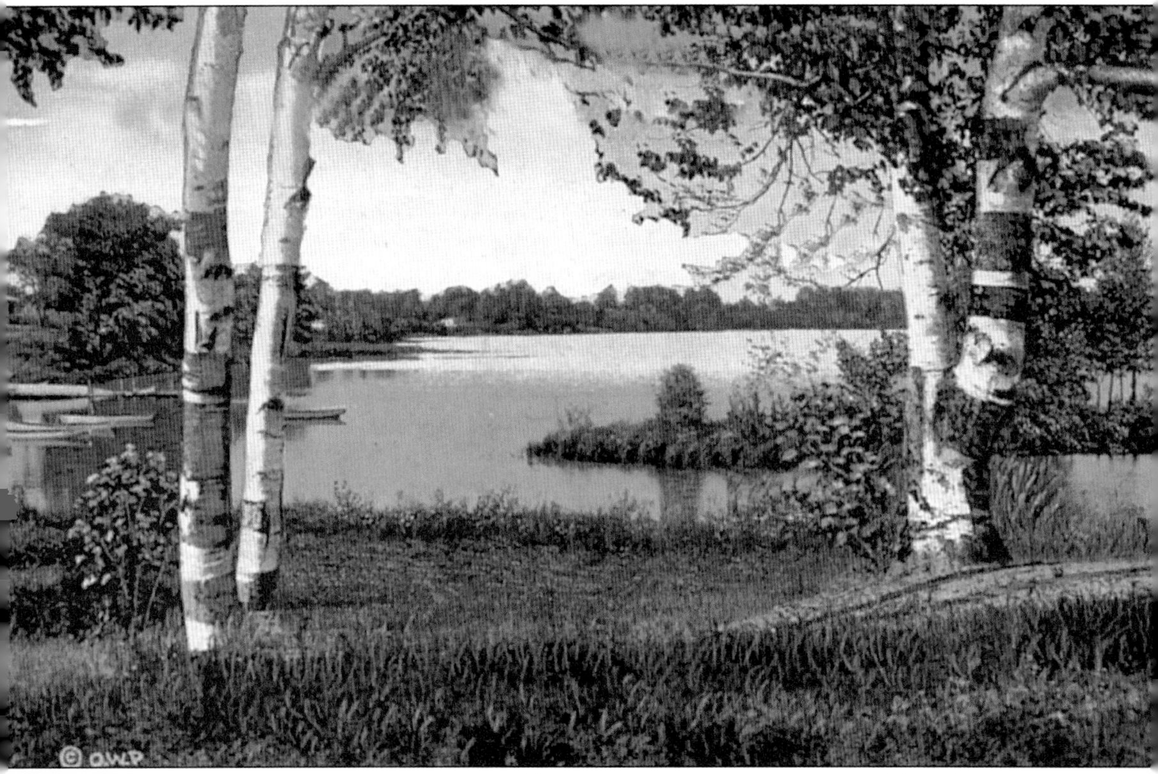

Silver Lake may be only one of 22 inland lakes in Grand Traverse County, although its proximity to town and its beauty make it one of the most popular lakes in the area. Located five miles southwest of Traverse City, just off North Silver Lake Road, the lake bustles with activity all year long. In the summer, there is boating, fishing, and swimming, and in the winter months, ice fishing is a popular pastime. While Silver Lake may not have the allure that it once did, the birches that line its shores still draw visitors.

(*Opposite, bottom*) Watching one of the many spectacular sunsets on Glen Lake after a long day out on the lake is one of life's moments that defy description. The sunset itself is worth the trip from Traverse City or any other location for that matter, yet for those who choose to stay a bit longer, a moonlit night on Glen Lake is beyond comparison. Rising majestically through the pines, as fireflies flit about and the chirp of crickets fills the night air, the moon slowly makes its ascent. Most of the area around Glen Lake is part of the Sleeping Bear National Lakeshore and, as a result, will always remain one of nature's untouched landscapes.

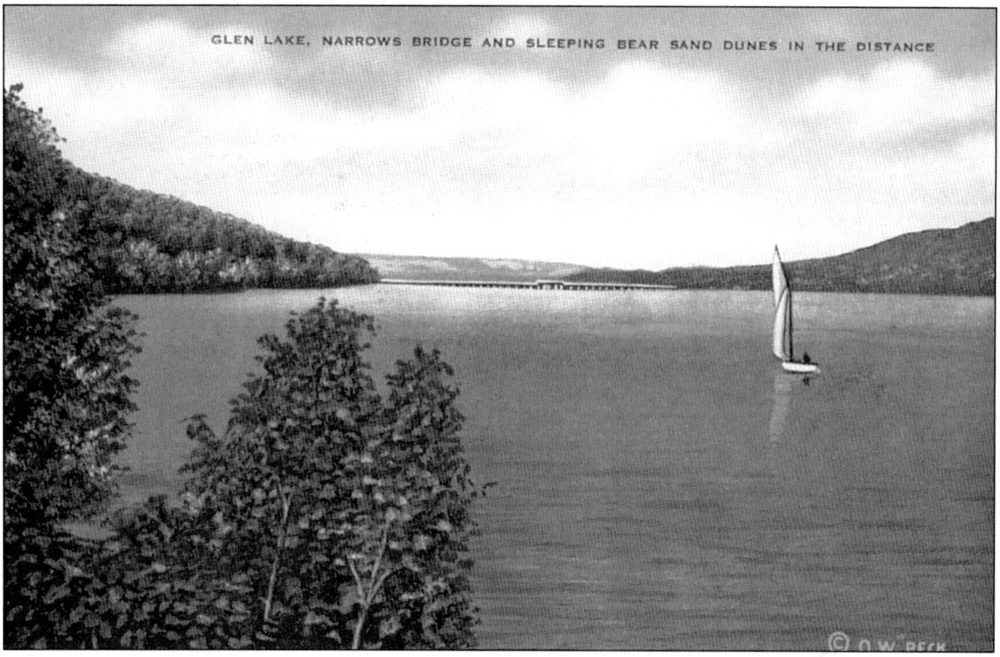

(*Above*) Glen Lake, picturesque as any body of water in the Grand Traverse region, is perfect for picnicking, sailing, or swimming. In the horizon, the Sleeping Bear Dunes National Lakeshore rises up to provide some of the most spectacular scenery in Northern Michigan. The narrows lie between Big Glen Lake and Little Glen Lake, and while they provide a means for transportation to cross from one side of the lakes to the other, they do not detract from their beauty. Many a summer resident prefers the quiet and natural beauty of Glen Lake, as do a number of residents.

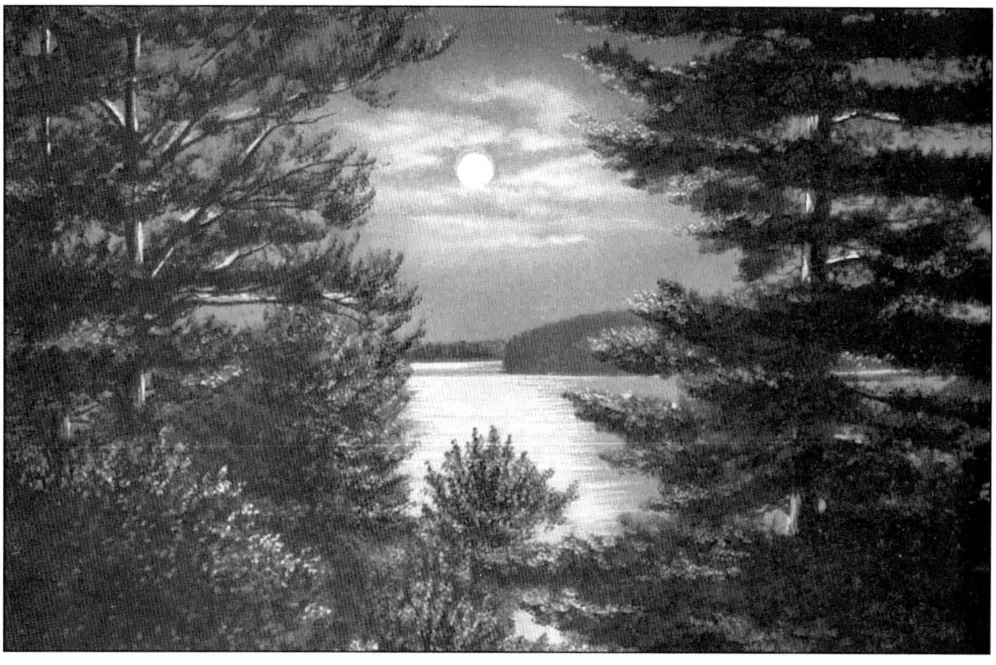

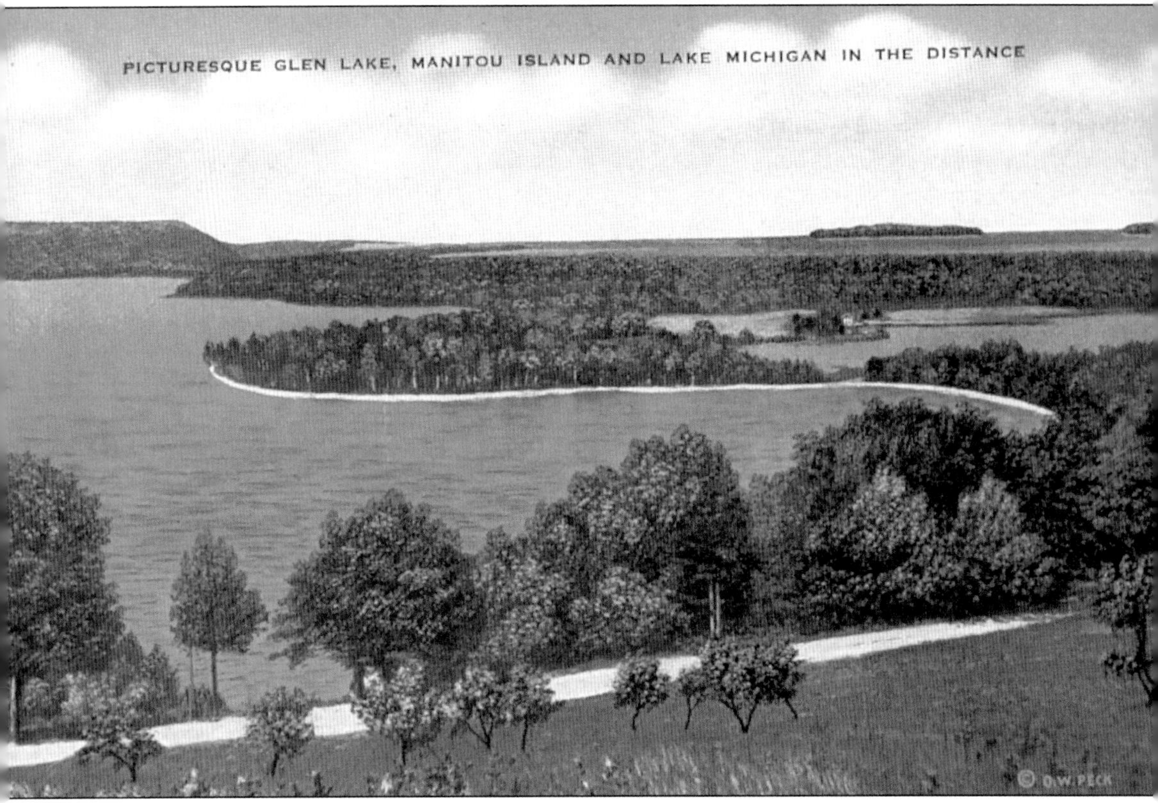

A scenic drive through the Sleeping Bear Dunes National Lakeshore gives visitors a breathtaking view of the surrounding area. From atop the dunes, it is possible to see out across the vast forests, Big Glen and Little Glen Lake, all the way out to Lake Michigan and the Manitou Islands. The dunes now encompass more than half of the Glen Lake area, which consists of mature beech and maple forests, as well as wetlands, lakes, streams, and bogs. Over 160 migratory species of birds nest in this area, lending credence to the claim that the area's value as a natural habitat cannot be overrated.

(*Opposite, bottom*) A drive along M-22, which leads out of Traverse City and north into Leelanau County, is beyond comparison. On the right side of the highway is the West Arm of Grand Traverse Bay. Every now and then the maples, pines, and birches that border the shoreline allow for a glimpse out over the water. To the left, after leaving the city limits, the surroundings change little by little, and soon there is nothing to see other than quaint country homes and orchards full of apple and cherry trees. To a great extent, still largely undeveloped, Leelanau County gives the visitor a chance to envision what the area was like during the first half of the twentieth century.

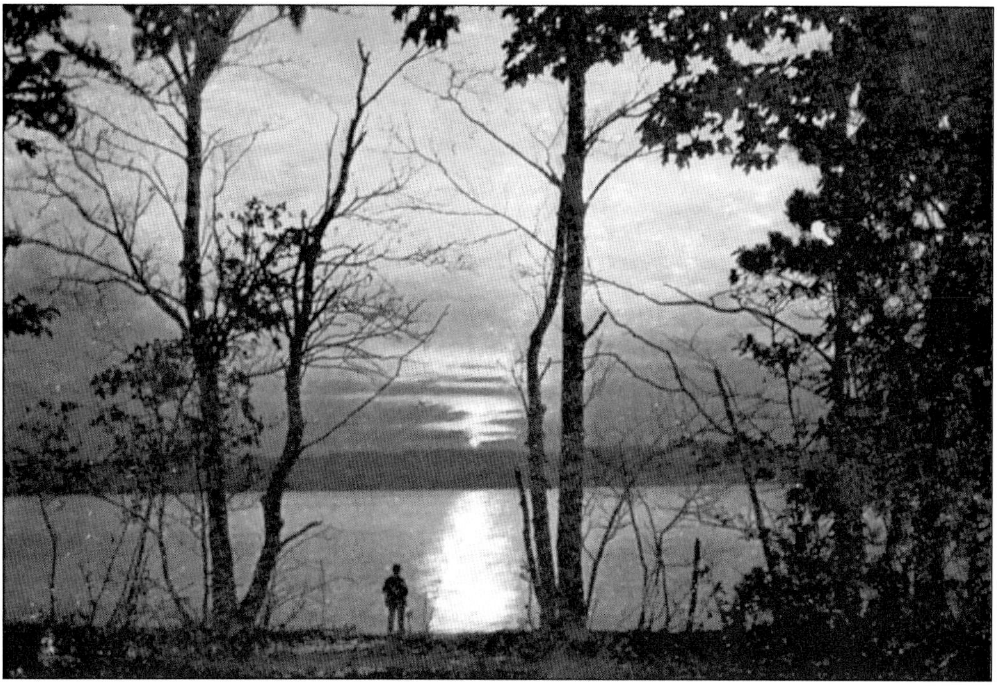

(*Above*) There is a saying in Traverse City that, "half your pay is a view of the bay," and residents and tourists agree that there is definitely some truth to this, especially after witnessing a sunset over Grand Traverse Bay. From virtually every vantage point in Traverse City, there is an unobstructed view of both the sunrise and the sunset, both of which leave the viewer awestruck. The light shimmers as it bounces across the glass-like waters and literally defies description, for like most of nature's wonders, the only way to truly appreciate it is to experience it.

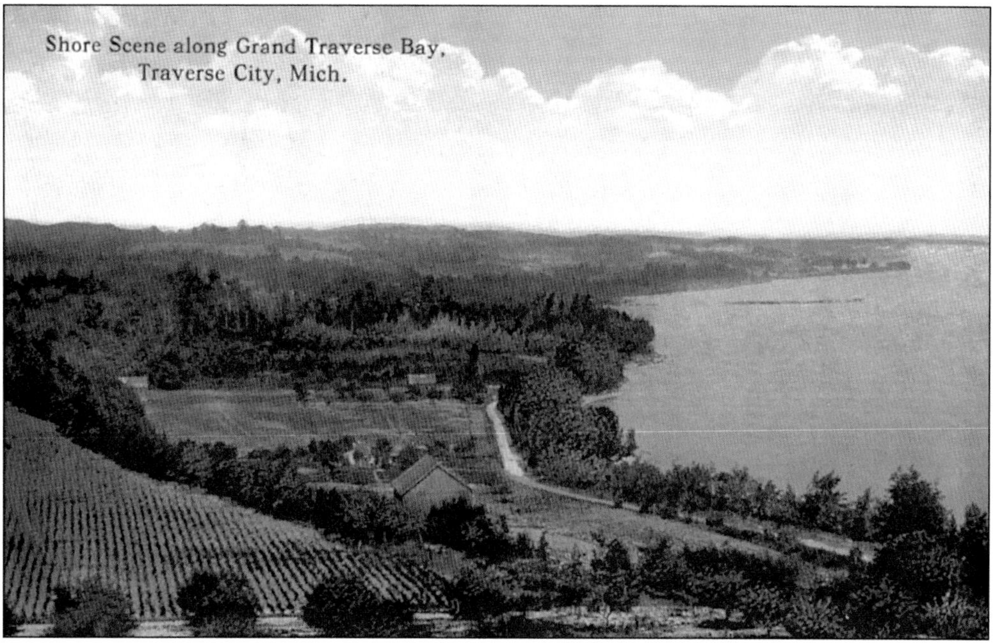

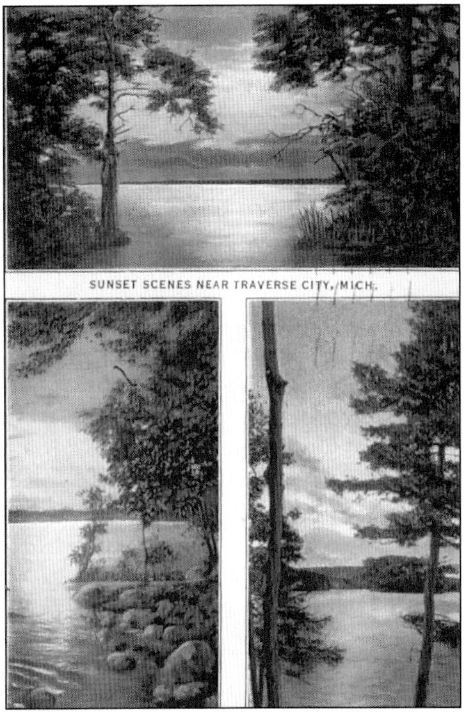

Sunsets in the Traverse City area are a feast for the eyes. Whether high on the Bluffs of the Old Mission Peninsula, down at Clinch Park, or out on Long Lake, the sight of the sun shimmering across the glass-like, blue waters, framed only by the birches, maples, and pines, leads some people to believe that this is truly a slice of heaven on Earth.

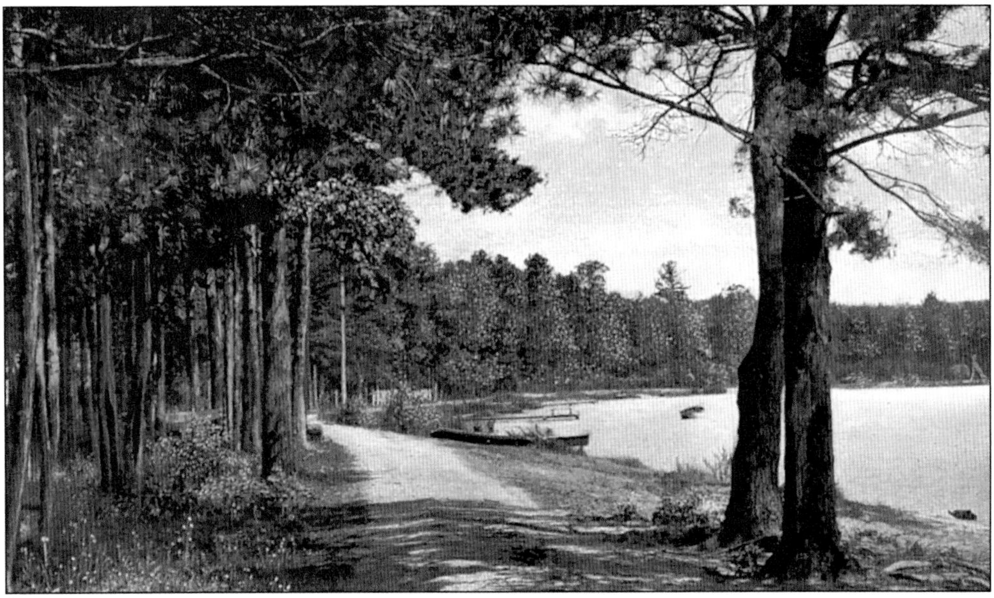

Birchwood Road, at the base of the Old Mission Peninsula, is nestled in a cove on East Grand Traverse Bay. Located just to the north of East Bay Park, formerly Milliken Park, this landscape offers up views of not only East Grand Traverse Bay, but also of the opposing shoreline. From this vantage point it is possible to scan the shoreline and gain a glimpse of the Tower at the Grand Traverse Resort, as well as Traverse City State Park. East Bay Park has a boat launch, picnic facilities, a children's playground and a sandy beach with a shallow swimming area. One of the most serene and beautiful spots in Northern Michigan, it is worth a visit.

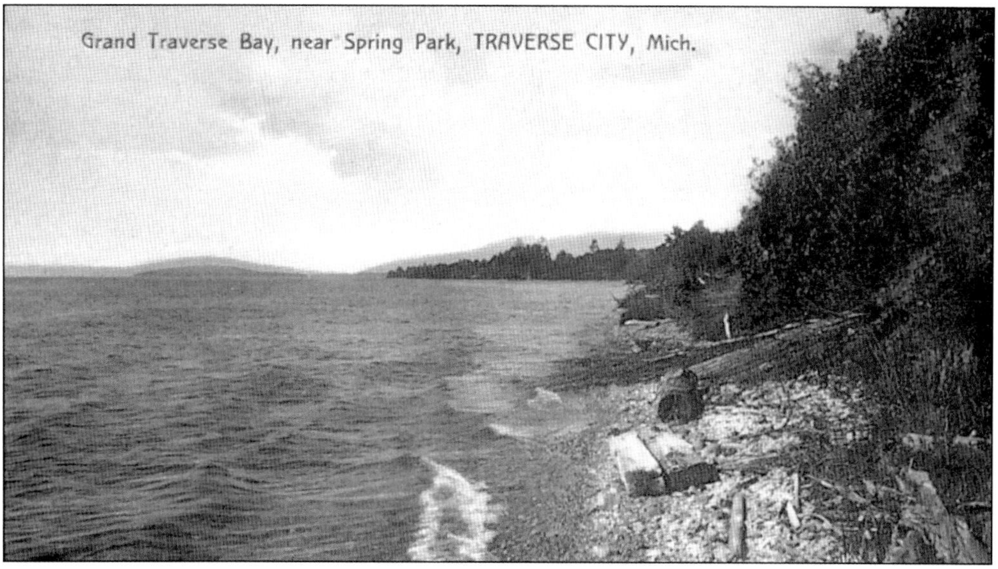

Spring Park, one of the forerunners of the modern park system in Traverse City, was situated on the eastern shore of West Grand Traverse Bay. The park afforded rustic surroundings—essentially a beach, brush, and woods, along with a view of Power Island, known then as Marion Island. While this park may seem isolated and uninhabited, it most probably was as popular as any other beach in the Traverse City area. The park system in Traverse City has changed somewhat over the years, and while many of the parks now offer playground and picnic facilities, there are still a number of rustic spots tucked away on the beaches of Grand Traverse Bay.

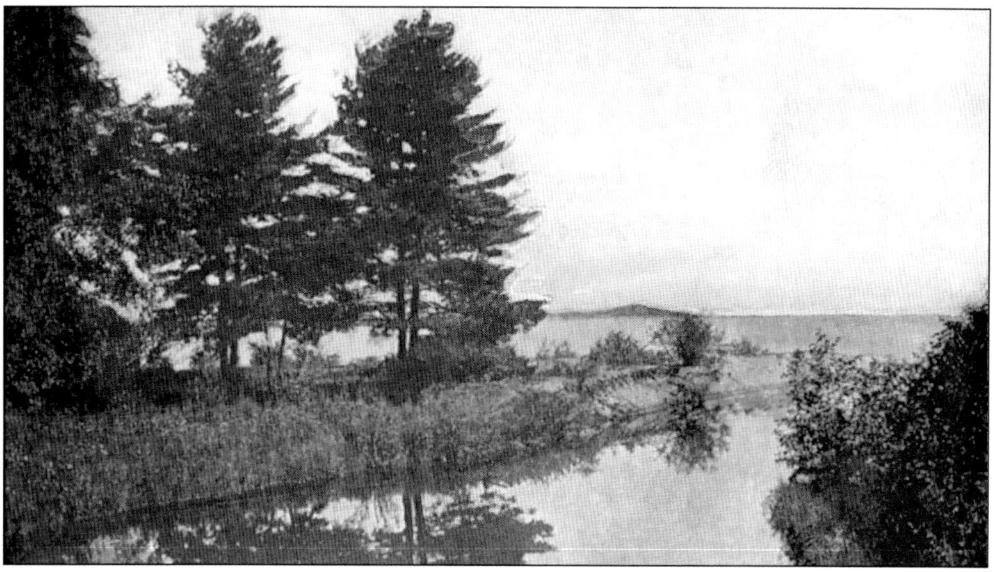

Beyond the Indian Trail Bridge, Mitchell Creek finds its way slowly to the headwaters of East Grand Traverse Bay. Located approximately three-quarters of a mile to the east of Traverse City, its course remains for the most part unchanged. A part of the old Indian trail that leads down through the Traverse City State Park, this little creek is known for its abundant brown and brook trout. A sandy beach sits where the flowing waters of Mitchell Creek meet East Grand Traverse Bay, and its shallow waters are perfect for an afternoon swim.

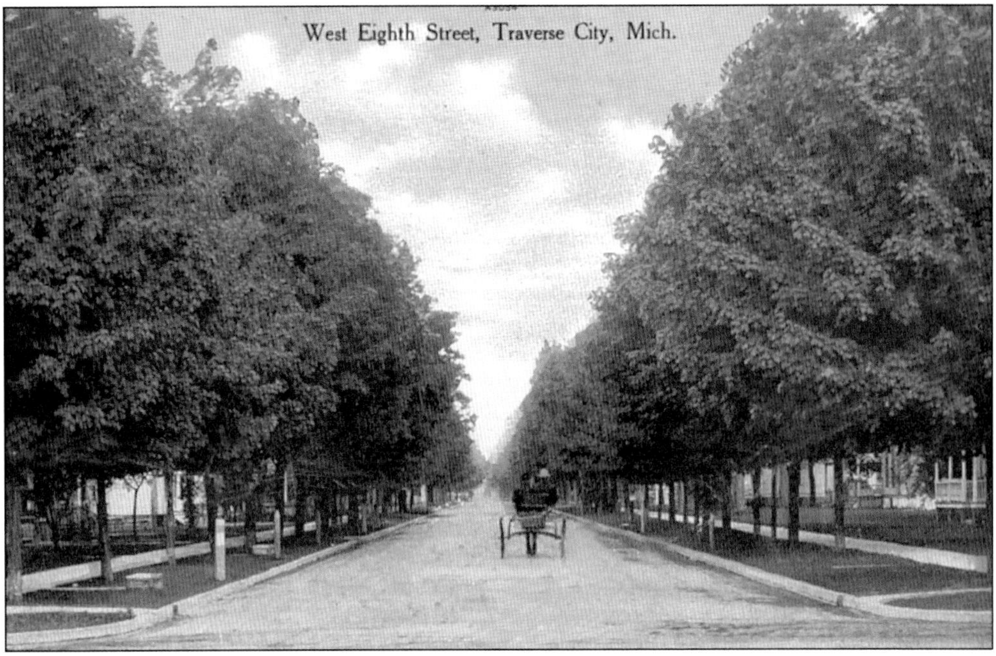

(*Above*) Nature, in its splendor, provides a canopy of leaves that hides the statuesque homes on West Eighth Street in Traverse City. One of the first streets to be completed, most probably due to its proximity to founding father Perry Hannah's home, there are portions of Eighth Street that are still made of the original bricks. A few blocks to the south is the site of the first golf course in Traverse City and to the north, Traverse City Central High School on Seventh Street. Just to the east of Eighth Street is Old Town Traverse City, a historic shopping district that stretches from Ninth Street to the Union Street Bridge.

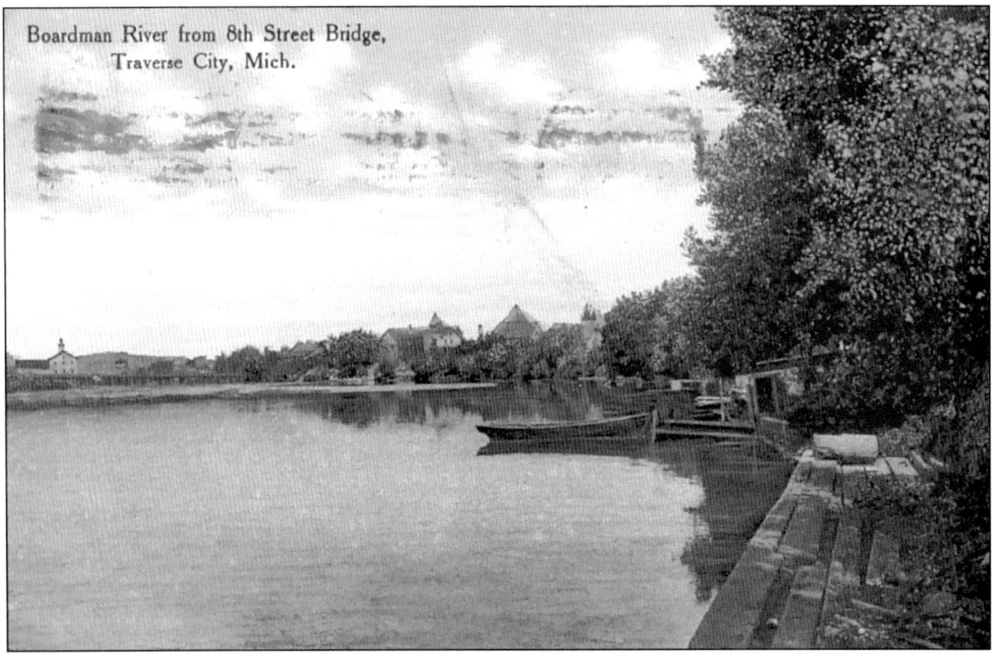

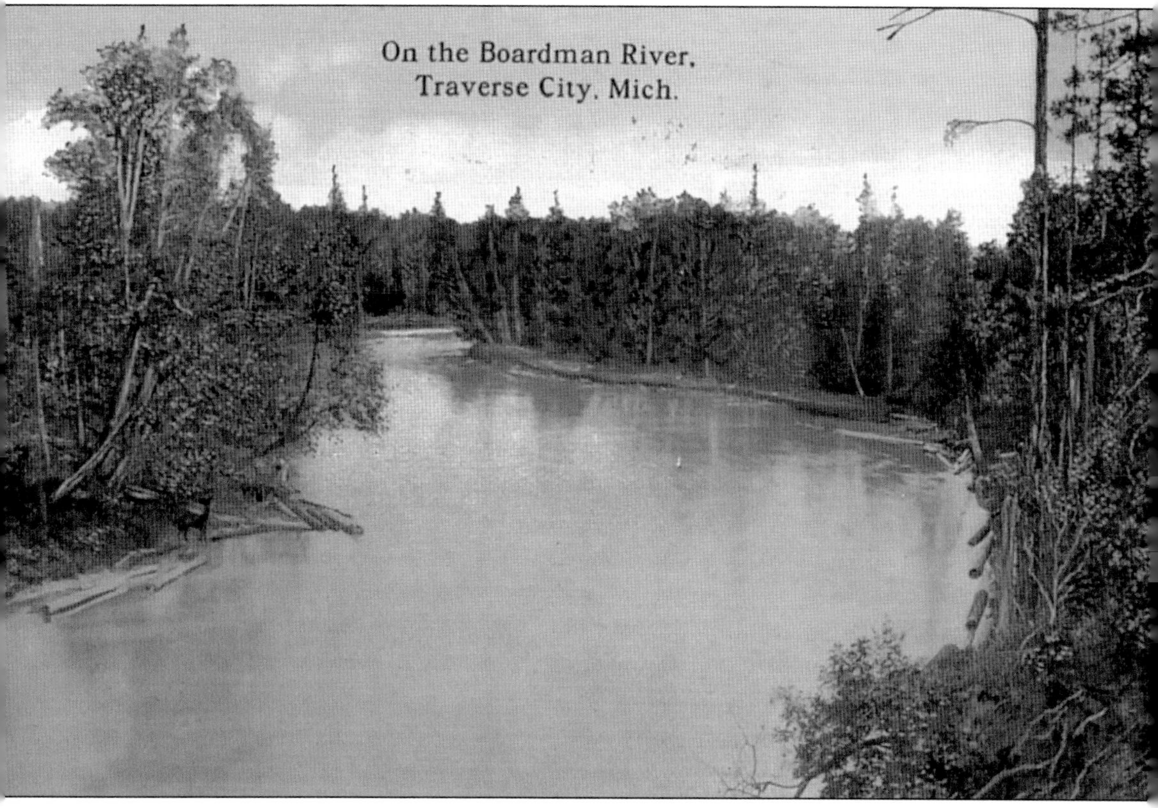

The Boardman River is not just poetry in motion; it has also played an important part in the economic development of the Grand Traverse area. Spanning over 130 miles, the Boardman River is the largest tributary leading into Grand Traverse Bay. During Traverse City's logging years, log drivers used the Boardman River to float timber down to the mill. The Boardman River is named for Horace Boardman, who built the first sawmill on Kid's Creek. It is also the birthplace of one of the most famous fishing flies in history. "The Adams," a fishing fly developed in 1922, was developed specifically for catching the big brown trout and brook trout of the Boardman River.

(*Opposite, bottom*) Flowing north out of Boardman Lake, the Boardman River winds its way toward Traverse City, passing under the Eighth Street Bridge. This view of the Boardman River is from the Eighth Street Bridge, and while much of the surrounding area has changed with the times, the river continues to meander its way around and through Traverse City on its way to Grand Traverse Bay. A favorite among sports fishermen, the Boardman River is teeming with fish of virtually every species indigenous to Northern Michigan. Despite the fact that a great deal of development has taken place over the years in Traverse City, the Boardman River remains one of the most awe-inspiring natural settings in the area.

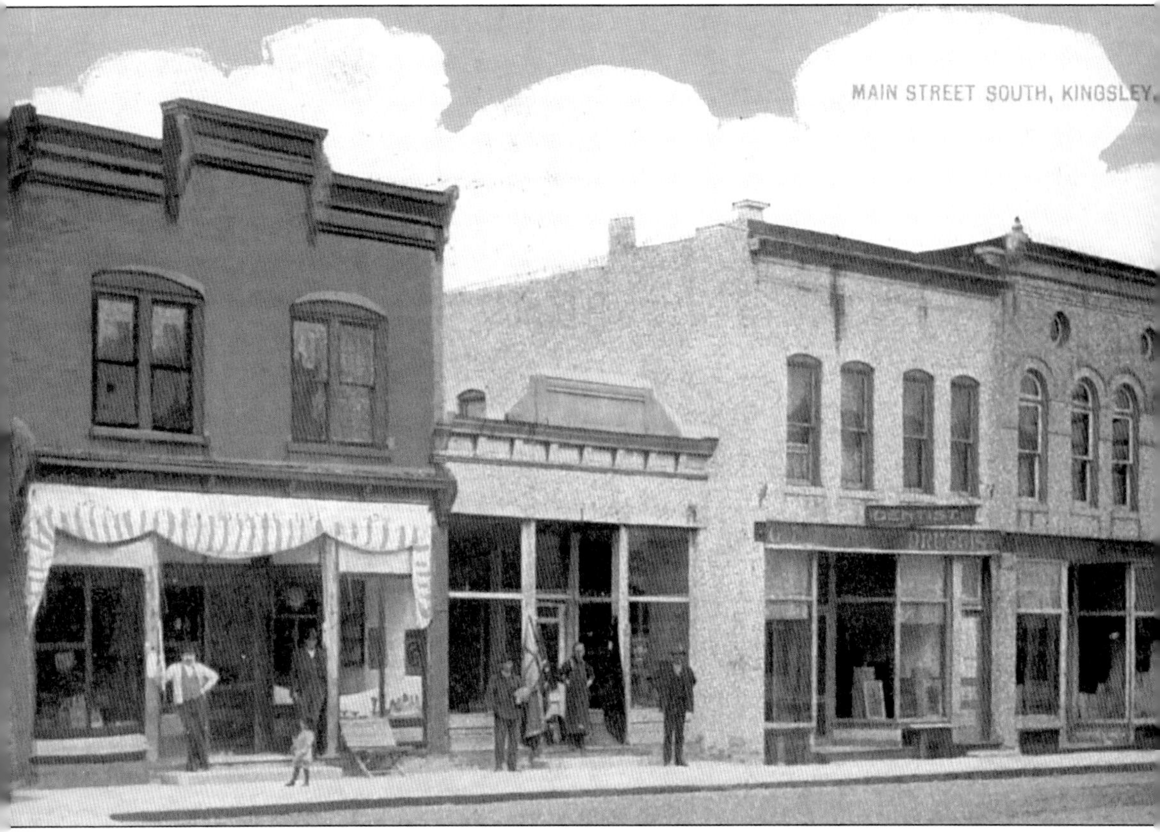

Kingsley was originally known as Paradise, a name taken from the township in which the village is located. Judson W. Kingsley and Dr. Myron S. Bronson platted and laid out property in 1874 and 1876, respectively. Initially, the rail station in Kingsley serviced the Grand Rapids & Indiana Railroad, starting in 1874. In 1890, the land was incorporated to form the village of Kingsley. Kingsley's early years were dominated by the lumber industry. When the lumber industry declined in the early part of the twentieth century, some residents turned to farming, while their neighbors found employment in larger towns such as Cadillac and Traverse City. Today, Kingsley remains a quiet, small village of about 700 residents located approximately 15 miles due south of Traverse City.

(*Opposite, bottom*) It isn't uncommon to see a whitetail deer grazing in a field, taking a drink from one of the lakes, or even nibbling on some cherries or apples, although until the 1880s there were more elk and moose in Northern Michigan than there were deer. As the cities were built in southern Michigan, the deer headed north and, as the lumberjacks cleared land, it made foraging for food all that much easier. By the middle of the 1880s, the elk and moose were disappearing from the Traverse City area, although the deer herd had swollen to over one million. Over the years, the Department of Natural Resources has developed a deer management program and, primarily through holding annual bow and rifle hunting seasons, actively engages in regulating the deer population.

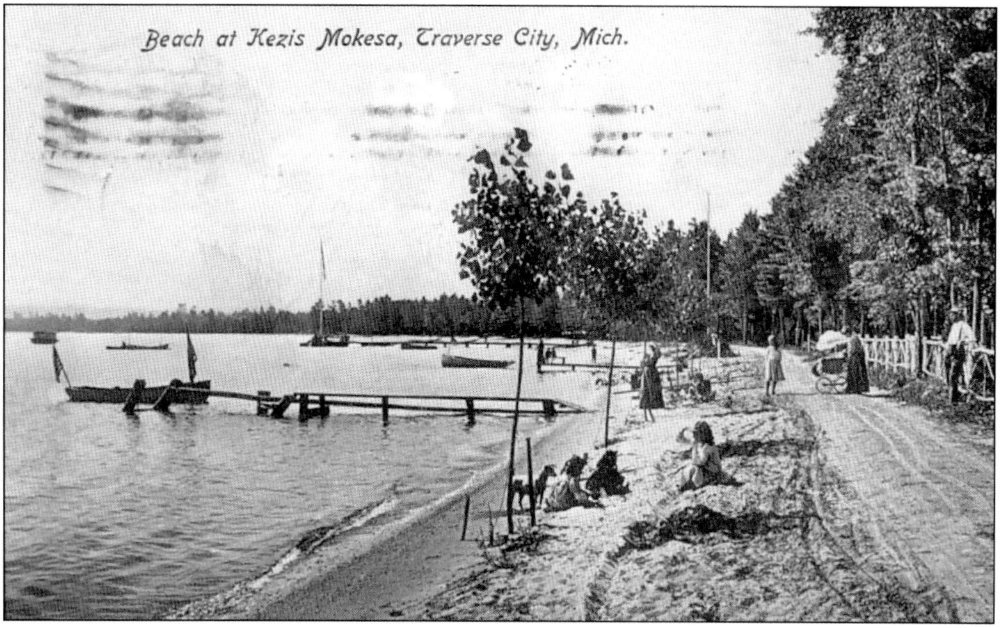

(*Above*) On the tranquil shores of the East Arm of Grand Traverse Bay is a beach area known simply as Kezis Mokesa, a Native American phrase of unknown origin. The trail, which follows the shoreline, is dotted with quaint cottages and homes on one side. There are boats, docks, and children playing in the sand on the beach. For those who enjoy taking in all that the outdoors has to offer, a walk from East Bay Park, formerly Milliken Park, past Kezis Mokesa and following the shoreline all the way to Mitchell Creek and the Traverse City State Park is a great way to spend a summer day.

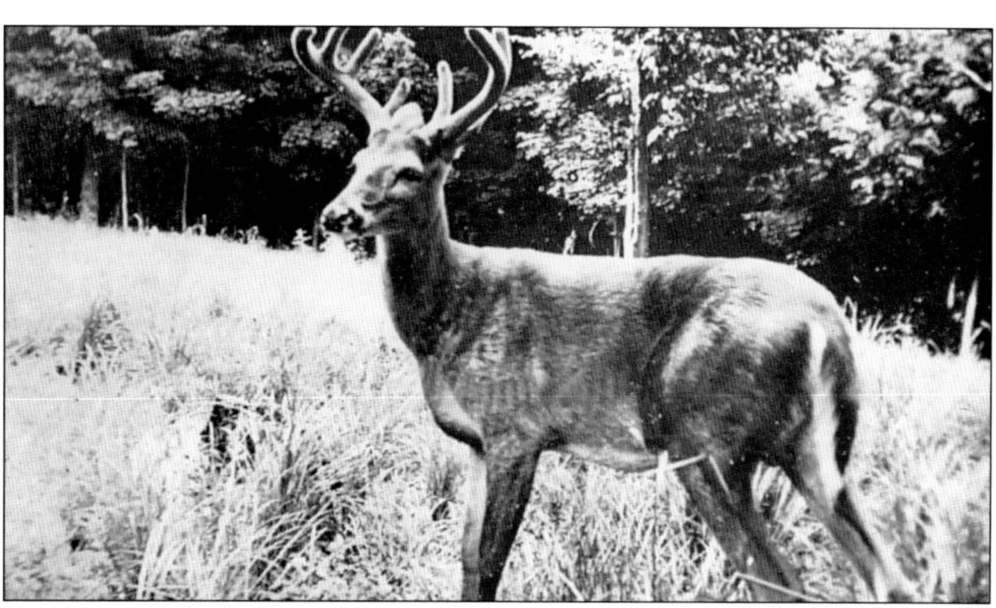

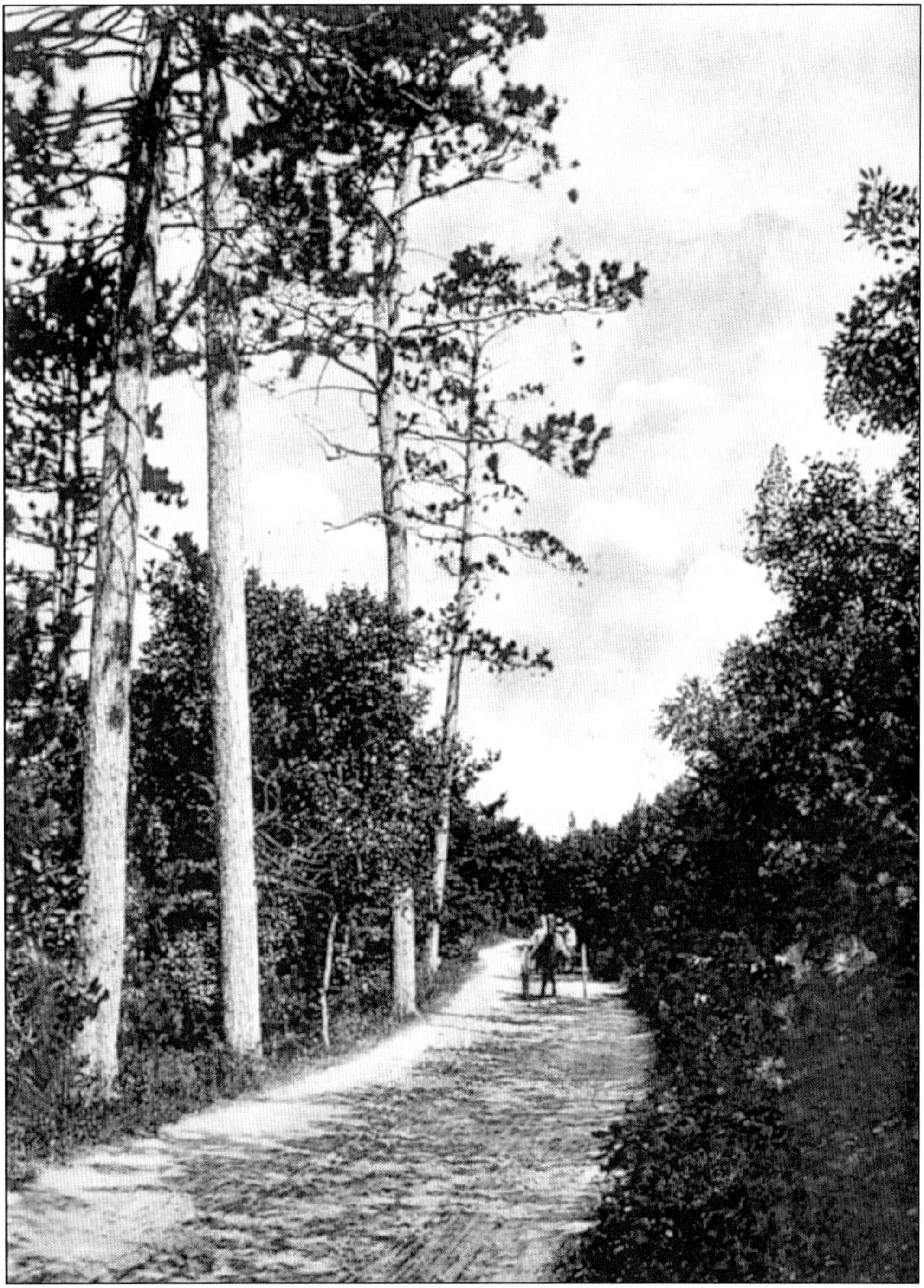

A lone horse and buggy makes its way down Bay Road, now known as East Bay Shore Road, in 1904. While still lined with trees, the area is somewhat more developed now than it was in those days. East Bay Shore Road begins in Traverse City, at Eastern Avenue, and continues out the Old Mission Peninsula until merging with Center Road. Now lined with homes, the winding road presents spectacular views of East Grand Traverse Bay.

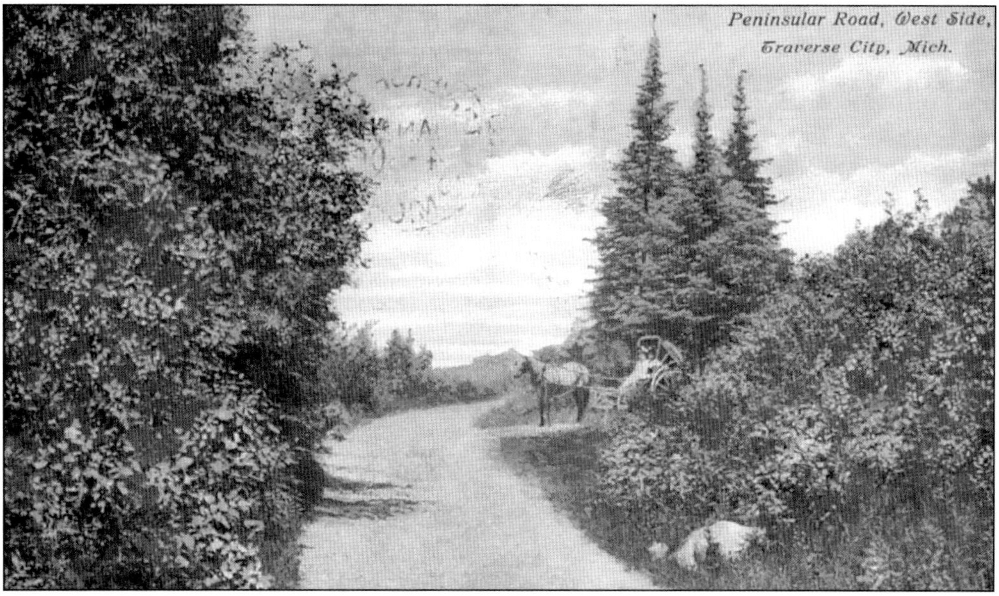

Starting in downtown Traverse City, Peninsula Drive, or Peninsular Road as it was referred to in earlier days, veers to the left of Front Street and heads out onto the Old Mission Peninsula. Not nearly as wooded as it once was, Peninsula Drive still offers up some of the most scenic views of any area in the Grand Traverse area. Passing by Bryant Park and heading out onto the Old Mission Peninsula, there are views of the West Arm of Grand Traverse Bay, Power Island, and cherry orchards in various stages of bloom. Wooded areas still exist on Peninsula Drive, many of which lead to the sandy beaches of Grand Traverse Bay.

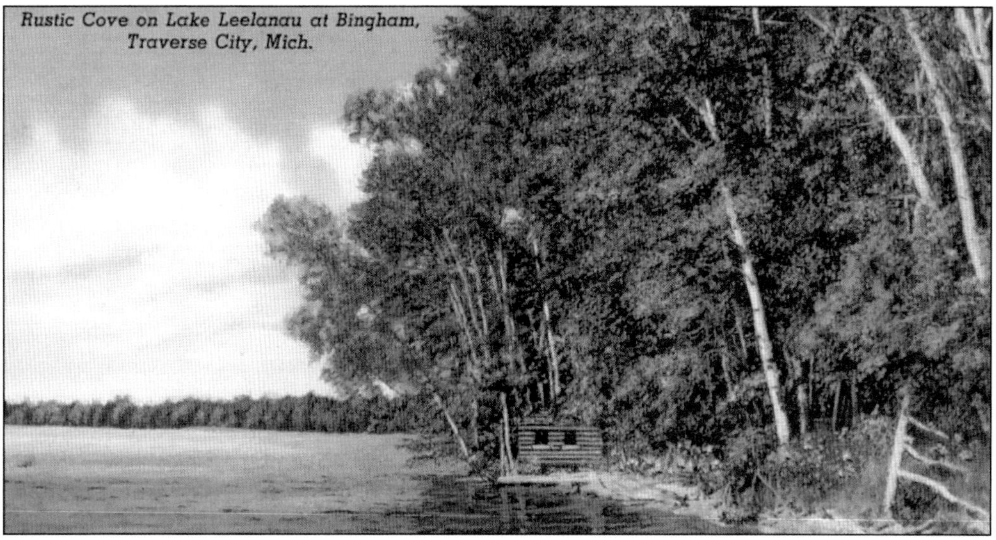

Trees lean out over the shoreline of this cove, as the waters of Lake Leelanau ripple ever so slightly, and small waves roll up on the beach. Much of Lake Leelanau is wooded, especially in Bingham Township, and there is no better place to commune with nature. The northwest portion of Bingham Township meets with the shores of Lake Leelanau, while to the east it cradles the west shore of West Grand Traverse Bay. Grand Traverse County and Leelanau County offer visitors not only numerous activities, but also some of the most spectacular views in the world.

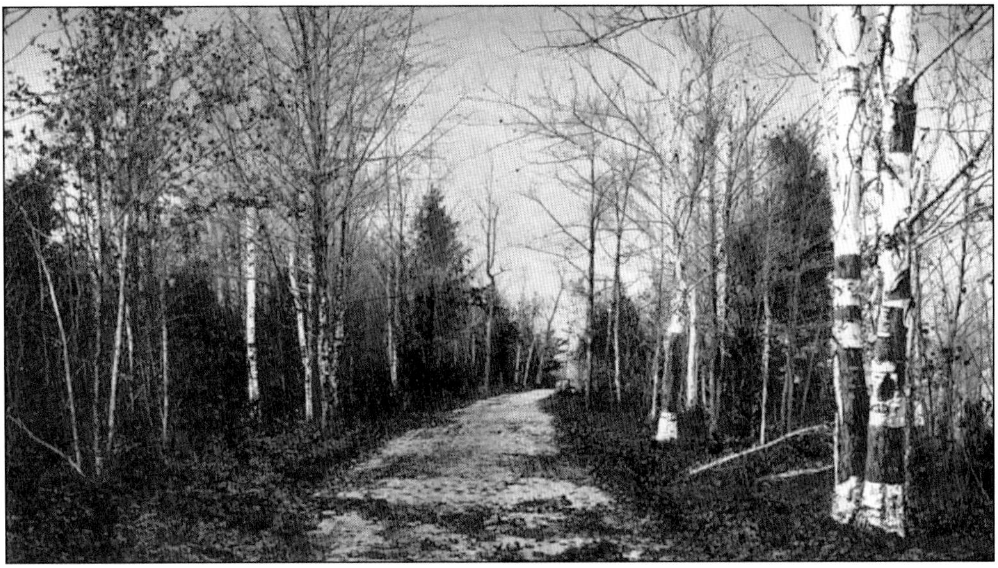

The onset of autumn is bittersweet in the Traverse City area; it brings with it the end of another summer tourist season, yet winter is just around the corner. For a brief time, the leaves of the beech, birch, and maple trees all turn to fiery colors and seem to light up the landscape in a dazzling display of nature's beauty. Cool air sweeps through the region and, for a brief time, it is Indian Summer. Within a few weeks, the trees take on an almost ghost-like appearance, their leaves having turned to a brownish color and fallen to the ground. Soon, the snow will fall, and once again nature's playground will be alive with activity.

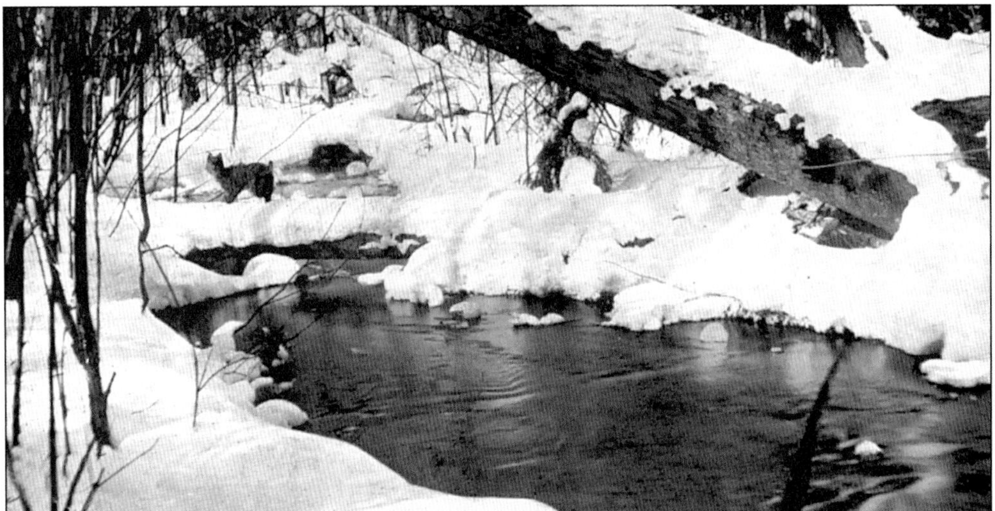

A blanket of soft, white snow transforms the landscape of the Traverse City area, and where once trees blossomed and birds sang, the woodlands now stand silent. The riverbed, once alive with activity, is now covered in the ice and snow. Fresh tracks mark the places where animals have come to drink and to play. Winter brings with it a certain air of peacefulness to the woods and forests, although it won't be long before spring will again give birth to the densely wooded forests of Northern Michigan. In the meantime, the water flows, unabated, downstream to the mouth of the river.

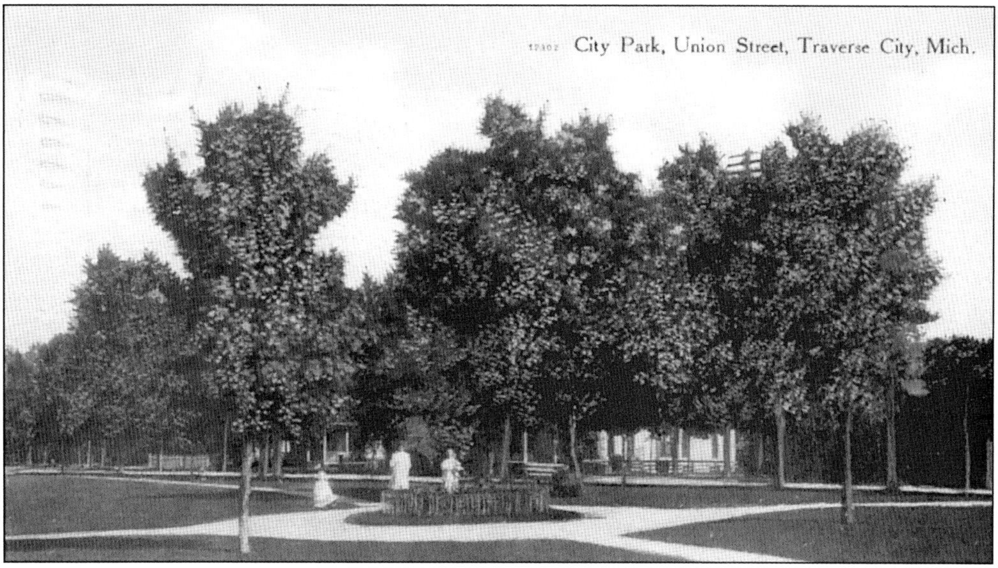

City Park, located on Union Street in downtown Traverse City, provided a place where people could take a break during the hectic day. Located in the historic Old Town District of Traverse City, City Park is one of the few parks in the area that is not located on the water. Instead, City Park was positioned between the shopping district and the neighborhoods of old Traverse City, just as forefather Perry Hannah planned. A benevolent dictator of sorts, Hannah had seen the necessity of combining business and leisure, and both City Park and Hannah Park are testaments to his foresight.

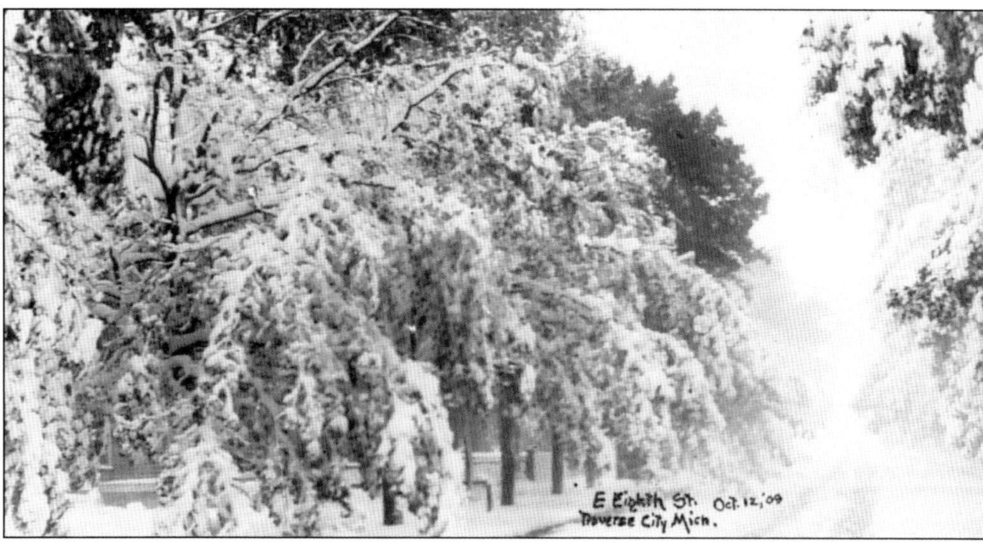

Winters in Traverse City can be long and difficult, especially with the cold north wind blowing in off of Grand Traverse Bay. Normally it is possible to get a clear view of East Eighth Street, although this unseasonably early snowstorm of October 12, 1909, tends to obstruct a clear view of the street. In the past, Traverse City has had record-breaking snowfalls of up to 20.5 inches in a two-day period, and residents are well aware that there does not need to be a heavy snowfall or exceptionally cold temperatures to make winter dangerous. The winters are not as severe as they used to be, yet it is wise to be prepared for any occasion.

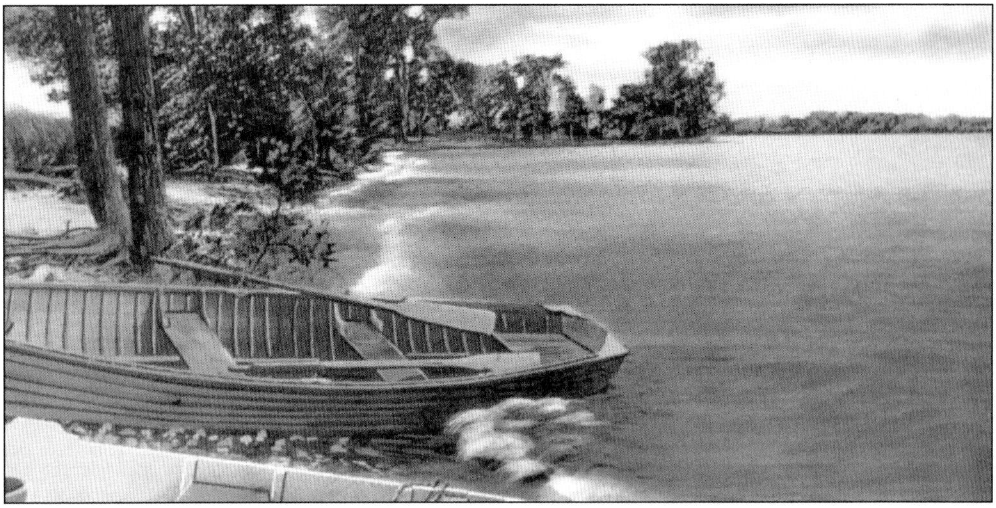

One of the most popular lakes in the Traverse City area is Long Lake. Home to numerous cottages, homes, and a Girl Scout camp, Long Lake is known for boating, fishing, swimming, and water-skiing. Located halfway between Traverse City and Interlochen, there are four islands on Long Lake, one of which, Long Island, has a picnic area. Well-known among local anglers for its walleye, there are also largemouth and smallmouth bass, as well as northern pike, rock bass, sunfish, and perch. Sandy beaches, shallow waters, picnic areas, and volleyball courts are just a few of the many reasons why Long Lake's public access sites, Gilbert Park and Taylor Park, are so popular. In addition, there is also the Crescent Shores Boat Launch and the Bullhead Lake Natural Area, a wetland area that provides a home for numerous species of frogs, birds, fish, and other wildlife.

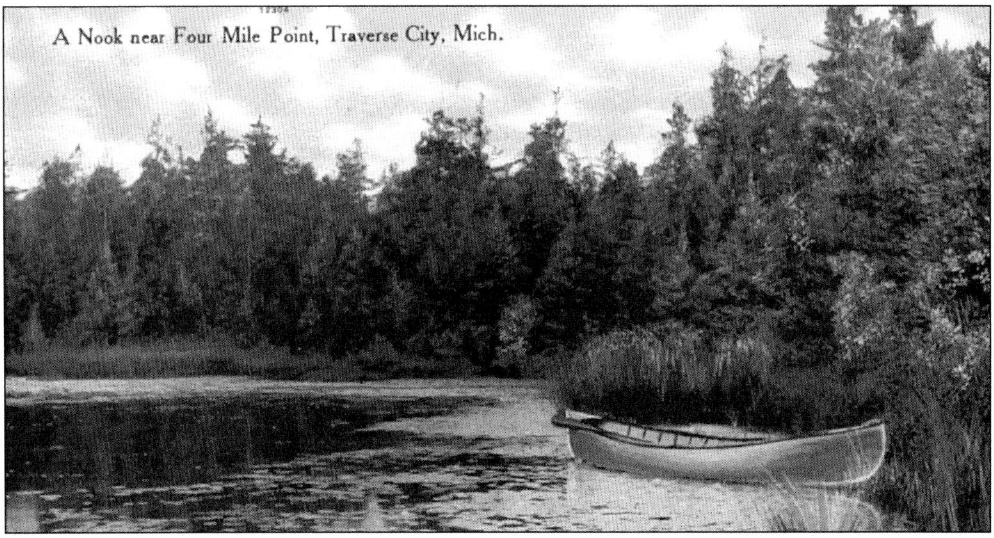

Tucked away in a cove near Four Mile Point, a lone canoe is pulled up on the shore of East Grand Traverse Bay. Over the years, a great deal of development has taken place out near Four Mile Point, which is located approximately one and a half miles from Traverse City. Peace and solitude can still be found on the beaches, although there are numerous resorts on the shoreline. Every once in a while, it is still possible to catch a glimpse of a boater pulling his craft onto the beach after a long day out on the bay.

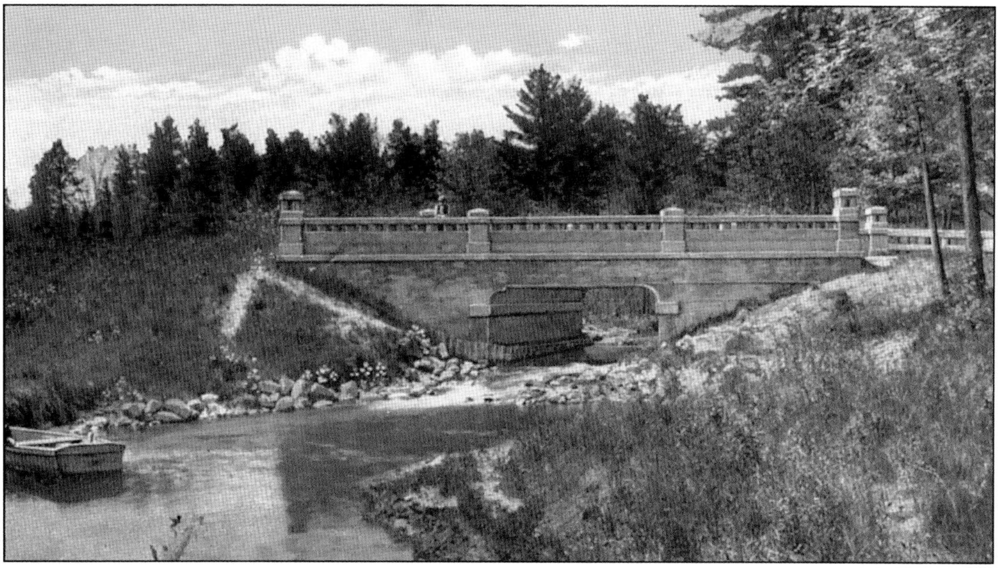

The Indian Trail Bridge, where Munson Avenue passes over Mitchell Creek, is approximately three-quarters of a mile east of Traverse City. Here, Mitchell Creek meanders its way, twisting and turning, until it reaches the East Arm of Grand Traverse Bay. The bridge itself is so named for the Ottawa branch of the Algonquin Indians, who were the original inhabitants of the area. Down the street is the Traverse City State Park, a 45-acre, 342-site campground, part of which is on Grand Traverse Bay. The campsites are located amidst a hardwood and pine forest across the street from the beach. The park features a swim area, picnic tables, a beach house, and a children's playground, while Mitchell Creek offers some of the finest trout fishing in the Traverse City area.

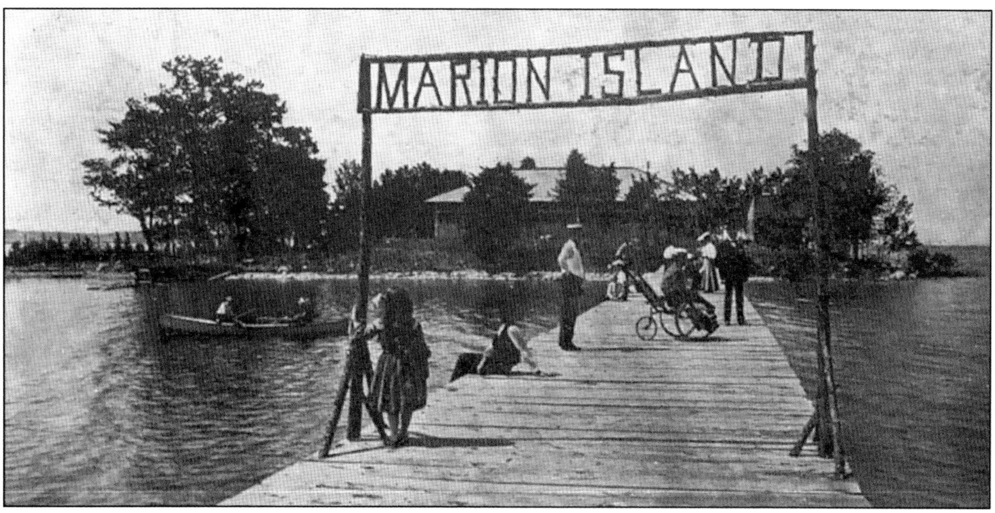

Since the early days, Marion Island, or Power Island as it is called now, has been a popular place to picnic, swim, and back in the days when the dance hall was on Bassett Island, socialize with friends. The island, which can only be accessed by boat, features restrooms, picnic facilities, and hiking trails, which wind through the island's interior. There are no squirrels, deer, or large animals that live on Marion Island, and as a result, the ground is littered with acorns. In the past, a log sign that towered above the pier greeted visitors arriving at the island.

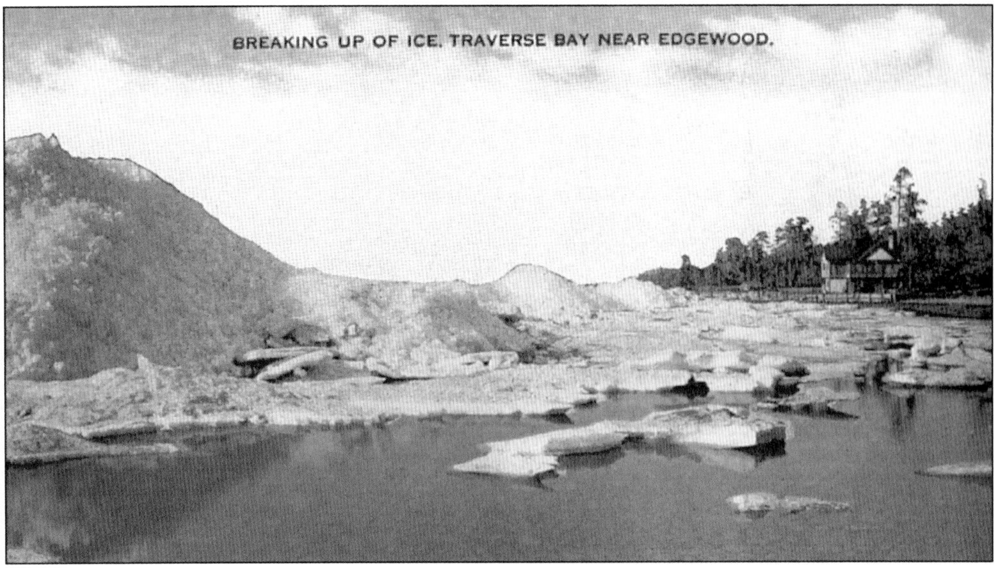

The coming of spring means not only melting ice and snow, but also the break up of ice on Grand Traverse Bay. Especially treacherous to those who dare to venture out on the ice, whether it is to fish, go ice boating, or merely to play, it also serves as notice that winter is nearing its end. In the past, all of Grand Traverse Bay, both the East and West Arms would freeze over completely, although in recent years that has become more and more of a rarity.

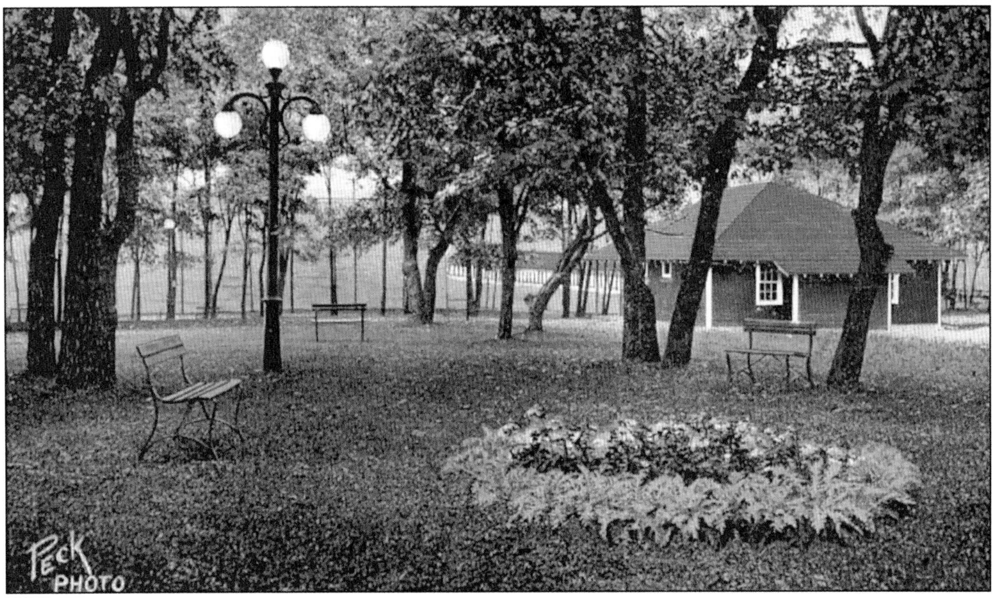

Sunset Park, located to the east of Clinch Park and right off of the Grandview Parkway, is one of Traverse City's oldest parks. The park has always been a favorite among locals, as well as tourists, primarily due to its central location. Outside of a white sand beach and well-kept restrooms, Sunset Park is a park with a number of trees perfect for climbing. Every week, the Central United Methodist Church holds church services at Sunset Park. While popular, Sunset Park does not get quite as crowded as Clinch Park, and as far as some people are concerned, provides a more relaxing atmosphere.

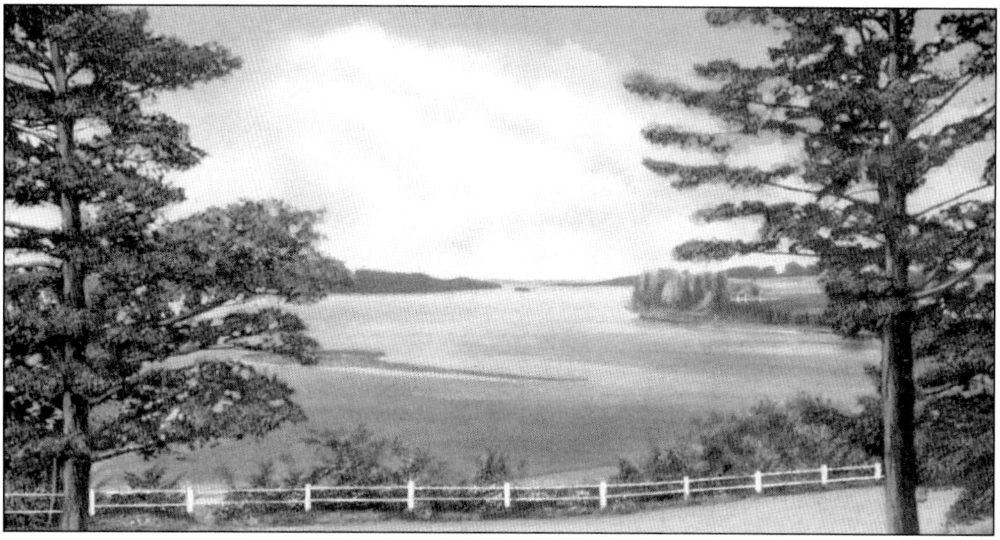

Silver Lake, so named for the silver birches that line the shoreline, is located five miles southwest of Traverse City, just outside city limits. While there are still a number of cabins and resorts located on the lake, a great deal of development has taken place in recent years. Silver lake has one public access site on the east side of the lake, primarily used for launching small boats. Over the years, the Department of Natural Resources has stocked the lake with bass, bluegill, and walleye. As a result, anglers have been able to reel in sizeable catches, five of them being worthy of Master Angler Awards. The largest fish on record that was caught in Silver Lake was a 12.25-pound bluegill. Silver lake, long and narrow, is one of the true gems of the Traverse City area.

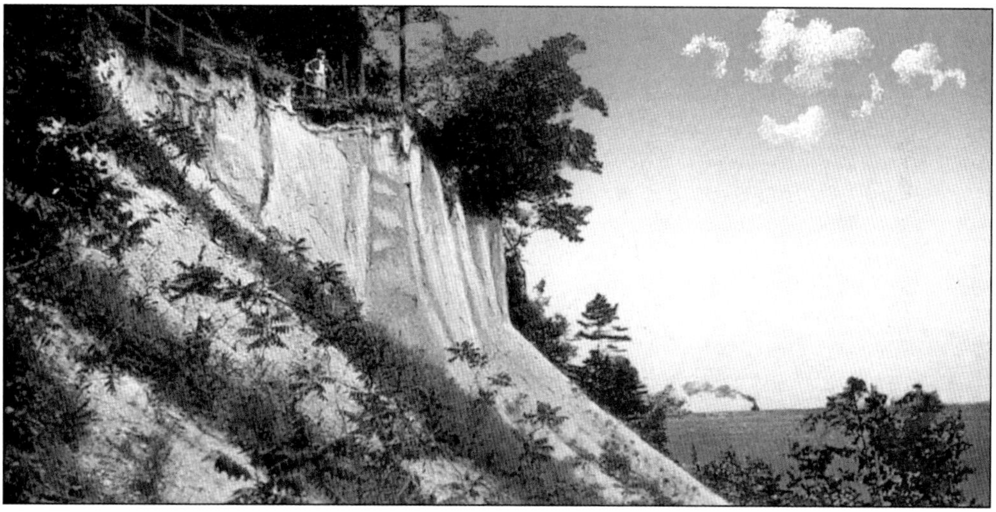

Bluff Road, located a short 10 minutes north of Traverse City on the Old Mission Peninsula, is home to Eagle's Nest Bluff. A drive out on Bluff Road is a feast for the eyes, not only are some of the oldest fruit farms in the area out there, but there are also sweeping views of the East Arm of Grand Traverse Bay. The Bluffs represent some of the highest points on the Old Mission Peninsula. It is easy to envision an eagle's nest perched high upon these hills. The panoramic view provided by Grand Traverse Bay and the Bluffs is evidence of the impact that the glaciers of the Ice Age had upon this area.

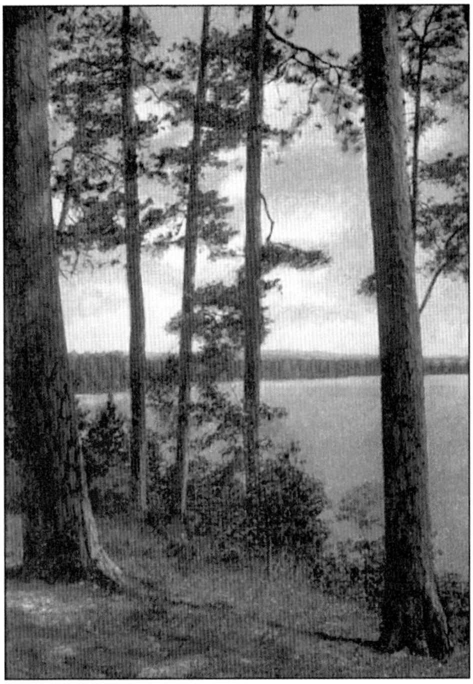

The area around Lake Wah-Be-Ka-Netta, or Duck Lake as it is commonly known, was once home to the Ottawa Indians. When lumbering came to the Grand Traverse region, nothing but a small forest of virgin pine on Lake Wah-Be-Ka-Netta was spared. For a time afterwards, a small cooperage and a resort occupied the land until the State of Michigan purchased it in 1917. This narrow stretch of land on Lake Wah-Be-Ka-Netta became known as Interlochen State Park.

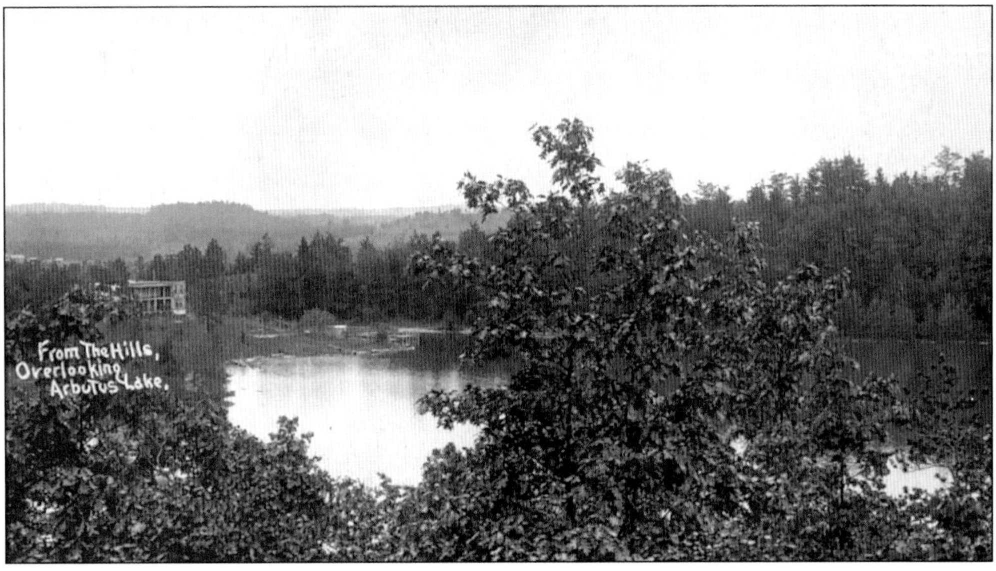

Arbutus Lake is actually a system of five spring-fed lakes, located southwest of Traverse City. There are 395 acres of water that comprise the lakes, and while fishermen are more likely to catch bass or bluegill than anything else, there are 11 species of fish. Camp Arbutus, still in operation today as a YMCA camp, was started in 1915 as a retreat for college women. It is difficult to believe that this string of lakes, the shoreline dotted with rustic cabins and resorts, is a mere seven miles south of the malls and parking lots which have sprung up in Traverse City. Recently, the Michigan Lakes and Streams Association designated Arbutus Lake as a "Wild and Scenic Lake"—due to 500 acres of undeveloped land on the lakes, as well as the loon habitat built by members of the Arbutus Lake Association.

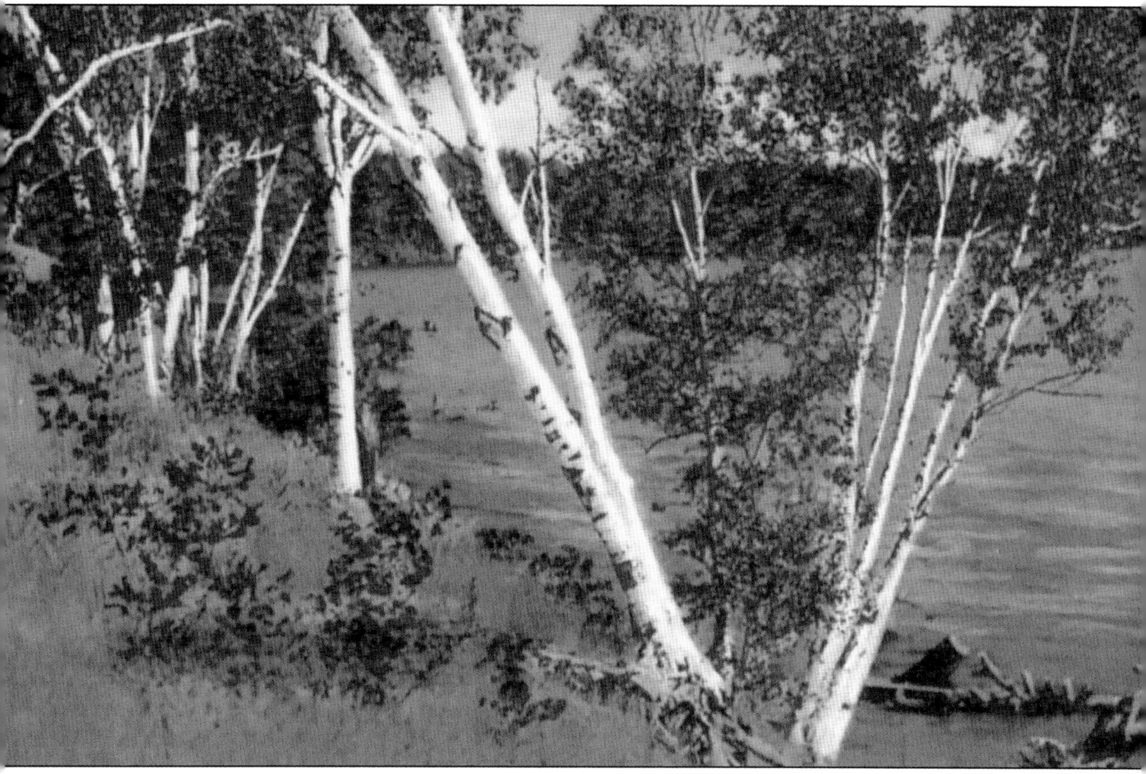

Platte Lake, which actually consists of Big Platte Lake and Little Platte Lake, lies approximately 30 miles southwest of Traverse City. Immediately to the north and west of Platte Lake is the Sleeping Bear National Lakeshore. Located in Benzie County, near Honor, the lake is only a short walk from the shores of Lake Michigan. Cottages, many hidden in the trees, dot the shores of Platte Lake, and it is quite common to see anglers fishing, children swimming, and boaters cruising the lake. Gone are the days when lumberjacks felled trees, floating them across Platte Lake and into the Platte River. Its natural beauty and use as a recreational area makes Platte Lake one of the Traverse City area's most popular destinations.

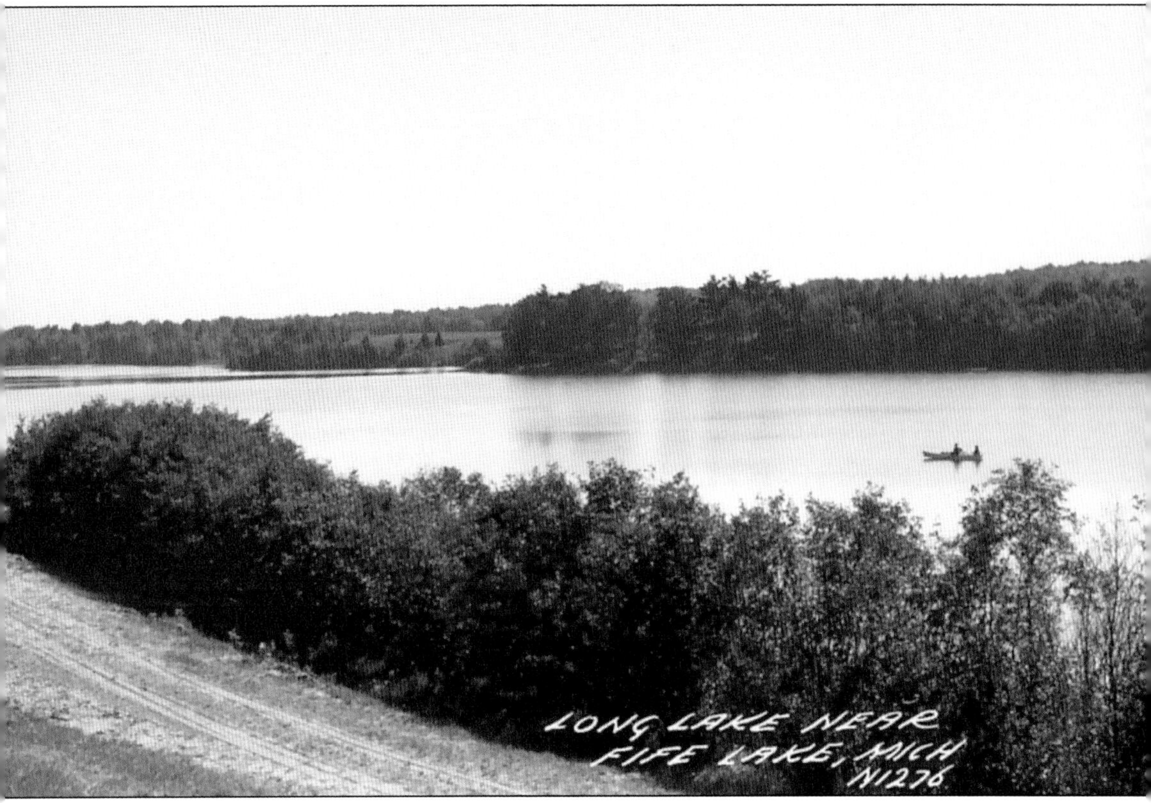

A lone fisherman casts his line on Long Lake, one of the area's smaller lakes near the Fife Lake Forest Area. Like many of the lakes in Grand Traverse County, Long Lake has a plentiful supply of bluegill, largemouth and smallmouth bass, perch, and sunfish. For those who prefer solitude, there are numerous small lakes in the Traverse City area such as Long Lake. While there is no listing of record fish caught in Long Lake, it is safe to assume that they do exist. Long Lake is located approximately 23 miles to the southeast of Traverse City, in Fife Lake Township.

Always pleasant and inviting, the natural beauty of Fife Lake has lured fishermen, hunters, lumberjacks, and sightseers for decades. Towering birches and pines surround the shoreline of Fife Lake. Almost all of the town's stores can be found on Main Street, and there are numerous resorts both on and off the lake for those seeking to take in the solitude of the area.

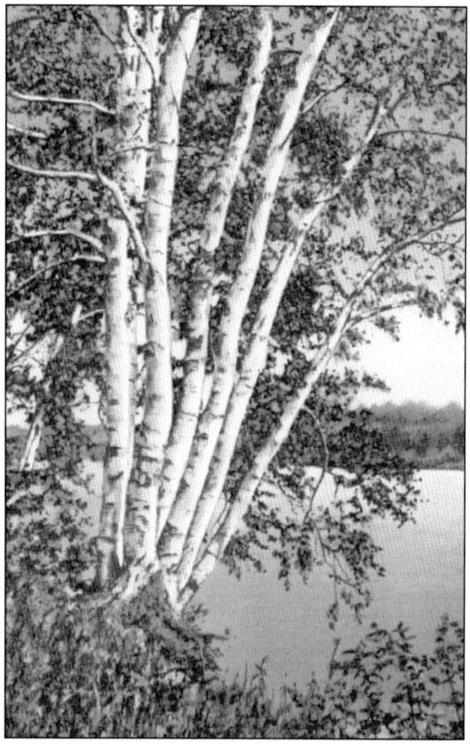

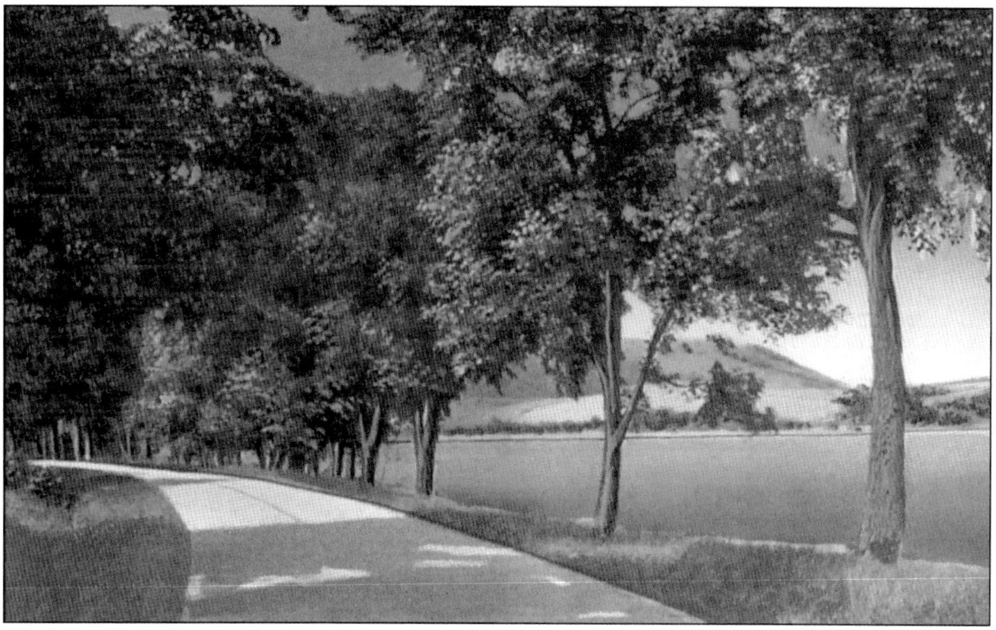

While Fife Lake is not as unspoiled as it may appear in this view, for the most part it has retained much of its natural beauty. A drive around the shoreline of the lake, especially in the spring when the trees are budding or in the fall as the leaves begin to change colors, is unequaled in its splendor. The beauty of the lake and the friendliness of the people are unequaled. That is, other than for the rest of Grand Traverse County.

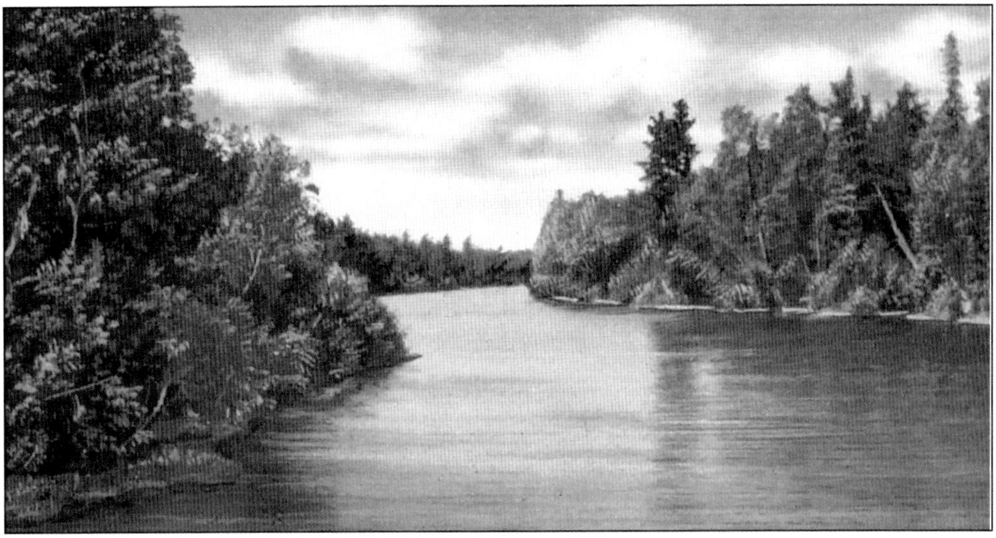

Viewing a lake from a distance, especially one the size of Fife Lake, creates an optical illusion. The lake, surrounded for the most part by trees, appears to be relatively small, although once on the lake it is easy to see how it could support an abundant wildlife population, including a number of species of fish and a loon habitat. Boating or canoeing on one of Grand Traverse County's inland lakes, such as Fife Lake, is an experience not to be missed.

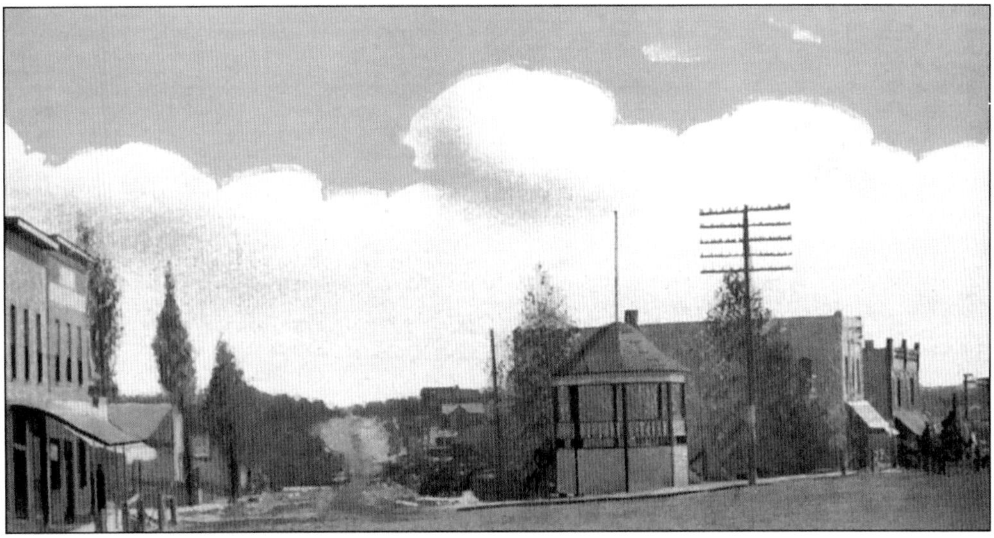

An 1867 plan to build the Midland, Houghton Lake, and Traverse Bay State Road offered to connect the east side of the state with the western portion. This road, which was to serve as a supply line for the construction of the Grand Rapids & Indiana Railroad, passed through what we now know as Fife Lake. At the time, Fife Lake was an uninhabited wilderness. The surveyor had the responsibility to name every lake and stream of importance, and by a vote of the survey crew, the lake was named after William H. Fife, commissioner of the Houghton Lake and Traverse Bay State Road. Fife Lake grew and prospered during the lumber era, although it is best known today for its plentiful fish and beautiful scenery. Situated seven miles west of Kingsley, or about 22 miles Southeast of Traverse City, Fife Lake looks very much the same today as it did around the turn of the century.

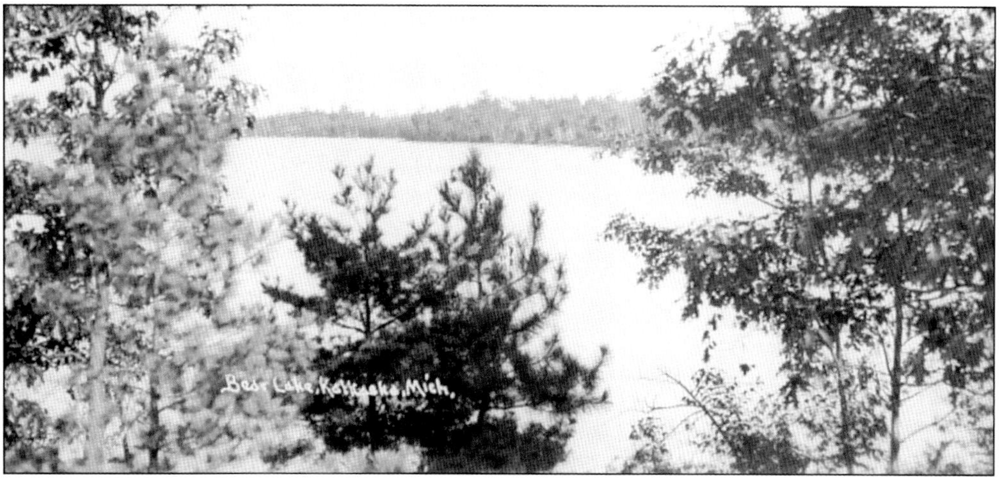

Peering through the tall white pines along the shoreline of Bear Lake gives an impression of what the first settlers in Northern Michigan saw when they arrived. Located in Kalkaska County, approximately 28 miles to the east of Traverse City, Bear Lake is situated between Mallard Lake to the north and Cub Lake to the south. Kalkaska County is home to the National Trout Festival and has long been known as a virtual paradise for fishermen and hunters. Bear Lake is teeming with brown trout, smallmouth bass, white suckers, yellow perch, rock bass, and bluegills. Like so many of the neighboring counties, Kalkaska was once home to a lumber industry that clear cut most of the area's timber. In recent years, Kalkaska County, like Grand Traverse County, has relied primarily on the growing tourist industry.

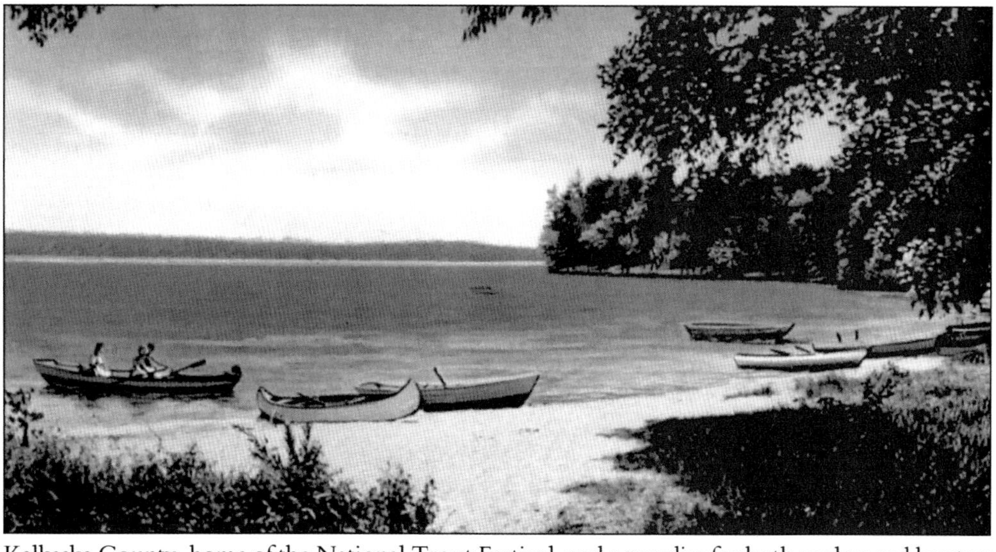

Kalkaska County, home of the National Trout Festival, and a paradise for both anglers and hunters alike, is located 25 miles east of Traverse City just off of M-72. Kalkaska is known as a land of lakes, streams, open space, and rolling hills. The county, which was originally named Wababasee, after a Potawatami chief, was soon changed to Kalkaska in 1843. Kalkaska is the Chippewa Indian word meaning "burned over" or "flat table"—obviously a reference to the landscape. The Pere Marquette Forest extends throughout the county, although there are a number of wetlands. A bonanza for sportsmen, the lakes and woodlands of Kalkaska are as bountiful with wildlife as ever.

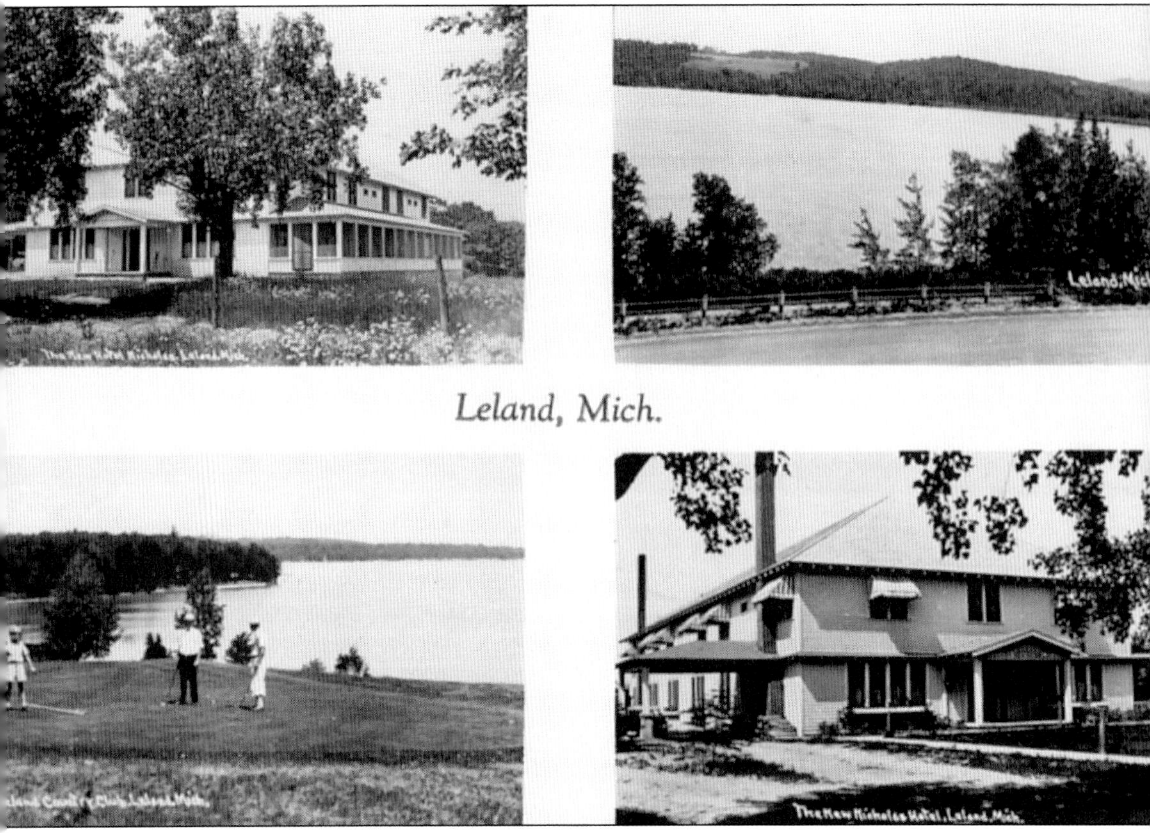

Leland Lodge, one of Leelanau County's oldest resorts, is located approximately 25 miles northwest of Traverse City. Overlooking one of the area's finest golf courses, the lodge is only minutes away from downtown Leland, as well as the sandy beaches of Lake Leelanau and Lake Michigan. Leland itself, founded in 1853, is nestled on a narrow strip of land between Lake Leelanau and Lake Michigan. Steamers and schooners brought settlers here, and in 1900, with a population of over 10,000, the town was named the county seat. Known as Fishtown, the town has historically maintained strong maritime traditions of boat building and commercial fishing, although the first tourists arrived on the heels of the settlers. To this day, the small village of Leland is known around the world for its smoked fish.

(*Opposite, bottom*) The northern tip of Lake Leelanau is one of the hubs of activity in Leelanau County, especially during the summer. The first European settlers initially called it Carp Lake, although Native Americans referred to it as Leelanau, meaning "delight for life." The north end of Lake Leelanau extends from the narrows, located at Lake Leelanau, northward to Leland. In total, the lake is 51 miles long and features at least a dozen streams, all of which are teeming with bass, trout, and walleye. Only the town of Leland, or Fishtown as locals call it, separates the north end of Lake Leelanau and the shores of Lake Michigan. Cottages and homes, tucked in along the shore of Lake Leelanau, bustle with activity during the summer months as boaters, fishermen, and swimmers take to its crystal clear waters.

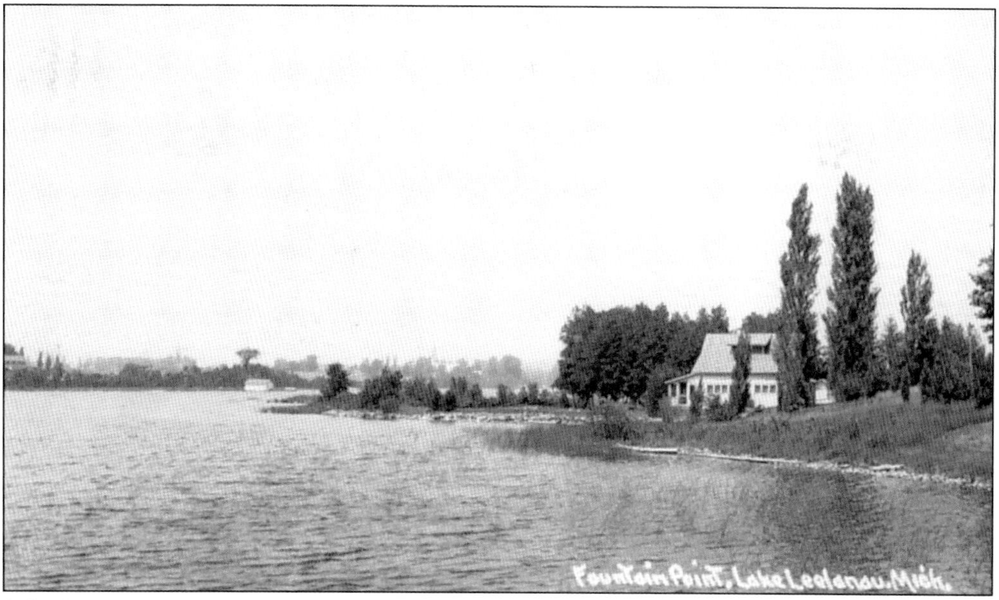

(*Above*) Fountain Point is located at the narrows that separate North Lake Leelanau and South Lake Leelanau. In the 1860s, a fur trader by the name of Andre de Beloit was trapping in the area and after a time, decided to purchase a tract of land. The land is situated on what was then called Carp Lake. Soon afterward, de Beloit began drilling for oil on his land, and in 1863 he struck a gusher—of water. The fountain at Fountain Point has been flowing ever since. Eventually, a woman from Cincinnati purchased the tract, and construction on the Fountain Point House, a three-story structure, was completed in 1899. Since that time, Fountain Point House has changed hands only once, having recently been restored in preparation for the next 100 years.

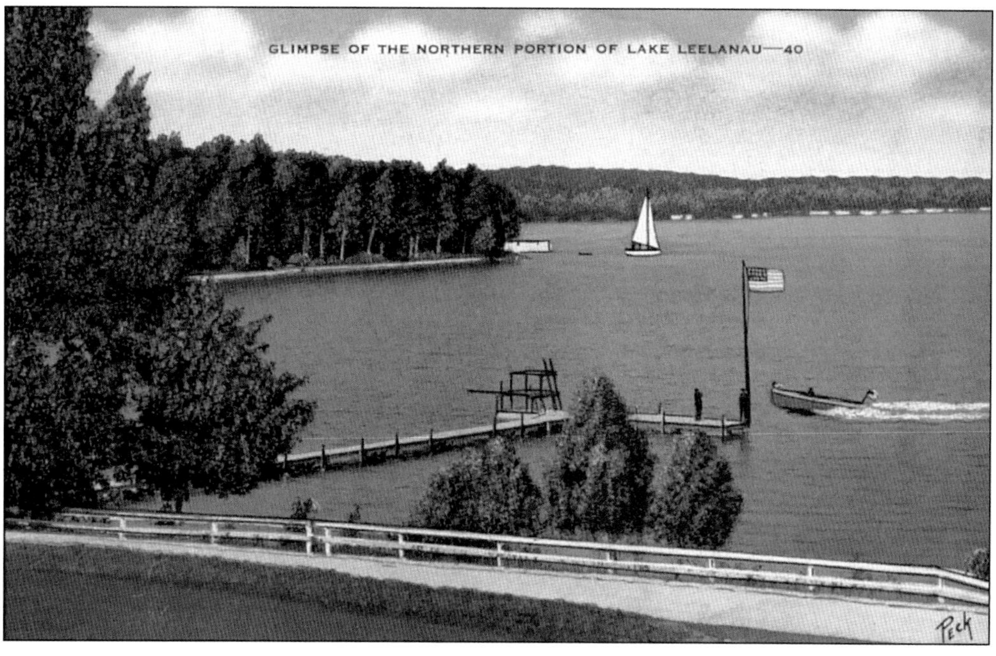

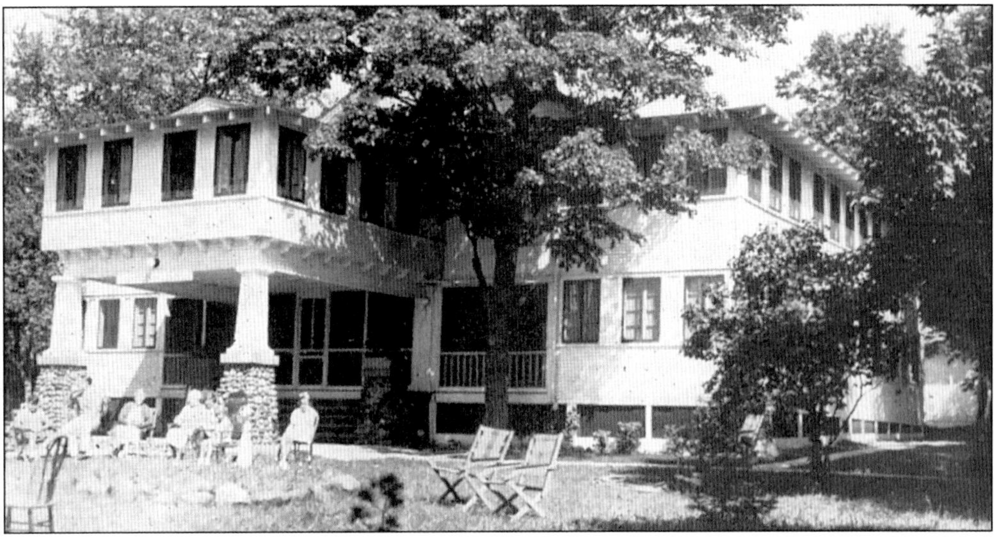

Back in the days when Traverse City was still a lumber and manufacturing town, the village of Omena had already played host to the local tourist industry. The Omena Inn, one of several summer resorts just to the north of the village, was billed as Northern Michigan's finest resort. The resort offered bathing, boating, tennis, golf, and horseback riding and was a hub of summer activity in Northern Michigan. Ships ferried passengers to the pier at Omena from such far-away places as Detroit and Chicago. Operating successfully from the turn of the century until just after the Depression, the Omena Inn has been restored and is now used as a private residence. Omena is located 25 miles north of Traverse City in Leelanau County, featuring historic cottages, summer homes, and of course Omena Bay.

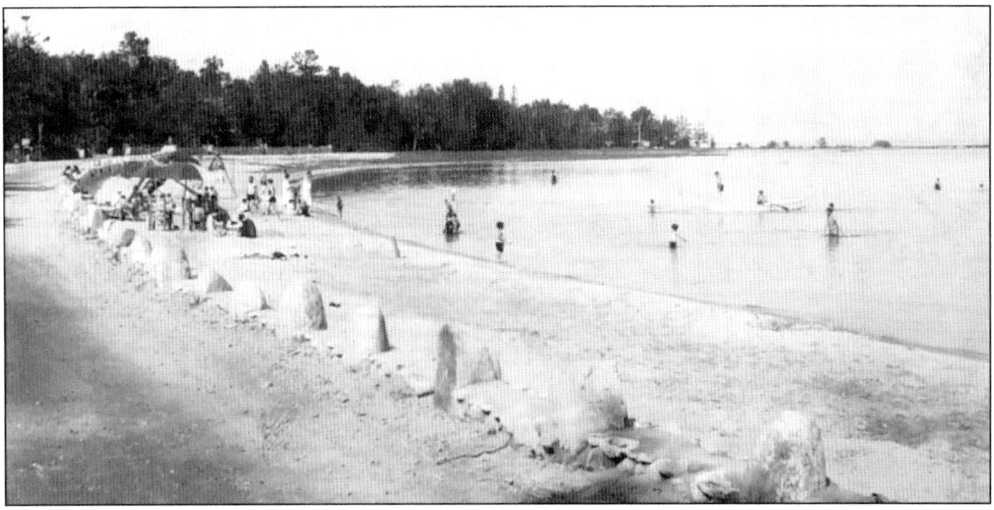

Northport Point, always a popular spot with swimmers, is located just north of the village of Northport, where Grand Traverse Bay meets Lake Michigan. To use a well-worn phrase, Northport is not the type of place that you get to unintentionally. After all, it is at the tip of the Leelanau Peninsula, and beyond it there is nowhere else to go, unless you are catching a boat. Just to the north is the Grand Traverse Lighthouse, located at the Leelanau State Park on the tip of the Leelanau Peninsula. The village of Northport is approximately 29 miles north of Traverse City on M-22 in Leelanau County.

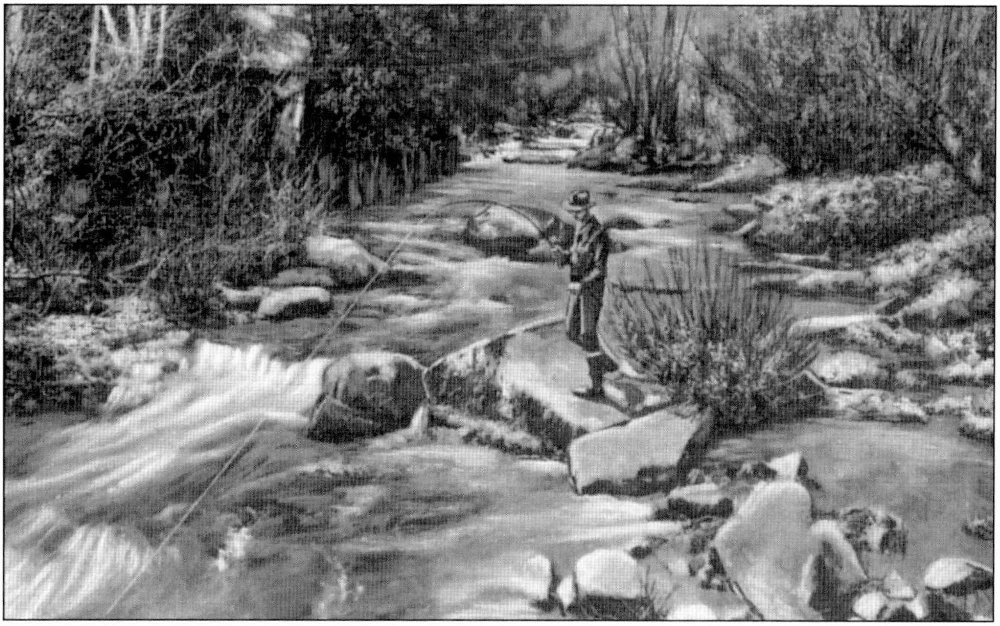

Kewadin, located at the northernmost tip of Elk Lake, is some 19 miles north of Traverse City in Antrim County. Places like Kewadin, where great stands of virgin pine still stand, and the streams meander through the woodlands, probably provide an experience similar to that of the Native Americans and the first settlers. Occupied solely by Native Americans until 1876, the village was known as Indian Town; eventually the name was changed to Kewadin in honor of one of the Indian chiefs. Known for its plentiful waterways, teeming with walleye, pike, perch, and smallmouth bass, Kewadin is also home to Camp Maplehurst, a private coeducational summer camp for youth ranging from seven to 17 years of age. Tucked away in the woods of Antrim County, Kewadin is truly one of Northern Michigan's jewels.

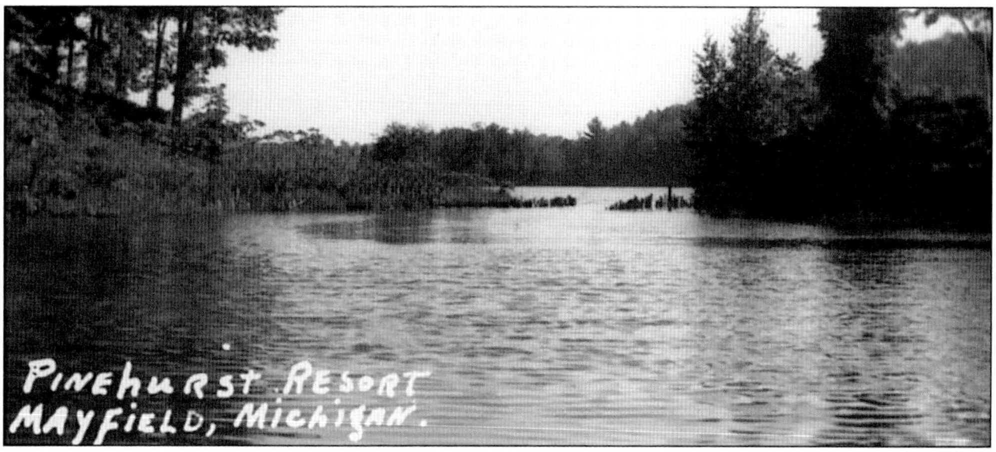

Mayfield is somewhat of a peculiar place. Situated among the pines approximately seven miles south of Traverse City, it remains a "diamond in the rough." A thriving village, Mayfield has become yet another commuter town. While the village of Mayfield, with its streams, ponds, and lakes, still has a great deal to offer, its glory days have passed. The days when the lumber mill and shingle factory were the predominant businesses are long gone. Now, it is primarily fishing and camping in rustic resorts that draw people to Mayfield.

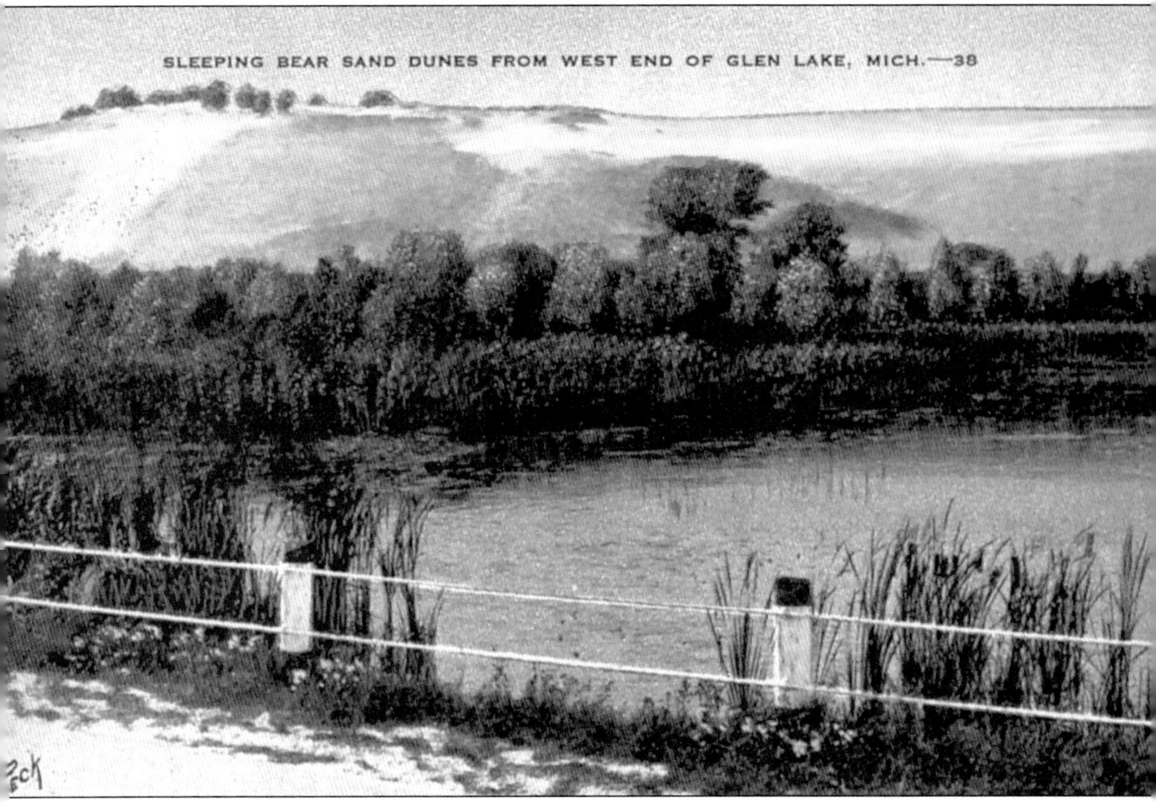

Peaceful and reflective, the sand dunes are now dormant, although they were formed during the glacial period and following that, millions of years of erosion. Gazing across Glen Lake at the sand dunes, one is able to gain a true understanding of nature. Beyond the lake lie a meadow, a forest, and sand dunes rising up out of the background. This little corner of Leelanau County offers up some of the most exciting activities found anywhere and include boating, hiking, swimming, fishing, biking, and cross-country skiing. First-time visitors, especially those with young children, make it a point to climb the front face of the sand dunes, if for no other reason than to run back down the hill.

(*Opposite, bottom*) The village of Elk Rapids, one of Traverse City's many neighboring communities, has undergone numerous transformations over the years. Founded in 1852, this quaint village was once a lumbering town. When the lumber industry began to decline, the milling efforts focused on smelting iron ore. Within a few short years, the Cement Works was built on the shores of Lake Michigan and began producing Portland cement. Eventually, Elk Rapids became home to a number of cherry packing plants, emphasizing agriculture over manufacturing. Today, the Village of Elk Rapids remains a quiet little town, just a mere 15 miles north of Traverse City.

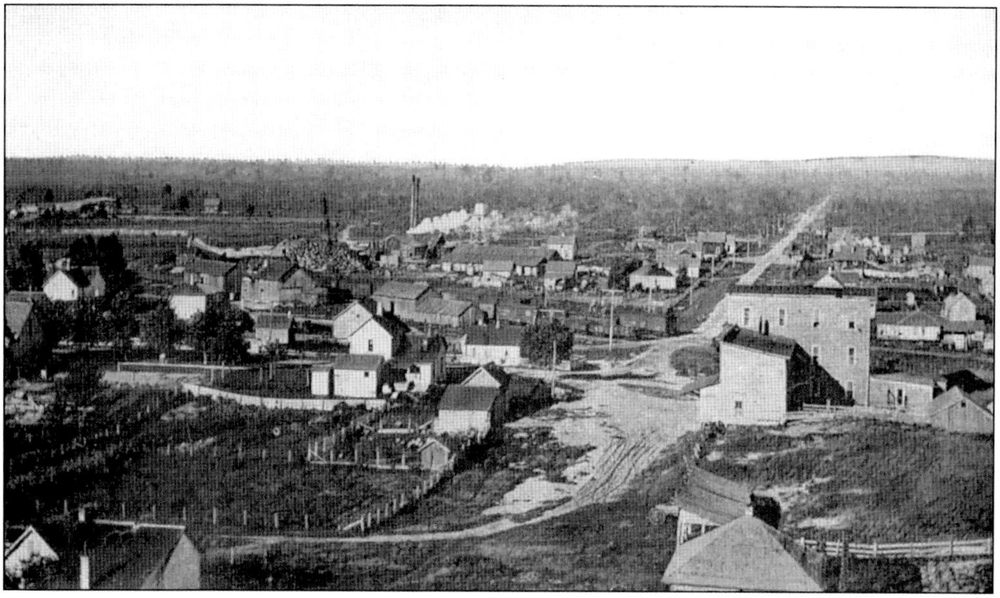

(*Above*) Copemish, organized as a village in 1891, is located approximately 40 miles south of Traverse City in Manistee County. In its early days, Copemish was a lumber town much like its sister city to the north, although as the lumber industry began to decline, it did not have the same financial resources as Traverse City. Agriculture played an important part in the development of the village economy, especially with respect to the apple crop; the nearby salt mines of Manistee have provided steady employment for many village residents. Residents of this little town of fewer than 300 people rely heavily on the neighboring towns of Cadillac, Manistee, and Traverse City to sell their crops and to buy life's necessities. The village name, Copemish, is a Native American word meaning "big beech," which refers to the idea of holding tribal council under a big beech tree.

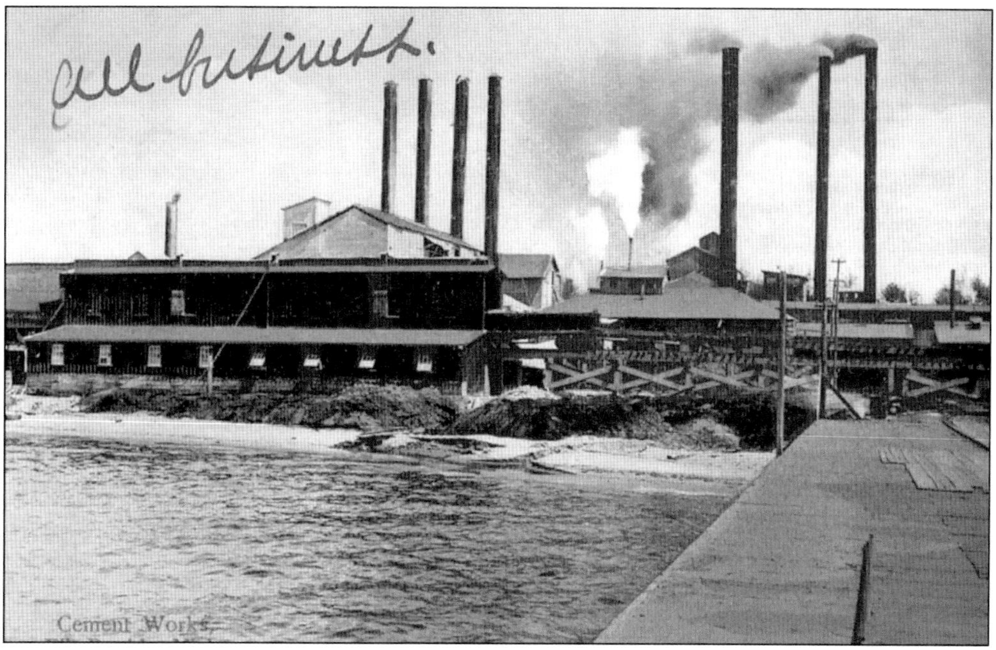

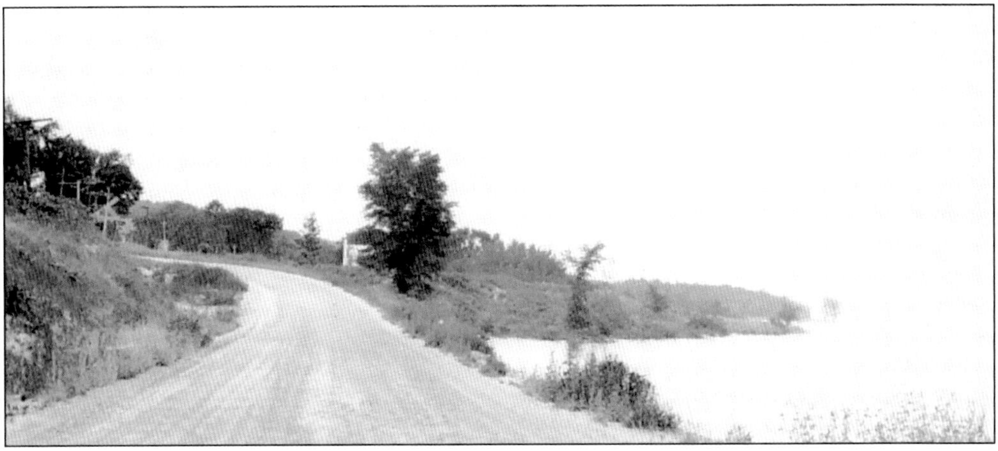

The drive along M-22 from Traverse City to Suttons Bay is no longer as pristine as it once was, although it is still one of the most scenic routes in Northern Michigan. Suttons Bay, named for Harry C. Sutton, an entrepreneur who set up a lumber camp that provided fuel for wood burning steamships, is 15 miles north of Traverse City. Quaint and charming Suttons Bay has changed very little over the years and has the feel of a town that time has forgotten. Whether merely taking a drive along M-22 visiting Suttons Bay or its neighbors Omena and Northport, this trip along the shores of Grand Traverse Bay in Leelanau County is a feast for the eyes.

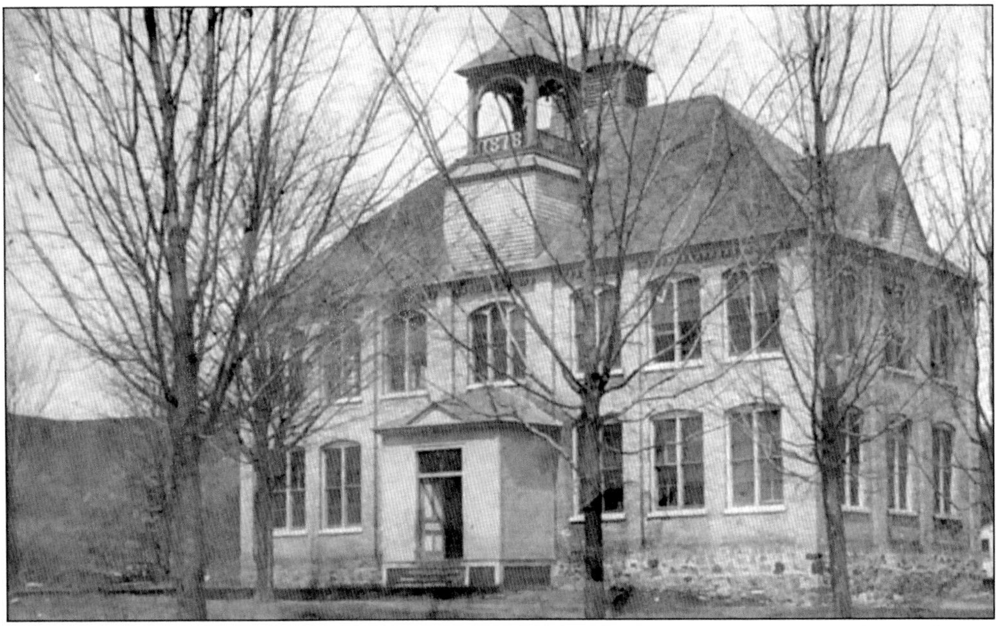

Founded in 1854 by Harry Sutton, the village of Suttons Bay, located on the west shore of West Grand Traverse Bay in Leelanau County, grew quickly and was soon in need of a school. Despite the fact that there was not a road between Traverse City and Suttons Bay until 1862, when the mail was delivered once every two weeks, the small lumber camp was soon in need of city services. In 1880, with a population of approximately 250, the village built its first schoolhouse. The relatively small schoolhouse soon experienced growing pains and was eventually replaced by a more modern facility. Presently, 85 to 90 percent of the students at Suttons Bay High School go on to college or some other form of higher education.

Five

Out and About in the Greater Grand Traverse Region

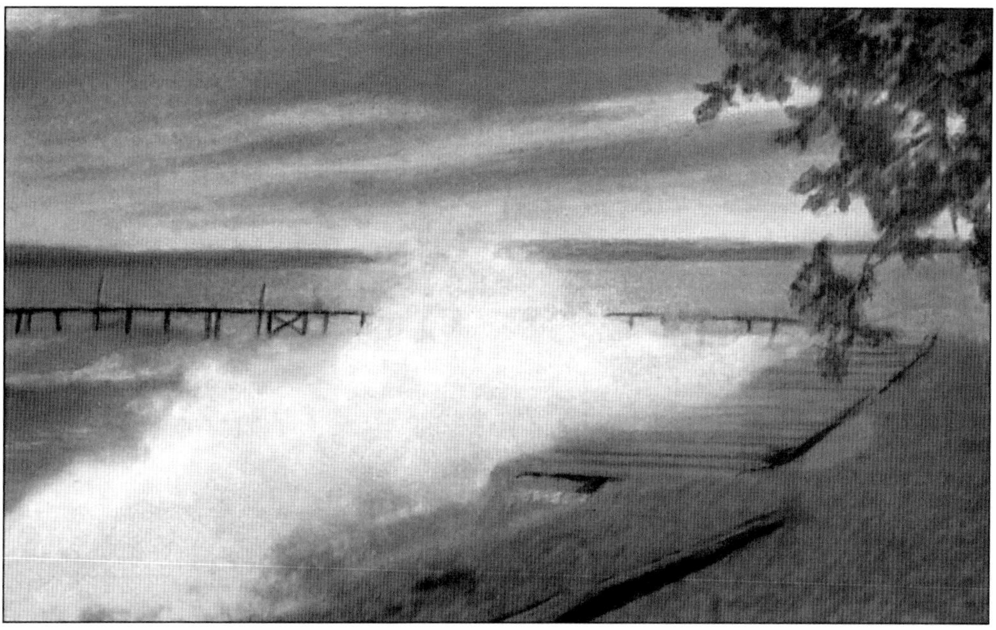

North of Traverse City and Grand Traverse Bay, near the town of Petoskey, is Little Traverse Bay. This inlet, which extends from Harbor Springs to the north, downward to Petoskey, and almost all the way south to Charlevoix, is well known for its beauty and its ferocity. It was here that ships from Detroit and Cleveland would make their first stop on Lake Michigan after rounding the northern tip of the Lower Peninsula.

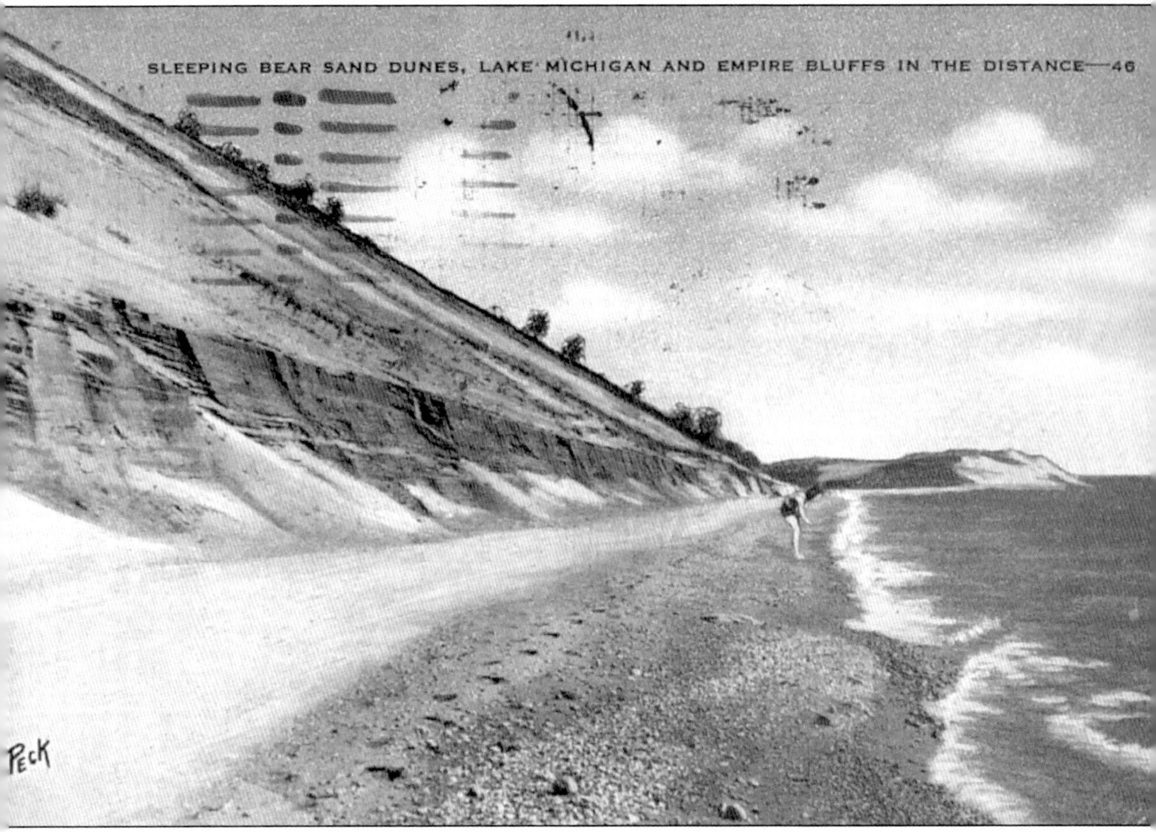

Sleeping Bear Dunes National Lakeshore, west of Traverse City near Glen Arbor, is a national park unlike any other, with over 61,000 acres of Lake Michigan shoreline and forests full of birch, pine, beech, and maple. There are also numerous lakes, rivers, dunes, and bluffs, not to mention North and South Manitou Islands. The dunes take their name from an Ojibway legend of a mother bear and her two cubs that were forced to swim Lake Michigan from Wisconsin to Michigan to escape a raging wildfire. While the mother bear made it to shore, the cubs had vanished in the waters of Lake Michigan. The Great Spirit took pity on her, raising North and South Manitou Islands to mark the spot where the cubs had disappeared.

(*Opposite, bottom*) The shoreline of Sleeping Bear Dunes National Lakeshore, with its magnificent views of Lake Michigan and the Manitou Islands, consists of over 61,000 acres of forests, beaches, and dune formations. The unique geological origin of the dunes, a natural creation of wind and water, is what convinced the National Park Service to designate it as a national park. The Manitou Islands, also part of the park, have a history that includes commercial fishing, logging, and lumbering. While the mainland offers camping, biking, hiking, and picnic facilities, the shipwrecks off the Manitou Islands are a favorite among scuba divers. To this day, a small village of descendants primarily of original settlers remains on North Manitou Island.

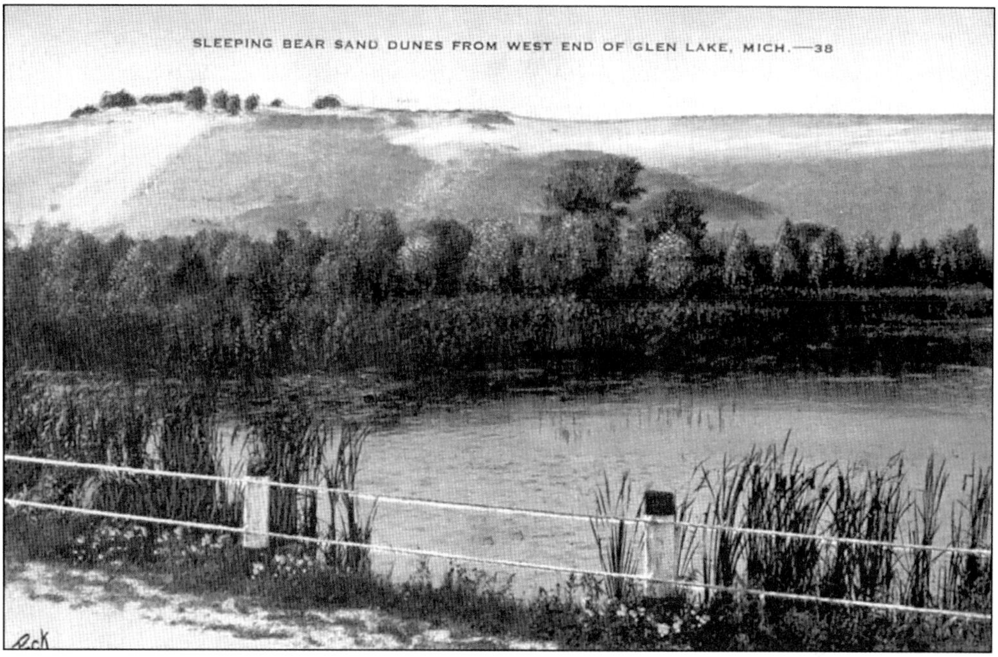

(*Above*) Since the 1970s, the west end of Little Glen Lake has been a part of the Sleeping Bear Dunes National Lakeshore. Regarded by some as the fifth most beautiful lake in the world, Glen Lake is much more than just another inland waterway. The lake, which has yielded some record fish over the years, is stocked with brown trout, lake trout, rainbow trout, and splake, offering some of the best fishing in the Grand Traverse region. In addition, there is a public access site with a boat ramp on the north side of Glen Lake, near Glen Arbor.

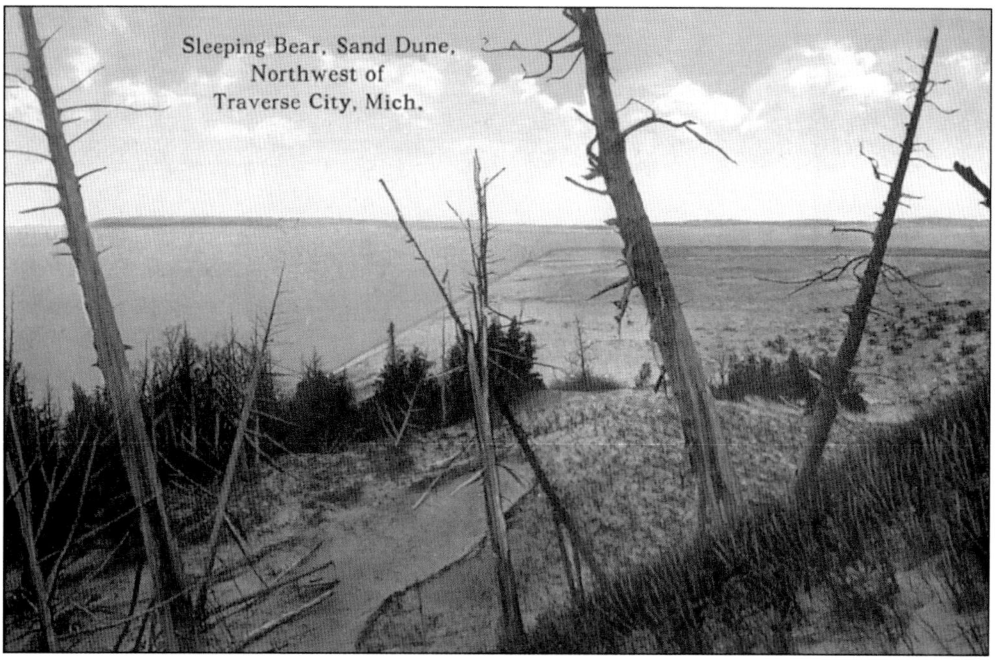

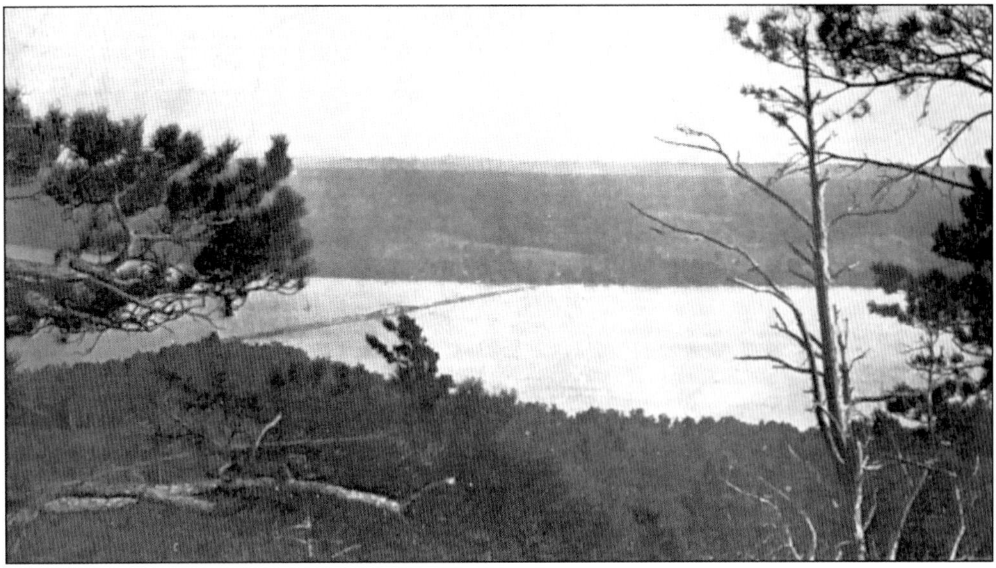

Big Glen Lake and Little Glen Lake, separated by "The Narrows," have been rated by National Geographic Magazine as ranking among the five most beautiful lakes in the world. The lakes, located about 25 miles west of Traverse City in Leelanau County, are surrounded by the hamlets of Glen Arbor, Glen Haven, Burdickville, and Empire. Much of the surrounding area is part of the Sleeping Bear Dunes National Lakeshore. A sweeping view of the lakes—as well as Sleeping Bear Sand Dune, Lake Michigan, and Manitou Island—can be seen from atop Inspiration Point. Designated as no-wake lakes, Big Glen and Little Glen Lake are favored by anglers out to catch their limit of bluegill, bass, perch, and trout.

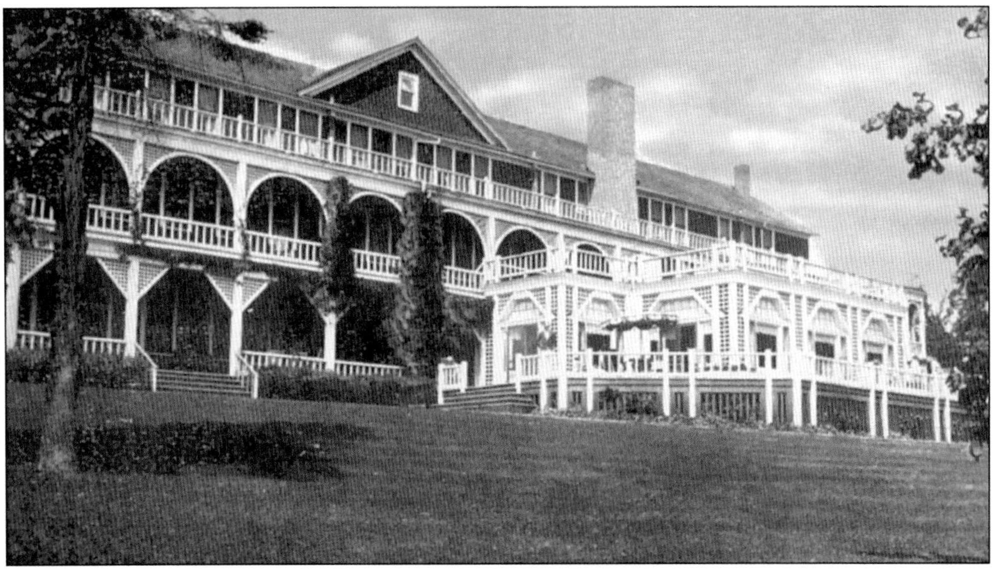

Breathtaking views of the countryside, as well as the surrounding lakes, are part of the experience for those who choose to play a round of golf at the Belvedere Golf Club in Charlevoix. Founded in 1925, the course opened for play in 1927, and the Belvedere has played host to the Michigan Amateur Championship a total of 38 times over the years. Known as a favorite among professional golfers, the Belvedere is located approximately 49 miles north of Traverse City.

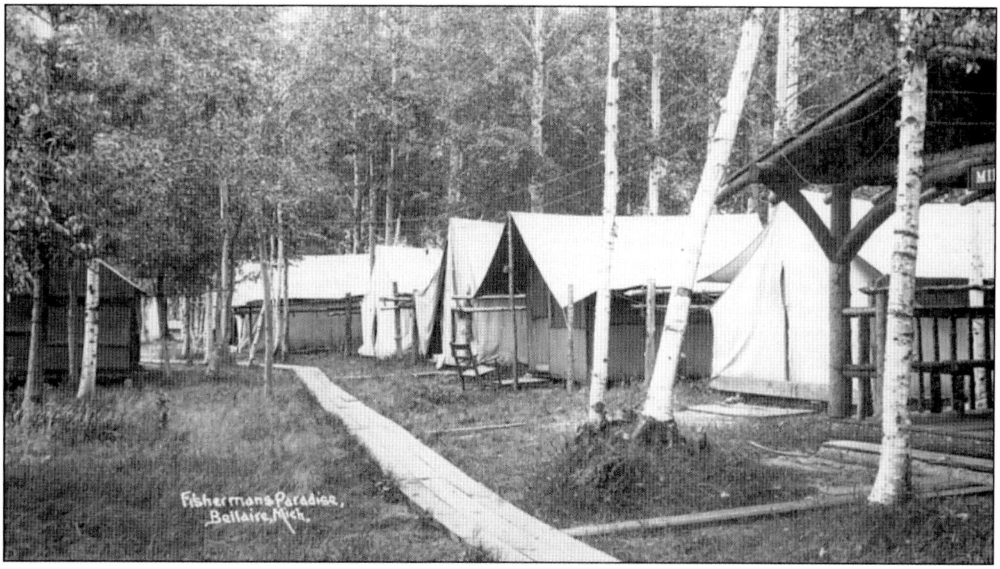

Bellaire and all of Antrim County are not only a fisherman's paradise, but also favorite hunting places. Lake Bellaire, Torch Lake, the Clam River, and nearby Intermediate Lake have been popular among fishermen for decades. Antrim County is one of the least developed areas of Northern Michigan, featuring vast expanses of forest and wetlands. Originally known as Keno, the name of the town was changed in 1879 to Bellaire, due to the clearness and purity of the air. In that same year, Antrim County was organized by the state legislature, and Bellaire was named the county seat. Located approximately 40 miles north of Traverse City, off of U.S. 131, Bellaire is still a favorite among fishermen, hunters, and in the winter, ski enthusiasts.

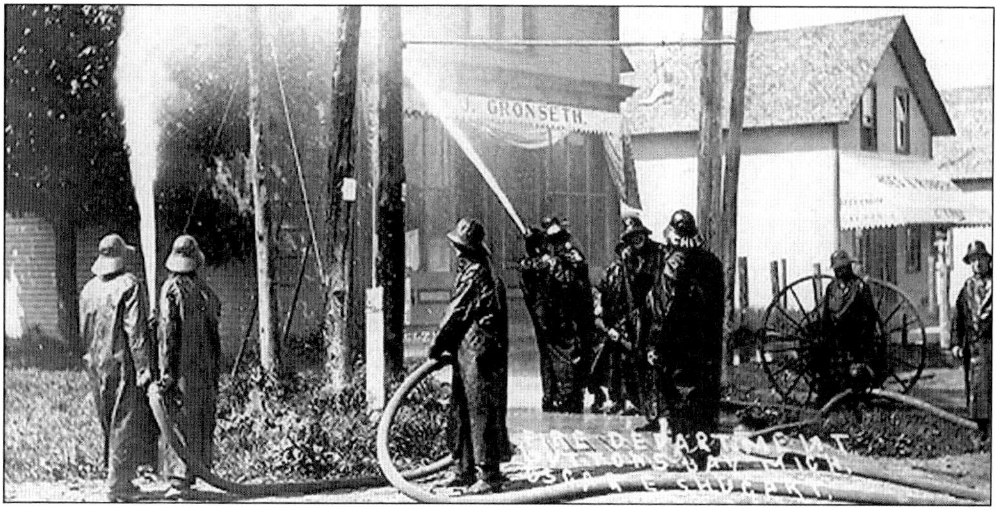

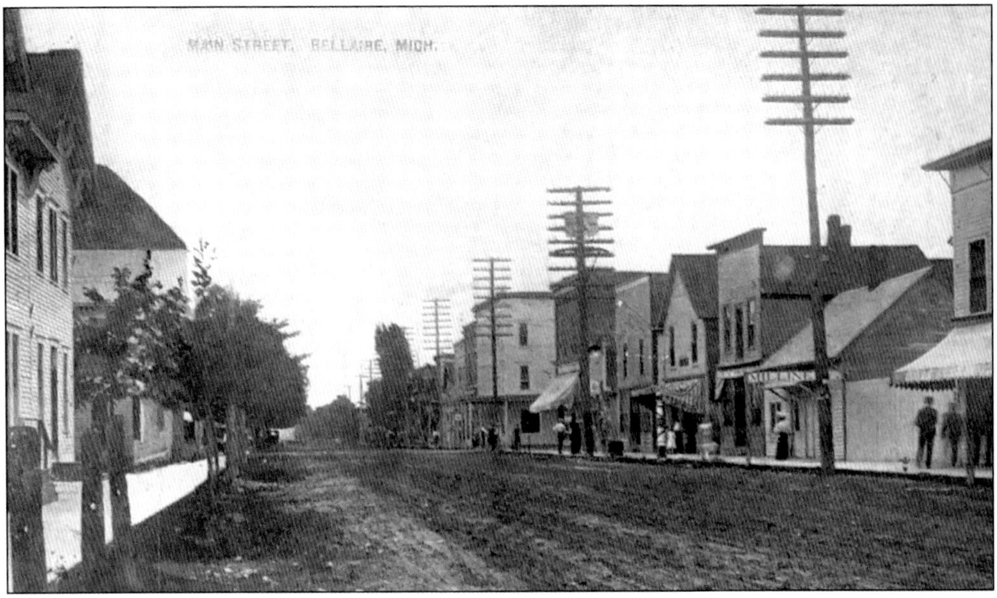

The town of Keno, located in the county of Meguzzee, was mapped out in the early 1800s. By 1843, the name of the county had been changed to Antrim, and at the suggestion of one of its leaders, Ambrose Palmer, the town had been designated as Bellaire to reflect the purity of the air and water in the area. In 1879, the state legislature organized Antrim County, and Bellaire was incorporated and named the county seat. Bellaire is still the county seat and one of Antrim County's most visited sites. Fishing, mountain biking, hunting, downhill and cross country skiing, as well as snowmobiling make Bellaire a popular year-round destination. Bellaire is located approximately 40 miles north of Traverse City.

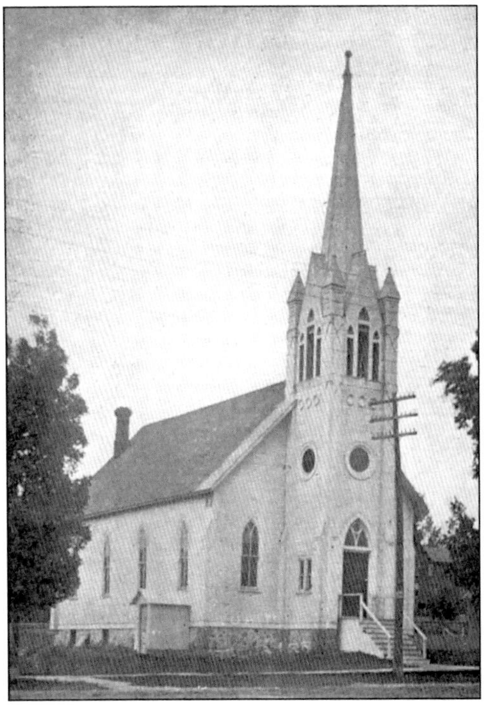

The First Methodist Church of Bellaire, now known as the Community United Methodist Church, is located on Bridge Street in downtown Bellaire. One of the oldest churches in Antrim County, it was also among a handful of structures left unscathed by the 1921 fire, which ravaged the town. Twelve buildings in the downtown area were lost to this fire, which started as a result of a cyclonic windstorm shorting out high-tension wires. The First Methodist Church may be one of the oldest churches in Bellaire, although it is not the only one. Today, there are 10 churches in town, representing most major religious denominations.

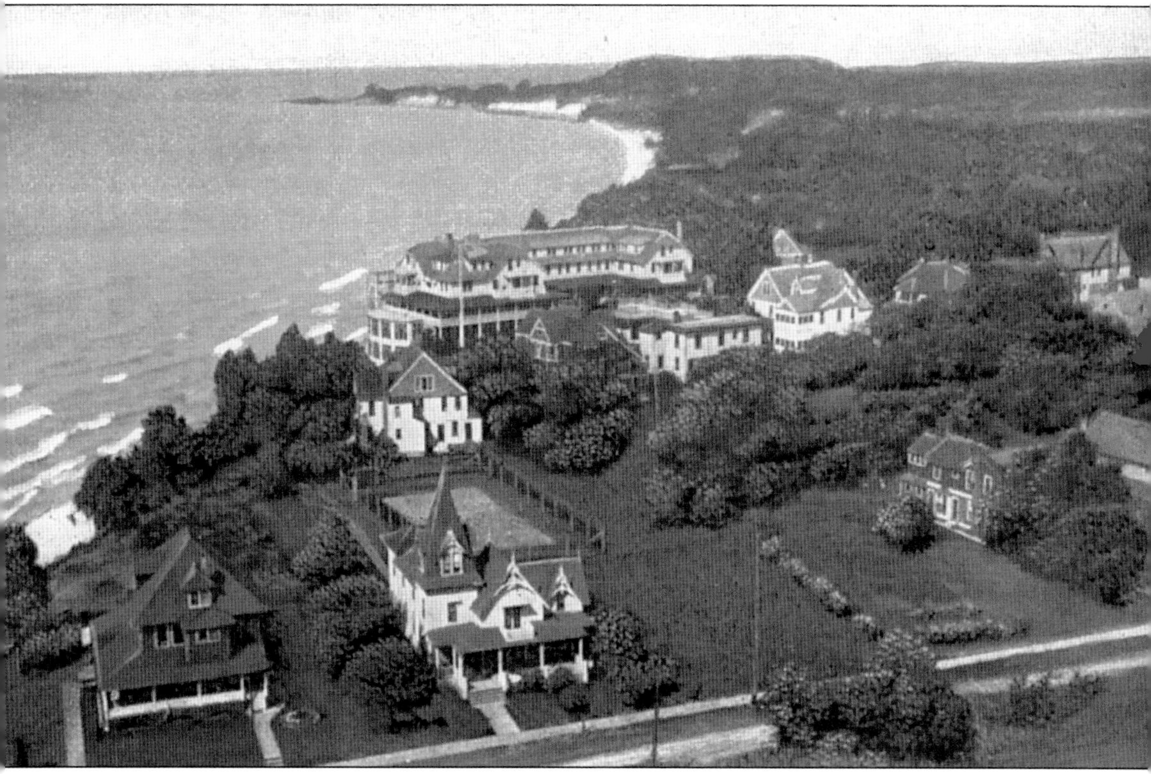

This aerial view of the lake and cottages in Charlevoix, north of Traverse City, shows just how popular tourism is in Northern Michigan. Charlevoix has been a resort town since its inception, and while it is almost 50 miles from Traverse City, these two towns have a great deal of shared history. Not only are they both resort towns—with Charlevoix swelling from its native population of 8,500 to over 30,000 in the summer months—but they were also both stopping points for passenger ships and railroads. In fact, the rail lines to Charlevoix and Petoskey were built prior to those in Traverse City, and almost every passenger ship on its way to Traverse City made a stop in Charlevoix along the way.

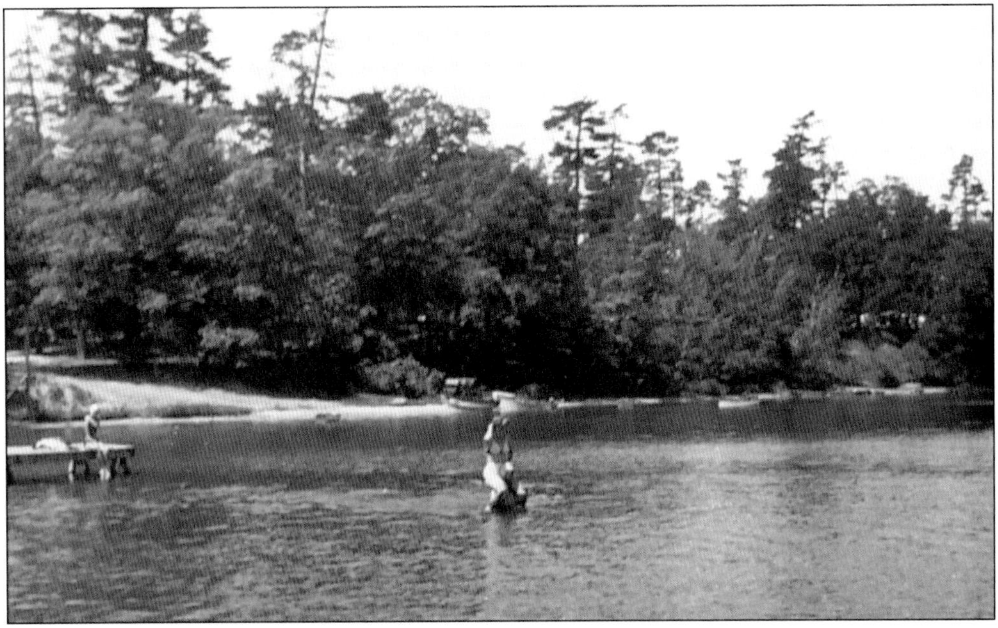

(*Above*) Lake Wah-Be-Ka-Ness, as the Native Americans called it, or Green Lake as it is commonly referred to, is the home of Michigan's oldest state park. Originally named Pine Park, the 200 acres that make up Interlochen State Park were purchased by the Michigan Legislature in 1917 at a cost of $60,000. In 1928, at the northernmost boundary of the park, the National Music Camp was established. Located on a narrow piece of land that separates Lake Wah-Be-Kah-Ness, or Green Lake, and Lake Wah-Be-Ka-Netta, or Duck Lake, Interlochen State Park is home to one of the few stands of virgin pine left in Michigan. A total of 490 campsites are available at the Duck Lake site, with a number of more rustic accommodations on Green Lake. Both sites offer a variety of water related activities that include boating, sailing, swimming, canoeing, and fishing.

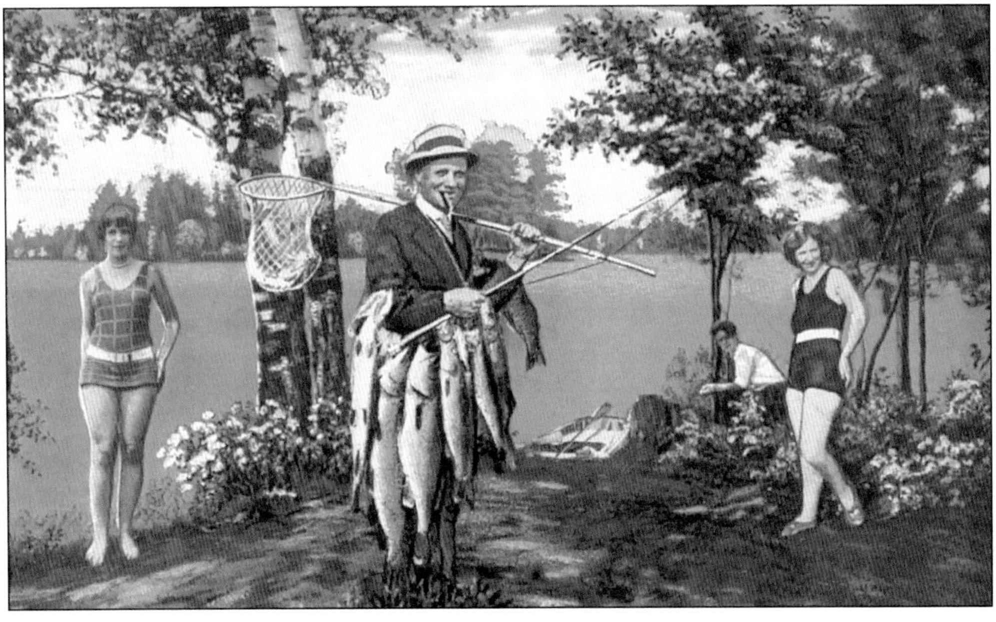

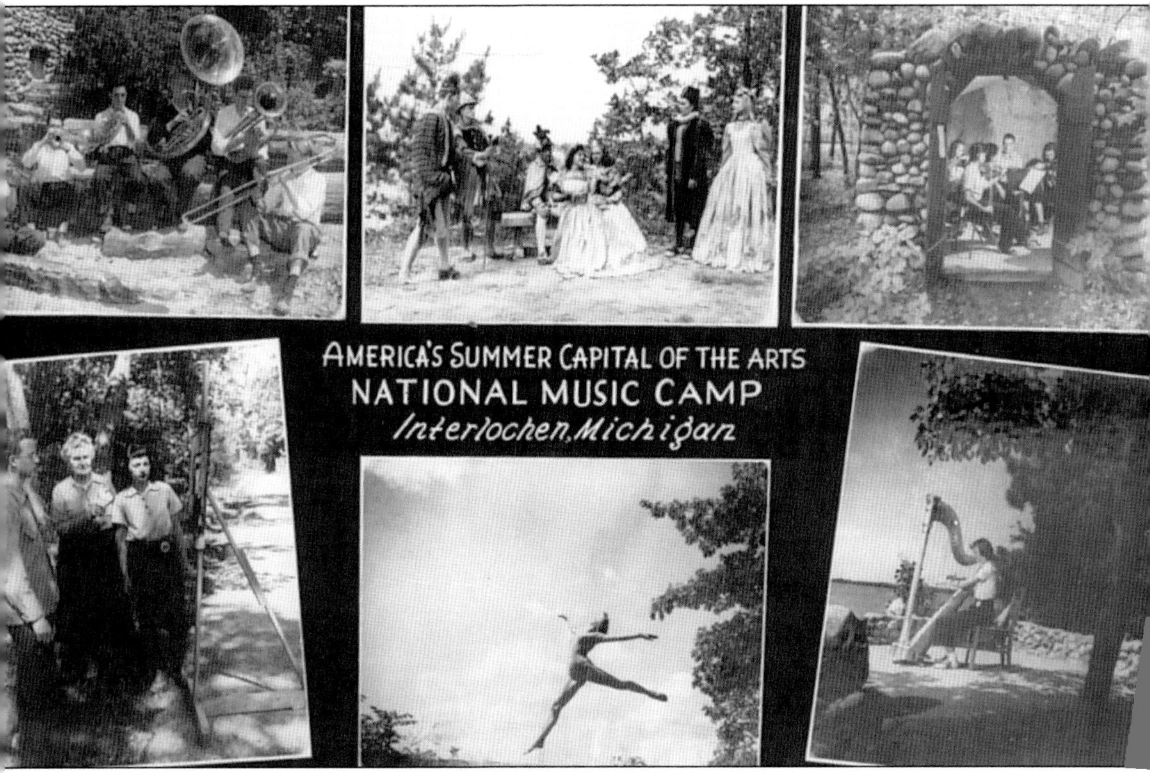

The National Music Camp at Interlochen has grown into a world-renowned center for the arts. In fact, the fine arts camp, started in 1928 by Joseph Maddy, has grown to become the oldest and most successful fine arts camp in the world. Professional guest artists such as Itzhak Perlman, Van Cliburn, and Andre Watts, as well as numerous dancers, educators, musicians, and writers come from around the world to perform and to teach at Interlochen. Now known simply as Interlochen Arts Camp, it was named one of the top 10 camps in the country in 1996, when the World Youth Symphony Orchestra made its debut at the Cultural Olympiad in Atlanta, Georgia. In 1998, Interlochen Arts Camp hosted the National Youth Orchestra Festival.

(*Opposite, bottom*) While the fishing and hospitality have always been top notch, this Bing Crosby look-alike may be overstating the case. Duck Lake and Green Lake, on the east and west side of Interlochen respectively, are both known to be popular fishing grounds. Stocked with northern pike, bluegill, walleye, gar, and bass, fishermen on each of these lakes have netted record catches. Just three years ago, a 41.5-inch Longnose Gar was caught on Green Lake, and in 1995 a 42.25-inch Northern Pike was caught in Duck Lake. Both lakes serve as breeding grounds and habitats for the common loon, a threatened species in Northern Michigan since 1987. Duck Lake and Green Lake are home to Interlochen State Park, Michigan's oldest state park, as well as Interlochen Arts Academy.

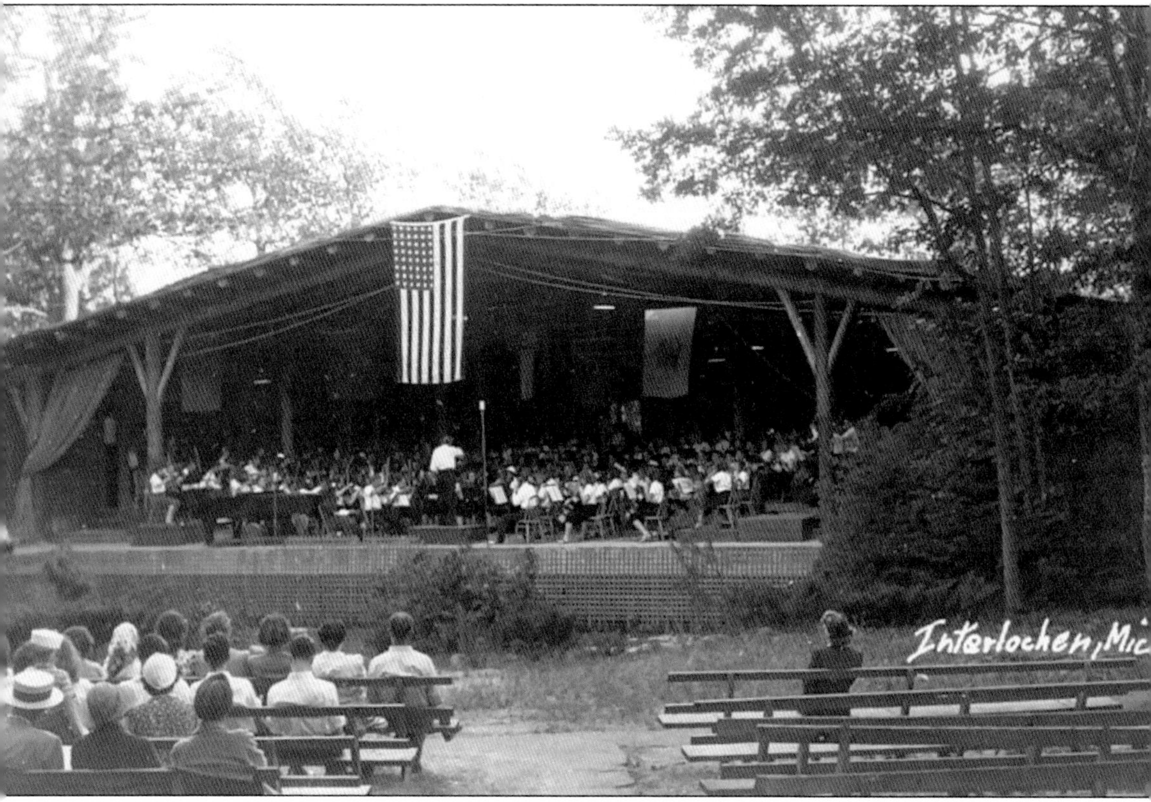

In the 1930s, the National High School Orchestra began performing at the Interlochen Bowl on the grounds of the National Music Camp. Many of the initial broadcasts were aired on NBC radio. The National Music Camp at Interlochen was founded in 1931. Willis Pennington owned Camp Interlochen, a summer camp for girls, as well as Camp Penn Loch for boys. Joseph E. Maddy and Thaddeus P. Giddings joined Pennington to found the National High School Orchestra Camp in 1928. Growing rapidly, the camp became known as the National Music Camp in 1931 and became affiliated with the University of Michigan in 1942. Chartered in 1962, the Interlochen Arts Academy provides year-round training in the creative arts. Interlochen Arts Academy is located on M-137, approximately 15 miles south of Traverse City.

(*Opposite, bottom*) Construction was completed on the Kresge Assembly Hall at Interlochen Center for the Arts in 1948. The hall, made possible by a donation from the Kresge Foundation, was "Dedicated to the Promotion of World Friendship through the Universal Language of the Arts." The center was founded in 1927 on 1,200 acres of land just south of Traverse City. Today, over 2,100 students from 50 states and 41 different countries attend the camp. Interlochen faculty, staff, students, and guest artists present more than 750 concerts, plays, dance productions, art exhibits, and readings every year.

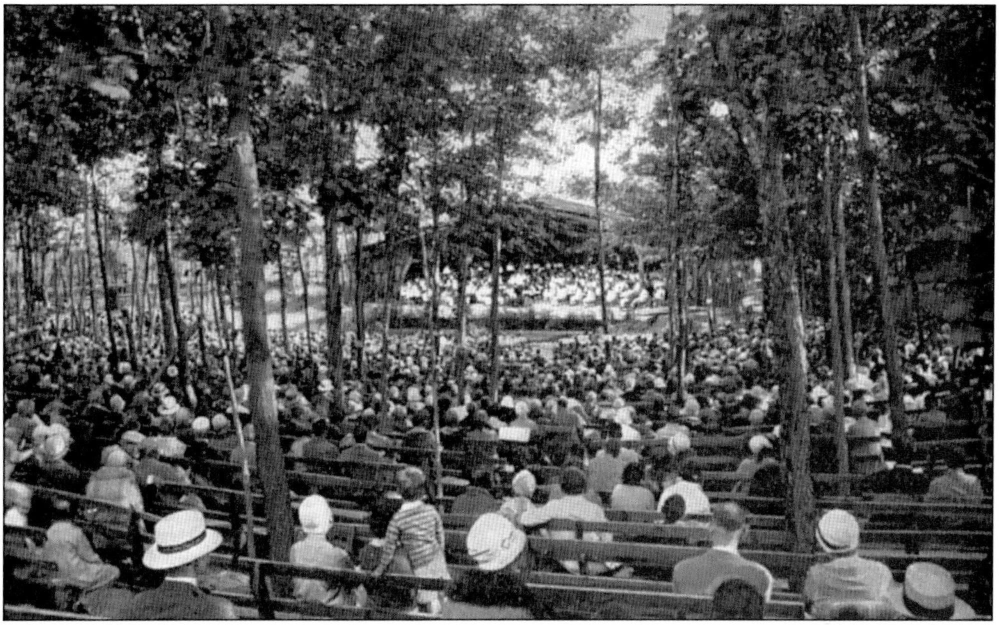

(*Above*) Sunday concerts at the Interlochen Bowl on the grounds of the Interlochen Arts Camp have long been a tradition for residents and tourists. Here, among a community of artists, scholars, and students come from around the world to study dance, music, theatre, visual arts, and creative writing. One of the oldest buildings on campus, the Interlochen Bowl, was built in 1928, and has hosted such luminaries as John Philip Sousa and Howard Hanson. Included in the long list of well-known alumni are newscaster Mike Wallace and Peter Yarrow of the folk group Peter, Paul and Mary, as well as child prodigy Lorin Maazel, an accomplished conductor and soloist and current Music Director for the New York Philharmonic Orchestra. National broadcasts from the Interlochen Bowl began in the 1930s and other than for a brief pause in the 1940s, continue to this day

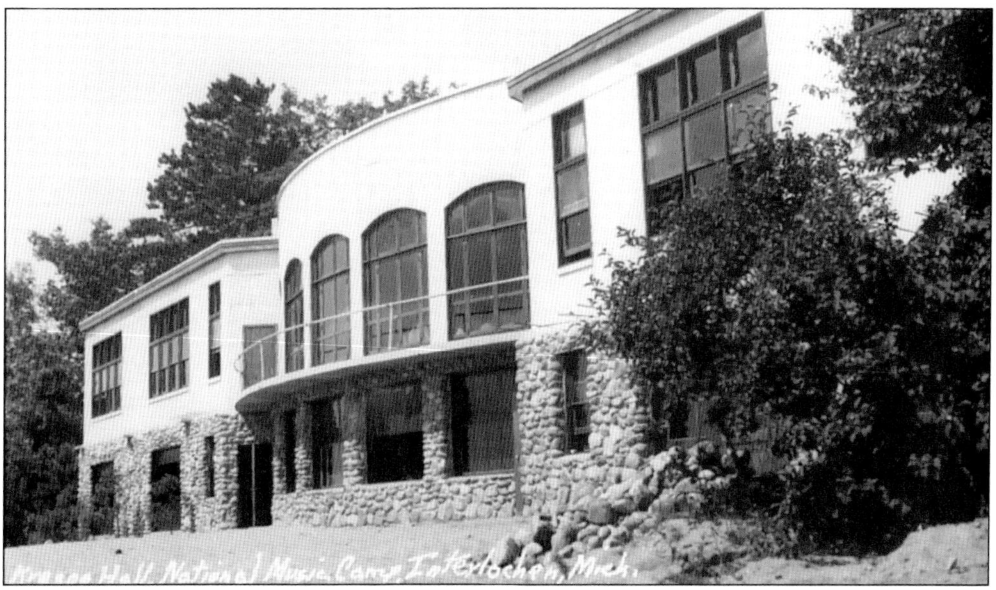

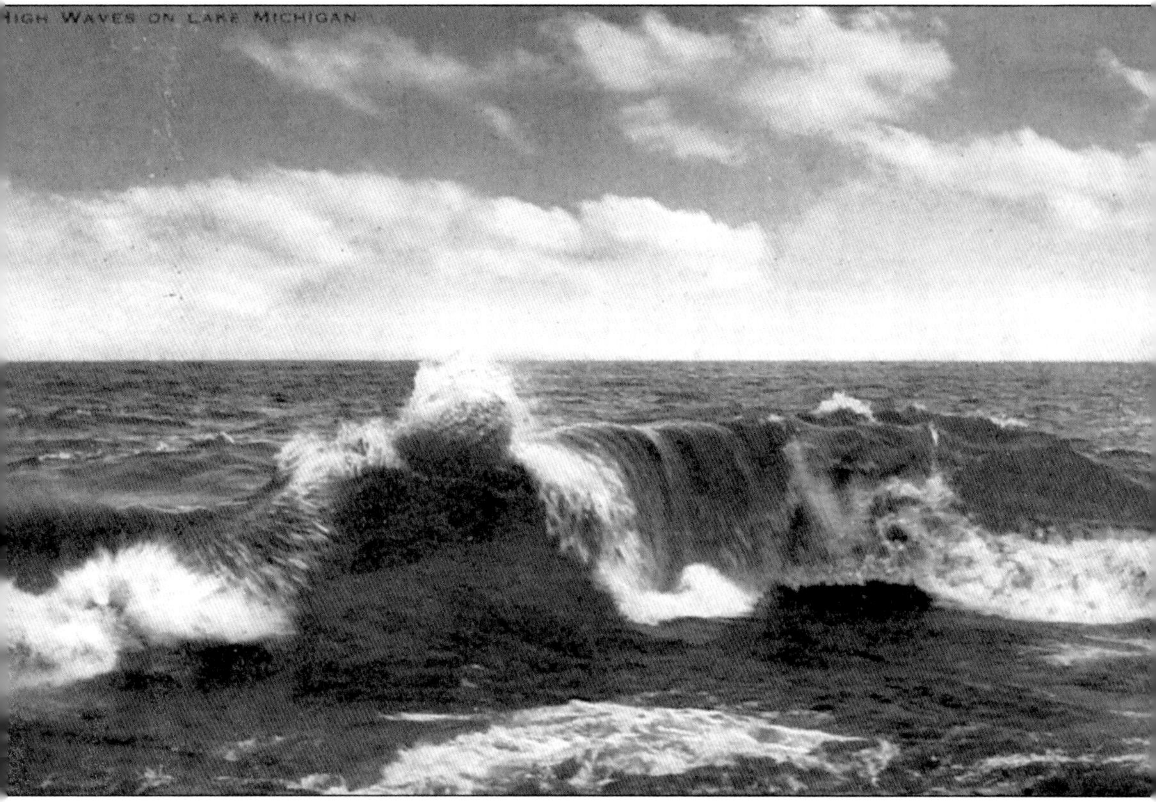

Whitecaps on Lake Michigan can be a great deal of fun if you are bodysurfing or swimming, yet the undertow created by these waves is often quite dangerous. Even experienced swimmers have difficulty maneuvering about in these waves, some of which can easily reach four feet in height. Experiencing the thrill of just watching these waves as they crash onto shore is one of the many wondrous sights that await the visitor to Northern Michigan. Yet, when whitecaps form on Lake Michigan, it is wise to keep your eyes on the horizon; it may be just the water spirits playing, or there could be a storm brewing.

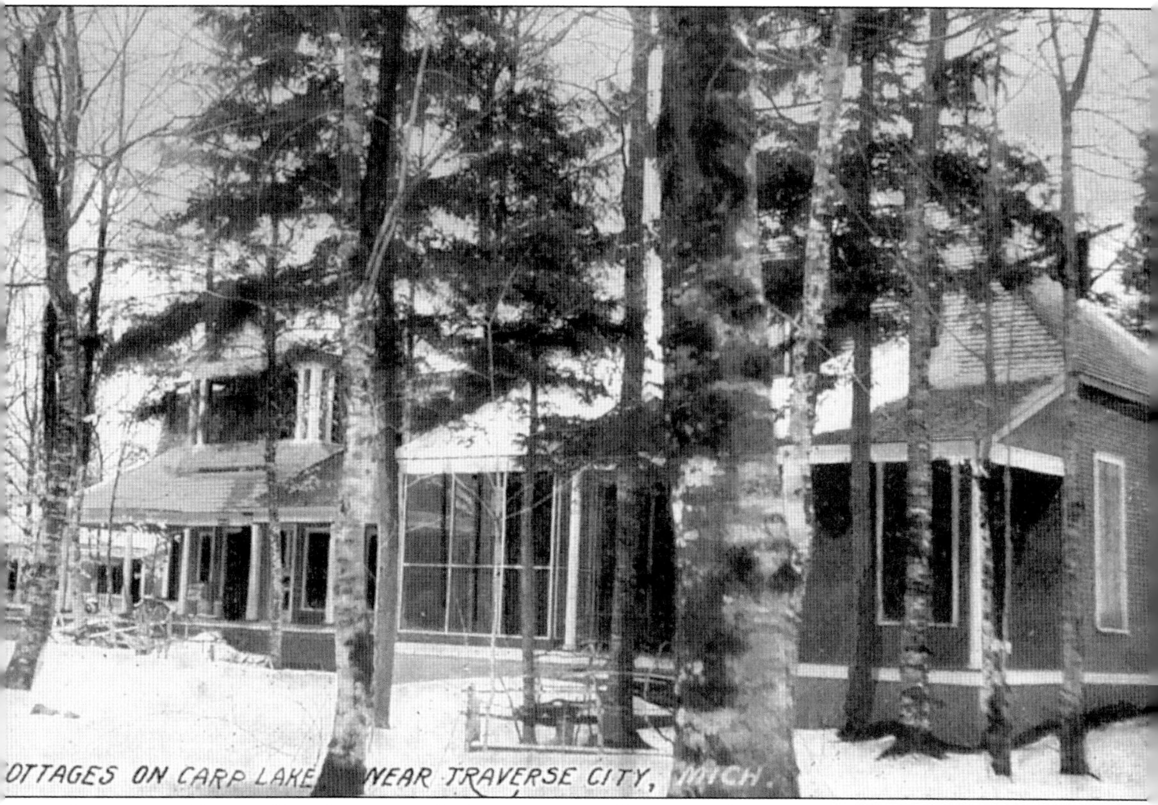

Cottages and homes line the shore of what we now call Lake Leelanau, although around the turn of the century, when it was called Carp Lake, it was used extensively by the lumber industry. A sawmill at the north end of the lake in Leland was the center of activity. Over the years, Lake Leelanau underwent a change, as did most of the area and is now known as a recreational lake. During the summer months, boaters, fishermen, swimmers, and a few folks who just like to relax and enjoy the view frequent the refreshing waters of Lake Leelanau.

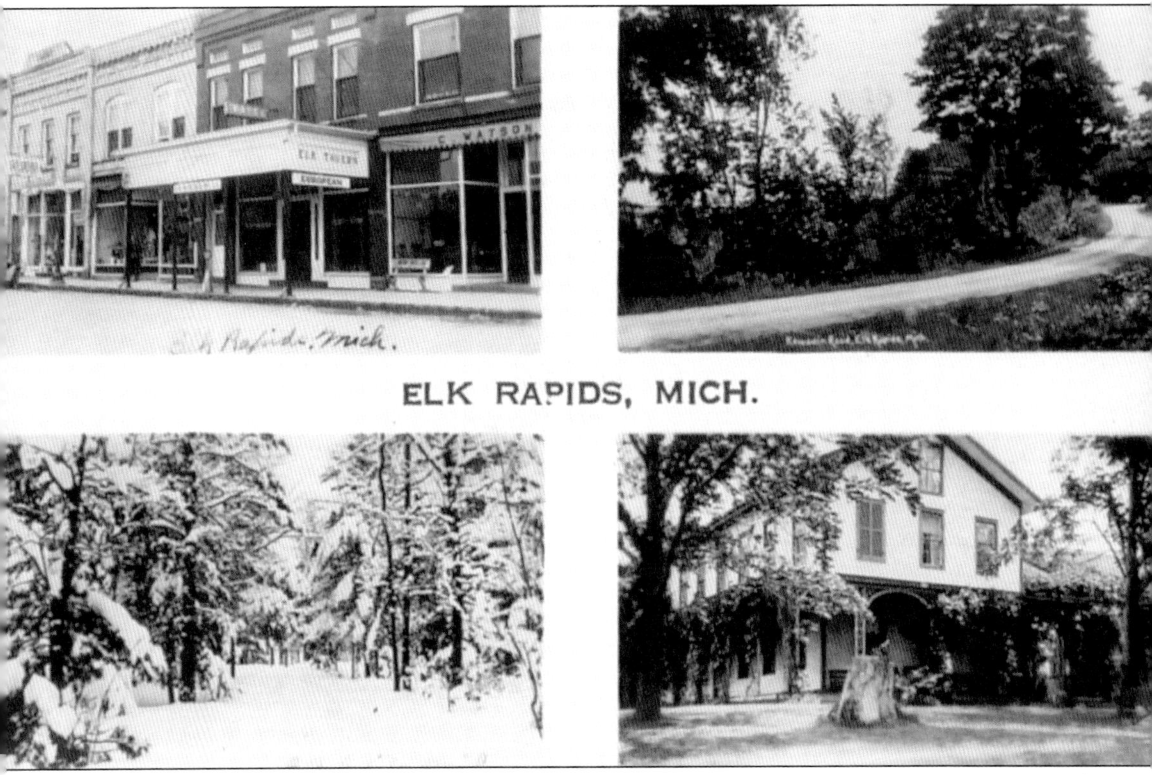

Elk Rapids is a sleepy little village located on the East Arm of Grand Traverse Bay, approximately 15 miles north of Traverse City. Today, this small town has all the charm that it did in its early days. While there has been a great deal of construction and renovation in the area, the pharmacy, tavern, and old general store are still in the heart of downtown. The road to Kewadin is built-up somewhat now, although residents have been careful to preserve the natural habitat. The picture in the lower left corner provides a glimpse of Elk Rapids after a mild snowstorm. Most of the homes in the village are rather quaint, modest structures, yet like any other community, Elk Rapids had its lumber barons and their mansions.

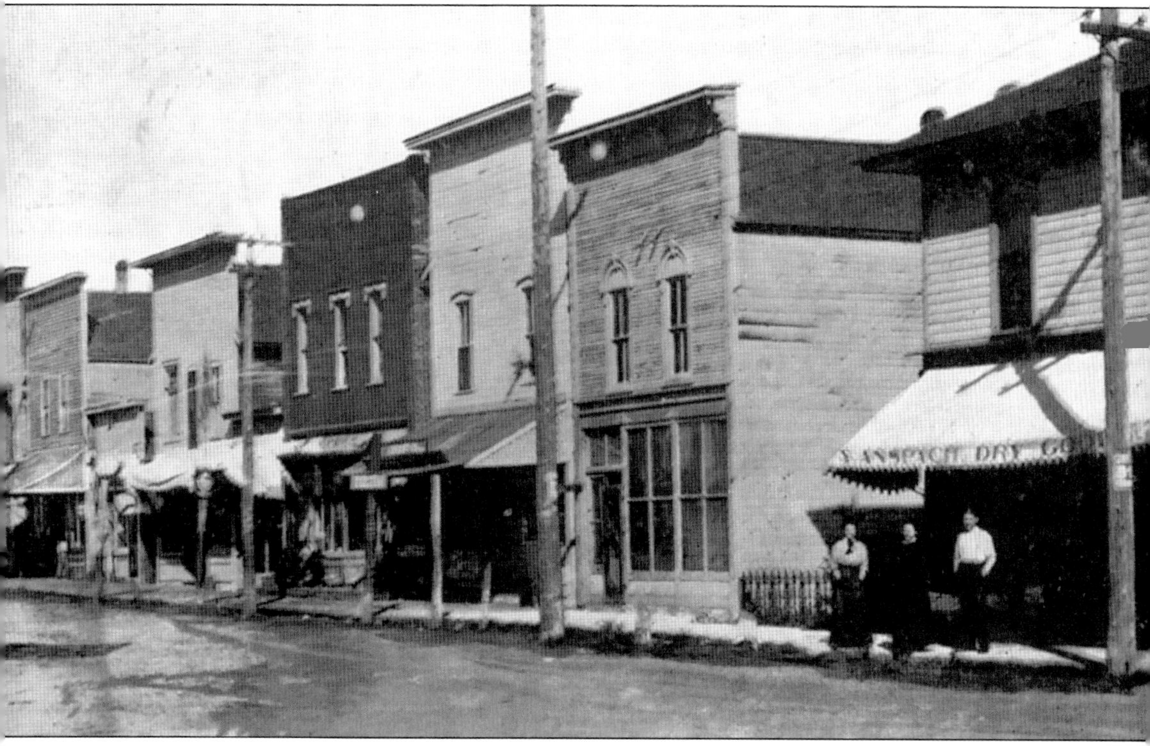

Initially known as Cedar Creek when it was founded in the 1860s, Manton was meant to be merely another stop for the Grand Rapids and Indiana Railroad. Due to financial difficulties, the railroad was unable to complete the track from Cadillac, or Clam River as it was known then, to Cedar Creek until 1873. In the process another tract of land was purchased and subsequently named Manton. Soon afterwards, a sawmill was erected, and logging operations began. As with most other Northern Michigan towns that relied upon logging, Manton suffered economically in the early part of the twentieth century and since then has relied, to a great extent, on tourism. Manton, approximately 30 miles southeast of Traverse City, remains very much as it was 75 years ago.

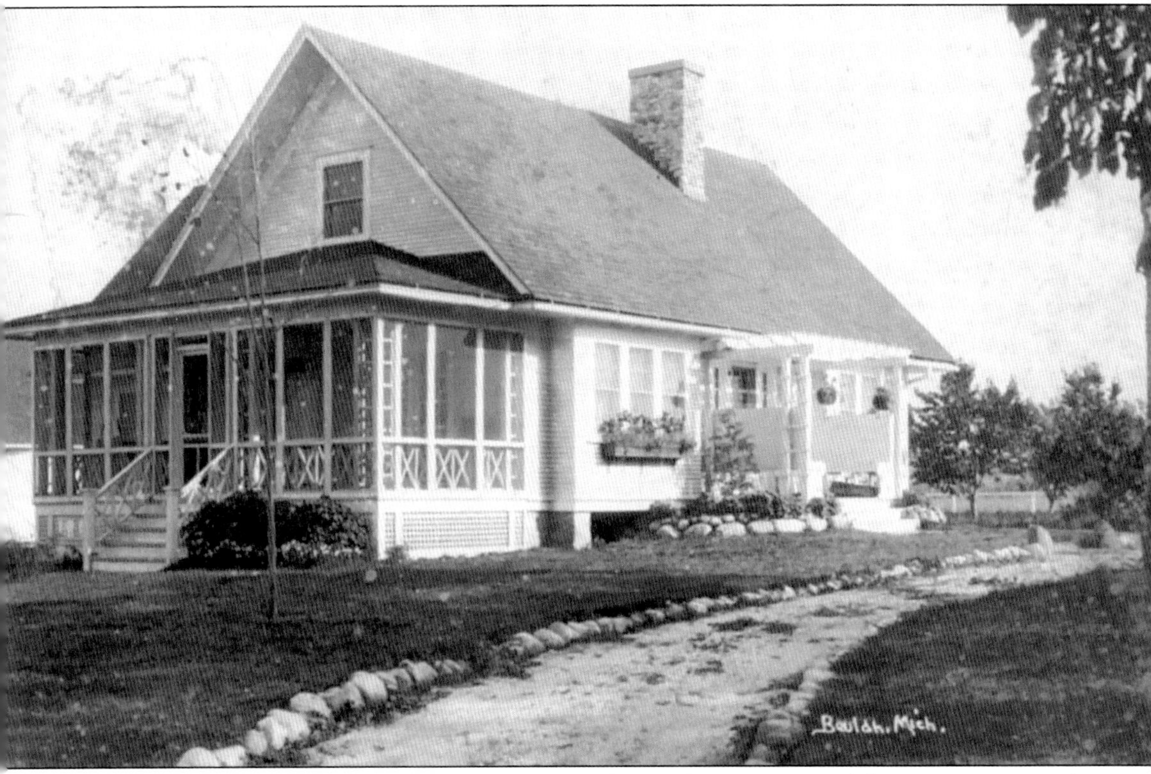

Cottages and homes of a clapboard style, similar to this one in Beulah, were very popular throughout all of Northern Michigan. Houses of this type, constructed primarily of timber from local lumber mills, were relatively inexpensive to build and easy to maintain. Beulah is located on Crystal Lake, in Benzie County, about 30 miles south of Traverse City.